Decisions Decisions Decisions

Marion Kline

Decisions Decisions Decisions

Marion Kline

iUniverse, Inc.

New York Lincoln Shanghai

Decisions Decisions Decisions

iUniverse books may be ordered through booksellers or by contacting:

iUniverse
2021 Pine Lake Road, Suite 100
Lincoln, NE 68512
www.iuniverse.com
1-800-Authors (1-800-288-4677)

ISBN-13: 978-0-595-39590-3 (pbk)
ISBN-13: 978-0-595-83994-0 (ebk)
ISBN-10: 0-595-39590-2 (pbk)
ISBN-10: 0-595-83994-0 (ebk)

Printed in the United States of America

Contents

FOREWORD

In these pages, Marion Kline tells the incredible story of a life that has spanned ten decades. It is the story of a feisty, independent, strong-minded, keenly intelligent, completely fearless woman of faith. From her beginnings in a poor and broken home in Seattle, through her struggles to get an education, through her faith struggles, through her pioneering as a clergywoman, through her exciting missionary service in the Philippines, through a whole lifetime of projects she has carried on since her "retirement," its hard to find a dull moment in her life! Scattered through these decades are her travels, which took her to scores of unusual places where ordinary tourists seldom venture.

Marion Kline thinks and acts "outside the box" of conventionality. She wants to know the truth, and when she does, she acts on it. I experienced this directly when both of us found ourselves on a public street corner in the weeks prior to the United States invasion of Iraq, carrying signs of protest. "Peace on earth" is far more than a slogan for Marion; it is the driving force of her life, exhibited daily in both what she says and what she does. This book tells her compelling story.

Jack M. Tuell
Bishop, The United Methodist Church
Retired

INTRODUCTION

It took Dr. Georgia Harkness and many hundreds of others to break the "glass ceiling" of the United Methodist Church. Finally, at the General Conference of 1956, the vote passed to let women have full clergy rights. Immediately those of us who were ready took advantage of that decision and became members of our Annual Conferences. I joined the Detroit Conference, which graciously made exceptions to some of their rules in order to let me in.

But there were more than just those times; there has been a whole life. Although many people had told me I should write my memoirs, it took determination on the part of my niece, Ann Clifton, to get me started. The course in Memoir Writing from Highline Community College was very helpful, both because of the teacher, Pat Tyllis, and also the students. Virginia Nunner has been an excellent proof-reader and editor. Howell Lowe's computer expertise made this project possible.

Join me, then, as my life unfolds, with God's Spirit leading, enjoying the diversity of God's wonderful people.

CHILDHOOD AND YOUTH

CHILDHOOD DECISIONS

I was sitting on a straight chair in the back of a dance hall in Fremont, a section of Seattle, Washington. The other children were playing games, but as a stubborn ten-year-old, I just sat there. My brothers, Walter, five years my senior, and Francis, three and a half years older, and I had been invited to this "Party for Orphans and Poor Kids."

I had not thought about being an orphan, though my parents were divorced. I was seven when our family went to Tacoma to join in the parade celebrating the end of World War I (1918). My father shouted loudly "The Marines Did It." His youngest brother had been a Marine and was killed in the war. Otherwise he was almost a nonentity, although he usually slept in our house. He was gone early in the morning, and came home late at night. Mother said he stayed in the pool halls evenings. He had set up an office with a sign as a chiropodist. Whether he ever had any clients, I did not know. Mother got the divorce for non-support.

Poor kids, yes. Before I went to school, Mother and I were home alone, and sometimes there was no food in the house for lunch. One day I had a penny, and went to the store about two blocks away, for candy. I tried to share it with Mother, but she insisted I eat it all. Another time she had a dime and sent me to the store for a can of tomato soup. The grocer put a can on the counter. I looked at it and spelled out v-e-g-e-t-a-b-l-e and said in my five-year-old haughty voice, "That does not spell tomato!" He quickly changed it. I spelled t-o-m-a-t-o, was satisfied, and walked out with my head high, wondering if he couldn't read.

When I went to school, Mother began to clean other peoples' houses to earn money, she told me later, to buy a piano for me. But from that time on my father contributed nothing to the household. Before long she was working full time. As soon as they were old enough, my brothers had paper routes. By the time I was nine I went home after school, made the fire in the old range, washed the break-

1

fast dishes, made the beds, and swept the floors. Then I played with the neighbor children, especially the girls next door, Zula and Zelda, or I played with my dolls. Somehow Mother managed to give me a doll each birthday and Christmas, often bought in Woolworth's Ten-Cent Store. When she came home she had only the dinner to cook, and we washed the dishes. We often read, but sometimes we played cards to keep the boys off the streets. As she had been a tailor before she married, sometimes she sewed, making clothes for my brothers and me from clothes people gave her. We moved from house to house as we paid no rent. Of course I did not put all these things together when I sat there in the dance hall, I just had known the stigma that is attached to the poor.

A man came to me and tried to get me to play the games. I didn't look at him, or answer him. As he left I could hear him say under his breath, "Oh, you poor kid." Poor kid Poor kid Poor kid Poor Kid. It was as if I had been branded. As we walked home, I DECIDED: I AM NOT ALWAYS GOING TO BE A POOR KID.

SCHOOL

School, at Daniel Bagley, had been easy, as very few of us could count to 100 or read. I skipped the first half of the second grade. It was then that we moved to Queen Anne Hill, and I went to North Queen Anne Grade School. Here I had no problems except in the fourth grade. I skipped the first half of that grade, and as it involved the beginning of fractions, I had to make it all up in the second half. The teacher was sometimes impatient, expecting me to know the part I had missed. A girl who had an artistic talent began a picture which the teacher especially wanted. The girl became ill, and the teacher asked me to finish it. I did a horrible job. She was terribly disappointed, and told me I was not an artist. I DECIDED: I WILL NOT TRY ANY ART AGAIN.

When I graduated we had a party. Another girl and I received the highest honors. Mother made me a dress out of new material, and bought pearls for me. The Principal, Miss Hurd, told me that in high school I should plan my courses so that I could go to college. College! When I told Mother, she said that is out of the question, we have no money. As I thought about it, I could work, I will find a way. I DECIDED: I WILL GO TO COLLEGE.

CHURCH

Four houses were grouped together, making our own little neighborhood. All of us children (not my brothers) went to the Sunday School near Seattle Pacific College. None of us had money to put into the offerings, and our teacher sometimes scolded us. We heard about the ghost that seemed to be lurking in the corners somewhere. When we told our mothers about that ghost, they said it was the Holy Ghost. We did not care how holy it was, we just did not want to meet up with it. It seemed that the end of the world was going to come immediately. We didn't want to die tomorrow. But it was when the teacher told us that she had seen Jesus, that we really became frightened. Our mothers decided we should not go there, and as one of them had been a Baptist, it was decided that we should walk up the hill to the Queen Anne Baptist Sunday School. After awhile some of the neighbors moved away, and my friends Zula and Zelda, and I walked by ourselves. We liked it, as there were no ghosts there, and no one made us afraid. One day, Dr. Richardson, the young pastor, told me that he had been very poor when he was a child. A load was lifted from my shoulders. He understands! It is all right to go to this church even if I am a Poor Kid! MY DECISION: I WILL STAY IN THIS CHURCH.

During the year before I graduated from grade school, my brothers left home to work, Walter in the Merchant Marine, and Francis in a logging camp. Mother and I moved to the west side of the hill. On Saturdays I went with Mother and dusted furniture. The woman gave me a dollar each time. I spent the first ones for a tooth brush and tooth paste, as I had learned in school that we should take are of our teeth.

When school was out and I was alone all day, I felt lost, having no friends in the area. After I finished doing what was needed in the apartment, I wandered around the neighborhood, and soon found Kinnear Park with its tennis court. As I sat and watched, often Agnes Samuelson came and sat beside me. Sometimes she loaned me her racquet so that I could attempt to play. Then with my Saturday dollars I was able to buy my own tennis racquet and balls.

Francis came home for a few days now and then in the summers, and Mother had him buy me a dresser set made of mother-of-pearl. It was beautiful and I used it for many years. She had him buy me some sewing scissors. I appreciated her choices.

Walter also came home a little more often, but not at the same time as Francis. He brought us gifts from the Orient, especially silk kimonos which delighted Mother. Just before I went to high school, Mother had him take me to town and buy me a pair of real shoes. Previously I had always worn just cloth Keds.

QUEEN ANNE HIGH SCHOOL

High school was a whole new experience. Agnes and I had all our classes together. I took Latin because Walter had enjoyed it so much. In the sewing class I was the only one who knew how to run the treadle sewing machine. Also I had used patterns, as Mother had bought some, so that I could make clothes for my large doll she had given me on my 12th birthday.

In Algebra, Agnes and I and some of the others were put into an accelerated class, beginning the start of the next semester. But this was a new plan, and we had to repeat that work. That made the whole semester boring so that when the teacher told me she thought I should become a math teacher, I DECIDED NO, I DON'T WANT TO BE A TEACHER.

In Chemistry laboratory once I spilled some acid on my legs. The teacher cleaned it up quickly and had me wash it off immediately. Thus I was not burned. At mid-semester I got a C in the course. That devastated me, but fortunately we had a new teacher the second half. I got an A at the end.

In a World History class, I was working hard, enjoying the class. Walter had sent me some pictures of Japan and I used them in a paper. But I got just a B for the first half. The second half I began to do nothing. When the teacher called me in one day to ask me why, I told him I had only a B, and I could do that without working that hard. He promised that if I would continue to work, I would have an A. So I went back to studying for that class.

One day, early in my third year, I was in the public library getting some mystery books for Mother to read. I started to read in various books about different occupations. I liked what I read about being a librarian. I told the high school librarian about that, and she asked me to help in the library during my study period. I enjoyed this the last two years.

During my second year I met Phyllis Borgen and several others who were members of the Girl Reserves, a YWCA group. Agnes was joining the group. I did not know how much it would cost, and as we had no money, Mother was skeptical. One evening a long-time friend of hers, Mrs. Shelton, came to visit, and she highly endorsed the Girl Reserves. Her daughter had been president during her senior year.

Phyllis's parents had a cabin at Angle Lake, way out of town to the south. The Girl Reserve group decided to go camping for a weekend, and this developed into many trips during the ensuing years. The five who went most often were Phyllis Borgen, Agnes Samuelson, Ethel Chivers, Judy Johansson (a friend of Phyllis from Lincoln High), and I. They skillfully arranged it so that I did not have to spend much money. We continued to be close friends for many years.

These friends did not smoke, but some of my other friends were trying it. I talked to Walter about it as he smoked a great deal. He told me he wished he had never started. That made such an impression on me that I did not try it. (When I told him that years later, he was shocked that I ever paid any attention to what he said). However, some time during these years Mother began to smoke. I was embarrassed but later came to realize that it was about the only pleasure she had in life.

During my second year the District Church Youth Fellowship had an oratorical contest. Our group pushed me to try out for it. We heard that one contestant planned to become a minister, so I was sure I had no chance. To my surprise, I won. Dr. Richardson said I was better prepared and that my delivery was much better.

Early in my third year, a friend who intended to become a lawyer asked me to join the debate team. I hesitated, but the church experience helped me decide. For the next two years the debates with other schools took a large part of my time and interest. I learned how important preparation is, for we had to prepare for both sides of the subject. I recall only one: Should the Philippines be granted independence? Our positive side won.

The students who had money were a group to themselves, going across the street to a grill for lunch, while those of us who did not have money stayed in the lunch room, including me with my 10¢ sandwich. One of the rich girls became a friend. When she became the President of the Girls Club, she maneuvered to have me elected Secretary. For one of the meetings we went to her house, and I realized that she lived in one of the mansions. She helped me realize that money, or lack of it, was not the most important thing in life. Still a Poor Kid—but it began to matter a little less.

In order to have a little spending money, I took care of children, 25¢ for the evening, 50¢ to stay overnight. Occasionally I worked for a woman who could not afford to have a maid, but who entertained now and then. I went about 5:00 P.M., made the salads, set up the table, and became her maid. She hired a Filipino cook who left before the guests came. I did all the cleaning up. I was paid $2.50 which was a big amount for me.

Dr. Richardson encouraged me at every point. We had a youth group which he organized, and a youth choir. When I was fourteen, the church built a new building. On the evening of the first service, a number of us were baptized by immersion. Our Sunday School was organized in such a way that we had fourth graders in the same class with high school students. I did not fit. During my second year I began to teach in the Primary Department. I loved it, and stayed with it through my Seattle years.

During the summers I cleaned the house, washed the clothes, and learned to cook. My Aunt Birdie (my father's sister, who took a special interest in me,) taught me how to make pies and other things. I also canned fruit and made the jams and jellies. And, of course, I played tennis with Agnes.

About a month before graduation, Miss Ethel Miller, the Librarian, told me that if I went to the University of Washington, I could have a job in the high school library. I was elated, and even Mother began to think it could be managed. MY DECISION TO GO TO COLLEGE at the end of grade school was now made possible.

When it came time to graduate, Agnes was Valedictorian, and I came in a close second as Salutatorian. At the senior picnic, Agnes, Phyllis, Ethel and I went rowing. We were accustomed to this in Angle Lake, but not on Puget Sound. We got caught in a small cove, and could not row out. Ethel took off her shoes and walked along the bank, pulling the boat. We finally made it back. The teachers were really worried about us—with two of the graduation speakers seemingly lost.

I needed a dress for the occasion and went shopping with the five dollars Mother gave me as a graduation present. I could not find anything that was suitable. It happened that one of my classmates and her mother were shopping also, and she realized my dilemma. She had me pick out a nice dress, paying $12 for it. I wore it for years, always remembering her kindness and my own determination to some day have it different.

I do not remember what Agnes talked about at the Graduation Ceremony, but mine was about vocational education, which was a new educational thrust at that time. Walter happened to be home, and sat in the back row. He said I was the only speaker he could hear. My debating experience had taught me to project my voice.

During the summer I worked for a woman who had fallen and broken her leg. With this and some money I had saved, I had enough for the fall tuition of $30.

Mother and I moved to an apartment on the east side of the hill with convenient transportation for both of us.

Graduation from grade school

With Mother and Brother Francis.

THE UNIVERSITY OF WASHINGTON

The University was a whole new experience, as it is for every student. The money for the tuition was not enough as I needed money for books. One of my friends graciously loaned me hers.

What do I write on for the paper due each week for English Composition? By the time I had settled down to study at all, and had finished the German and English Literature it would be at least 10:00 P.M. My mind was blank. After about a month the Dean of Women told me to drop the course until the next year; the work and housework would not allow me to take a full course from then on. This meant extending my course to five years.

I needed two foreign languages for Library School. German was easier for me than French for I never did learn to speak it or understand it. I discovered that Shakespeare was exciting. During my fourth year I was required to take a reading course for Library School, which with literature classes meant that I was reading three or four books a week. I found it quite a load.

The Sunday School teaching and the youth group took me away from home a good deal on Sunday. Mother did not have so much work to do, but she kept busy, and resented my being away. As always the church continued to be a gap between us. The term "religious fanatic" was devastating.

Confusion abounded when Mother had a stroke at the end of my third year. She was in the Harborview Hospital a couple of weeks then went to a county nursing home, known as a "poor farm". The Depression was well under way, and good summer jobs were impossible to find. Finally I found a job in a home doing the housework and taking care of a three-year-old girl. On Sundays I went to visit Mother, and evenings I went to Youth Fellowship.

At the end of about two months Mother was able to take care of herself and we moved back to the apartment. The next winter was difficult. Mother had worked so hard to help me get this far that she was not willing to have me stop, nor was I. Often she spent time with a neighbor, Mrs. Shingles who had family problems of her own, but took good care of Mother. Walter sent money home for groceries and expenses, sometimes a check for me. When the City of Seattle went bankrupt my little checks were cashed by a man for whom Mother had worked. Francis was out of work much of that time, came home off and on, and in the early spring brought his bride, Cecelia. He discovered a food bank in Fremont from which we were able to get staples.

Mother decided to give me a birthday party as she thought it a good way to introduce Cecelia. I invited friends from the church. We played cards and had a good time. Mother was disappointed in Francis' choice of a wife, but she determined not to say anything, as her mother had chosen her mate, and it had not worked out.

In order to get into Library School, I had to take two more courses in summer school. I realized Mother was getting weaker and I spent as much time with her as I could. Church friends said I should pray for her to get well. I was confused. There was no possibility that the damage caused by the stroke, and later smaller ones, could be canceled. Should I pray for her to continue suffering? So I just prayed for her, admitting to God that I did not know how to pray.

In early August I came home from school and discovered that Mother was in the Hospital with another stroke. As the doctor termed it terminal, I spent the next week at the hospital with her. As she went into a coma, I sat looking out at the beautiful sunset over Puget Sound. I had an intense experience of the presence of God which gave me courage in the days ahead. She died that night.

As Mother's family had long believed in cremation, even when it was considered "heathen", we had her cremated. Dr. Richardson persuaded the mortuary to do the service half price so that Mother's small insurance paid the expenses. Finals that next week meant extra studying. Francis wanted the furniture which we left with Mrs. Sprinkles until he could move it to Shelton. As soon as Francis and Cecelia left, I went to Phyllis' home to stay for about a week until school started again.

As Library School was too intensive for me to work, Mrs. Shelton loaned me the money I needed for the year, knowing I would get it from my insurance on my 21st birthday. Cynthia, also in Library School, and I rented a furnished apartment in the University District. I had the dishes and other things that we needed.

That year of Library School kept us busy. We would be given assignments for a week ahead. I would do them when they were assigned, then do the required reading of books. Others would let them go, do a quick job, then complain that my grades were better than theirs. My roommate had a real struggle with the lessons, and sometimes I would help her, not actually giving the answers.

Cynthia lived in Bremerton, and went home weekends. I continued to go to the Queen Anne Baptist Church, taught Sunday School, then went to Ethel's home for dinner. They had a dog who would sit on the porch, and when I was a couple of blocks away he would start to bark. Then they knew it was time to mash the potatoes and do the last minute things to have dinner ready.

At the church one day I was talking about Mother to a woman whom I knew well. She said, "Oh, Marion, stop feeling sorry for yourself." I closed up, and did not talk to anyone about it for a very long time. I did not want pity, just someone to share my grief.

I went to two campus Bible study groups, one "liberal" taught by our Baptist Chaplain, Jim, and one "conservative" because Agnes wanted me to go with her. This helped me think through by own concepts and doubts. Jim was a wonderful, steadying guide. Through his influence I was made chairman of an interdenominational worship committee, and thus had charge of two very large all-campus worship services. Both were well attended and went well.

Dr. Richardson, as always, was very helpful. When I asked him questions he loaned me books by Harry Emerson Fosdick, a well-known "liberal" pastor of the Riverside Baptist Church in New York City. Also he questioned if he should have been a Chaplain in World War I, and in other statements planted pacifist ideas in my thinking.

It was during this year that I had a boy friend. Howard was chairman of the Baptist Student Fellowship. He and I went to all the Jeanette McDonald and Nelson Eddy movies. When Kirby Page came to town we followed him from place to place, fascinated by his socialism. For a person from the poverty I knew, his ideas seemed to be the entire solution to the economic problems of the nation. He was the speaker for one of the all-campus worship services. After I graduated Howard and I did not keep in touch with each other. He had another year before he graduated.

Agnes was teaching school at Pasco, which at that time was a wide spot in the road. During Easter vacation I went by bus to visit her. She was rooming with a farm family who laughed at me, for it was my first time on a farm, and I enjoyed doing their chores. We drove back to Seattle in the Model A Ford her parents had given her for graduation from the University. We went into a snow bank on Snoqualmie Pass, and sat there, not knowing what to do, until someone helped us out.

Winter Quarter I went to Portland to do my practice work at Reed College. I thought I did all the work well, but got a C for that semester, the only one through the college years. While in Portland I contacted the family of Mother's sister Anne, meeting my cousins for the first and only time.

During spring semester I went to see Mrs. Sprinkles. Two of her children had the mumps, but as I had had the disease I went in. Later I had a terribly sore mouth; then Cynthia became ill, and it was mumps. By the time she was out of the infirmary the end of the quarter was near. I felt so guilty about being the one responsible for her illness that I helped her with some of the assignments. So we both cheated, but we did get her graduated.

About a month before graduation the five of us, Agnes, Phyllis, Ethel, Judy and I, went to the First Presbyterian Church in Seattle, sitting in the balcony. For me, as for many others, the song "Just As I Am" struck a chord. I was a nobody, not worth anything, with no talents. But could God use me, just as I am? I struggled against the idea, but also realized I would find no peace until I gave in. I DECIDED, GOD, IF YOU CAN USE ME I AM READY.

Graduation itself, in 1933, was lonely. Other graduates had family there to clap and demonstrate for them, but although I graduated cum laude it did not matter to anyone.

And now, homeless, alone, what was I to do? Richardsons invited me to stay with them until I found work. There were very few jobs during the Depression, and none at all for Library School graduates. I walked the streets, but all I could find was housework. I was "over qualified," but got the first one after I did not mention the University.

I kept the house clean and made good meals. Pies were a specialty. There was a two-year-old boy to take care of, and we got along well. I got him to eat, which his mother had not been able to do. My lady was happy with it all, as she was free to play golf, and play cards with friends, etc. But I was depressed. Mother had worked hard all those years so that I would not have to do housework, and here I was. All my struggle for an education had been in vain. The idea of doing some kind of service for God seemed a day dream. I was still a Poor Kid!

I had worked about six weeks when I decided to talk with the Counselor, Jim. For the first time I told him about the experience that Sunday morning. It happened that Dr. John Bailey, a professor from the Berkeley Baptist Divinity School, was in Seattle. Jim made an appointment for me to see him. In a few days I was told that I had a scholarship and a job at the Seminary starting in September. Ruby Richardson would also be going. She had her masters degree but no job.

I went on with my work with new vigor and new dreams. This was not going to be forever after all. My friends decided I should have a little free time before I left. I stayed with Phyllis about a week. Then I went to Ethel's to take care of the house while her mother took a much needed vacation. Ethel had found a job and the other children were able to take care of themselves. There was no salary, but I was happy to have time to sort my things, pack a second hand trunk, and store the rest in the basement of Mrs. Shelton's home. I thought that in another year I would come back and take care of them.

We had a big party at the church before we left. I was given a pair of Chinese soapstone bookends. A few friends went to the train to see us off, giving us some sandwiches and fruit and stuffed dates to eat along the way. When we arrived in Oakland Dr. Bailey met us and took us to the Seminary

AMERICAN BAPTIST DIVINITY SCHOOL

During the first week I was offered work in the library. This gave me a total of tuition, room and board, and a little spending money. Who wouldn't shout thanks to God when no one could hear?

With my lack of self esteem I was a natural for practical jokes. When I was on duty in the library in the evenings, one of the men did some silly things. I was deeply hurt for I needed to be built up rather than torn down. Before long the faculty heard about it, and he stopped.

Some of the courses were fascinating, some just mediocre. The Old Testament course was one of the latter. We had to outline the whole Old Testament. We just copied the headings, without reading it. There was no information on how it all got put together. I had learned much more from the course in the Bible as Literature at the University.

The New Testament course was excellent. Dr. Bailey was a scholar who shared his knowledge and his appreciation for the New Testament. Church History was completely new to me, and I enjoyed reading the works of the early Fathers. I also enjoyed the Missions class. The public speaking course was very helpful. At first, if I held my notes in my hand, my hand shook so much it was difficult to read them. The professor helped me to gain security, and to make what I was saying come alive. There were a number of Christian Education courses, some rather ordinary, some really fun. I learned much from a woman who had prepared for elementary school teaching.

It was during the first year that Harold began to pay attention to me. I was told that at a faculty meeting we were discussed, as some thought I had come to the Seminary to find a husband. I was shocked. As the year went along it seemed to me Harold was trying to train me to be the kind of minister's wife he thought I ought to be. I was too independent, and did not train well.

During the Christmas vacation of the first year I went to Catalina Island to visit Mother's sister, Ollie. She and her husband had come to visit Mother a number of times, and Aunt Ollie had come while Mother was ill. My cousin Claudia was fourteen and we had a good time riding on the glass bottom boats, free, as my uncle was the Captain.

During the summer I decided to go to the University of California as I was feeling constrained by this small school. I easily found work with a family including two boys, ten and five. One course I took was Developmental Psychology. I found it so helpful in Christian Education that later I taught such a course. That was a memorable summer with a polio epidemic and a general strike, closing everything.

One day in the fall of 1934 an English woman, Muriel Lester, spoke in Berkeley. That day I joined the Fellowship of Reconciliation, a peace group begun in 1914. A small group of University students and I met once a week reading together her works. We all felt close together for several years afterward, though we were separated by work and graduate schools. The F.O.R. has been a mainstay throughout my life.

Another group which was meaningful was a small prayer group at the local Baptist Church. We spent 15 or 20 minutes in silence, then the balance of the time praying for people we knew. Off and on others joined us, but they could not take the silence. Thus our number stayed at five or six.

Sophie, my roommate, and I had some fun experiences with two brothers of one of our students who lived in Berkeley. They drove us to Oakland, then parked the car in the middle of a three way intersection. They got out of the car, one of them going to the front and opening the hood, the other to the back. Then they called to each other in Swedish, testing peoples' reaction to immigrants. No one offered to help, but almost all swore at them, and some telling them to go back home. Finally they put the hood down and drove off. Only then could we burst into laughter.

Another time they sent us into a restaurant, and told us not to know them. We ordered coffee and a sweet roll, and when they came in they sat at a different table. Talking in Swedish, they started flirting with us, but we ignored them. The restaurant owner pleaded with us to be nice to them, they were nice men, and new to this country. So we made friends with them in time for them to pay our bill. But it was their brother I fell in love with, to no avail.

A good deal of time during the second year was spent working on my thesis for my Master's Degree. I was certain that I wanted to be a counselor at a state university, and I was also convinced that the state university offered a broader and more challenging education than the small Christian colleges that many of our students had attended. I did lots of research and made many tables. It had to be typed perfectly, with no erasures. In preparation I had taken a short evening typing course to rid my typing of the errors accumulated since high school. My thesis was all typed and turned in about a week ahead of the date due. In order to have money to rent a typewriter I had agreed to type the thesis of one of the students. I did not know what I was getting into. When I started typing it, he had not finished writing it. We sat up all the night before it was due, typing it as he dictated. The Dean was very angry. He did graduate, but the Dean confided to me that it was because of his prominent family, and the faculty were certain he could not get a church to serve, anyway.

The Graduation Service was held at the Berkeley Baptist Church, June 1935. I received a degree in Master of Arts in Christian Education.

Soon after graduation Sophie and Fred Owen were married. I was the maid of honor. It was held in Dr. Warburton's home as he conducted the ceremony. No one had money for a reception, so the only people there were the wedding party. Sophies' family lived in central California, but they did not approve of her choice and refused to come.

I was hired by Dr. Bailey to work in his home. His wife was not well, but now and then she liked to entertain. I tried to plan all the menus in such a way that she thought she was doing it. A luncheon for twenty was the largest I ever cooked, but it went very well. The salary was small, but I had my room and board, and the encouragement from Dr. Bailey was wonderful.

Although jobs were still scarce two came my way. One was as a Director of Christian Education in a church in Portland. Dr. Bailey thought it was too con-servative for me to be happy there. The other was as Librarian of Westminster College in Salt Lake City. Dr. Bailey had been a speaker there the year before, and he thought it was an excellent opening for me. Ironic that it should be a church college! The salary was small, but it was work. I appreciated the Library School recommending me.

A few years after I left Berkeley I wrote these words and sent them to Dr. Bailey:

> Sometimes I wonder why you had faith in me,
> But no matter why—your having faith was enough for me.
>
> When others doubted me until I began to doubt myself
> Your reassuring smile gave me confidence.

When those in authority wondered where my ability lay
And I wondered what use God could make of me—
You hired me.

And now when people say: "You are doing a fine work out there"
You smile at me—is that the way you smile to your own daughter
when you are proud of her? And I smile back,
for I know it is just because you had faith in me.

With Borgen, Gangmark, Johansson and Samuelson

Librarian, Westminster College

WESTMINSTER COLLEGE

Arriving in Salt Lake City by train, I was met by the Secretary of Westminster College. This was a Presbyterian Junior College, servicing the Protestants who were struggling to keep alive in the largely Mormon communities. About half of the students lived on the campus. There were three new faculty members that year: Helen Hamilton, Music; Beulah Hart, Physical Education; and myself as Librarian. Helen had sciatica, making it difficult for her to get around. Helen and Beulah and most of the older faculty members lived on the first floor, but the Dean of Women and I lived on the second floor with the women students. This had its problems—how to relate to the students as a faculty member, living so close.

When I first arrived a friend sent me a dress. It was quite new, and one I really needed. But I had worn other peoples' clothes all my life. I DECIDED: I WOULD NEVER WEAR ANY MORE SECOND-HAND CLOTHES.

The Music Faculty put on a beautiful concert for the general public, and all the faculty dressed in formal gowns. The only one I had was the very cheap one I had bought for Sophie's wedding. The second year I made a deep red velvet formal. The faculty loved it.

Although this was a Protestant school about one-fourth of our students were Mormon. When I asked some of those who worked for me in the library, they said they were "Jack Mormons", that is, they had been baptized but they had never gone to church, and did not consider themselves of any religion. They were delightful and excellent workers.

I spent a good deal of time correcting errors I found in the records. The second and third year we received a grant to buy new books. This was great fun, working with the faculty for selection of books, processing them, and persuading the students to use them.

Especially in the first couple of years, but somewhat in all of them, I had a problem with discipline in the library. Part of the problem was that some of the students were with me in the youth group at the Baptist Church and they refused to cooperate. That was hard enough, but added to that the criticism of the older faculty who had their own ideas about the library. My own insecurity added to the problem. I was making the shift from being a student to becoming an adult.

Helen was lonesome, and the second year I began to take piano lessons from her but practice was so boring that I did not do well. I went with her to the New York City Opera when they came on tour. I learned much about opera and other music from her.

Beulah and I played tennis every day that the weather permitted. On Sundays we substituted ping-pong inside, as to have fun on Sundays was considered some sort of sin and not to be seen by neighbors.

Another form of recreation was the "Poison Ivy Club", a group of faculty and students who climbed the mountains in the Wasatch Range. Starting at 4,000 feet, we climbed to about 10,000 feet, and one mountain of 12,000 feet. There was brush to hold on to for a good part of the way, but we did some climbing with ropes. On some there were trails, on others we followed the deer trails. Only once did we see a poisonous snake, and it was easy to get around it.

Because we were a church-related school some parents who could not control their children sent them to us to be reformed. We had about five or six of these each year. They would become a little clique that spent their time in "nicotine gulch," the wooded area where students were allowed to smoke. Perhaps the closest one to being changed was a girl in my last year who hated all teachers. The teachers returned the feeling. After some time of prayer, I realized God could give me love for her, even if I didn't have my own. I began to treat her as I did the others, and before she left she told other students that I was "O.K." I wondered what changes might have come about for these incorrigible ones if I had asked God to give me a little love in previous years.

The Physical Education Faculty changed every two years. Beulah left at the end of the second year and was succeeded by one who was very different. Helen attached herself to her immediately. I was busy with other things, but I did miss the tennis playing. The third one to come was Dorothy Schlappy. The students called me "Klinky" and her "Happy". We got into the tennis routine. She was fired because she was not a formal member of any church.

I joined the Baptist Church as soon as I arrived, and was active in the youth group, the Girls' Guild, and soon became the leader of the Primary Department of the Church School. At the regular meetings of the teachers I taught a course in Christian Education. One who responded most I sent to a Methodist training session and she loved it. After several years I left the department in her hands.

It was during my second year that Check and Dorothy Ramsey came as Baptist home missionaries. Check gathered together a group of anti-war people, and we met each week to talk together about growing tensions with Hitler and Stalin.

Valuable as these years as a faculty member of the college were for growing up, gaining personal security, learning to have fun along with work, and other facets of living, it was the vacation times that really strengthened my understanding of people.

My first Christmas Beulah drove me to Pasadena stopping on the way at the YM-YW camp at Asilamar. This was a pivotal experience for me, as we not only had inspiration, but also names and addressees of organizations to write to for volunteering during the summers.

The summer of 1936 I went by bus to a six week Quaker Work Camp in southeastern Ohio, in the town of Dillonvale. The Quakers set up camps where young people could study how non-violent methods could be used in situations, such as labor disputes. We were in a mining town where the mines were closed. It was the strong Cooperative which brought us there. Our work projects were varied. The men constructed a very fine playground for the children, including a soft ball court, wading pool and other facilities. Tom and I taught in Vacation Church Schools organized by Antioch College. The other women did the cooking, washing, painting of the garage, and various things they found to be done. We paid all of our own expenses.

There were eight men and eight women, the Director and his wife and two children. We lived crowded in a house, with the men sleeping two blocks away in very spare rooms. One of the women had just graduated from high school, one of the men had just finished his Ph.D. in Economics. Most of us were pacifists, one a communist. The latter and I, sleeping next to each other, argued constantly.

Most of our study time was spent on Cooperatives. A workshop was held one weekend with about 100 people present, which gave us a splendid introduction. The men went to meetings of the mine operators and miners. The women could not go because it would interfere with the language the miners were accustomed to using.

My work was in several small towns, teaching the only class in the Vacation Church Schools. The school buildings I was supposed to teach in were such wrecks I could not imagine anyone using them so I held my classes out-of-doors. One day as the girls and I were hiking I tore my dress. I stopped at Margaret's house which, like the others, was a shack. Margaret went in to get some thread while I discreetly sat on the porch. Her mother came outside and sat with me, chatting about little things. Soon her father came and we talked for over an hour about cooperatives, the international situation, and domestic politics. If I had ever thought that people who used poor grammar and lived in shacks were ignorant I was certainly educated that day.

Having Bill, a black man, with us was a new experience for all of us. One day we decided to go to a pool in West Virginia to go swimming. On the way, someone, perhaps Bill himself, realized that he would not be allowed to swim there. At every pool we were turned down until we found a mud hole in a cow pasture. It did not look very inviting, but finally we decided if it was good enough for the cows it was good enough for us.

We were on a field trip to a mine in southern Illinois. We went down into the mine to learn from the men what the work was like. Afterward Bill and I were walking up the street together. I asked Bill why people were staring at me. He chuckled. "Don't you know?" "No." "Don't you know that a nice white girl would not walk on the street with me?" I straightened up my shoulders, took his arm, and we walked on together. Let them stare!

We went on a field trip to Arthurdale, West Virginia, a special project of Eleanor Roosevelt, knowing that she would be there that day. Each of us shook hands with her for she was very interested in what we were doing. We felt honored.

We were told that when she had lunch at the home of the mine superinten-dent, a miner's wife came to the door. The maid turned her away in disgust but quickly Mrs. Roosevelt went to the door, was very gracious to the woman and accepted her garden flowers. She was certainly a different First Lady.

At first I went to the Presbyterian Church in Dillonvale but visitors, especially our kind, were not desired. Thus with some of the others I went with the Hamil-tons to attend a Quaker Silent Meeting about thirty miles away. Sometimes some one would be moved to speak, and perhaps others would build on it. When Rufus Jones, A Quaker leader, was expected to come, all were cautioned to let the Spirit move him. It did and he was tremendous. I grew to appreciate the Quakers for their freedom from dogma, their simple living, and their social thought and action.

When the camp was over in August three of us drove to Philadelphia. I went to Springfield to find my uncle Ed Leighton, my mother's brother, his wife Mary, and their son Edward. I argued with Uncle Ed for he blamed God for all the wars. I wandered around Philadelphia on my own until after a few days my brother Walter came and took me to New York. We went to two plays, "Boy Meets Girl" and "Idiot's Delight." He took me to many of the tourist sights.

I went on to Washington, D.C. by myself, staying with Ethel Chivers who had found work there. We went to church at the Episcopal Cathedral, and went also to Mount Vernon and Arlington Cemetery. Here I felt depressed, for these men had died thinking they were ending all wars and instead we were heading for another. While Ethel was working, I took a tour of all the government buildings.

I returned to Salt Lake City by bus, going through Denver and the beautiful Berthoud Pass.

◆   ◆   ◆

The Emergency Peace Campaign took the summer of 1937. One of our Con-gressmen, looking at the world, thought we were like children fighting each other. He organized the Emergency Peace Campaign as an educational program, sending out young people into communities all over the country to educate about peace.

Five of us young women were on a team in a small town in Northern California. We had a booth at the county fair, talked in all the churches that would have us, clubs such as Rotary, etc. One day I spoke to a men's group and afterward went to the bank. The teller said "I didn't hear any Communism in that." "Did you expect to?" I asked. "Well, that is what everybody was saying." That prompted us to try to make a special effort to let people know that we were not Communists but simply people who felt that war might come again, and we did not want our country to get involved.

At first we had difficulty finding a place to live but we were able to stay in the home of a woman who had gone on vacation. Before we left, we washed her clothes, scrubbed the floors, and left it really clean. We were not sure why, but that seemed to prove that we were not Communists.

◆   ◆   ◆

My friend, Nelle Wright, a Deaconess for the Methodist Church, asked me to direct Vacation Church Schools for her during the summer of 1938. I lived at the Deaconess home when in Salt lake City, and was paid $35 per month with room and board. In each town I gathered together our students and had them help. I discovered that people expected them to know a lot more than they did, just because they had been to school at Westminster. I found it an excellent experience to know the towns our students came from.

In one church there were a number of young people, which gave me an opportunity to have a class for them at night. At the end of the school one of the teachers came to me excited, saying that this one girl, who had been so rebellious that they had almost given up on her, had now signed a statement that she was going to tithe her money. That not only made my day, it also helped my reputation.

As a Baptist, a faculty member of a Presbyterian school and now working for the Methodists, some of the pastors called me "Hash". Hash is good, I told them.

◆   ◆   ◆

The Christmas of 1938 was an exciting one. The Presbyterian mission at Ganado, Arizona, among the Navajo Indians, had a program for young people. If one paid the transportation, they paid the room and board for working. I had just enough money to pay the bus fare across the petrified forest. I arrived on Saturday night, and went to church on Sunday morning. I was surprised to find a choir of forty Indians. They gave an excellent cantata in the evening. The next day I went with a missionary nurse to some of the hogans. They were made of logs put together with sod, and had sod roofs. As we visited we found there was a hole in the roof for the smoke from the stove to escape. There was no window. In one, a mother with TB, lay with a baby on a sheepskin on the sod floor. There were at least twelve who lived in that one little home.

In the evening the Indians who were already gathering for "Kishmus" had a dance. I could watch from the window only. The next day, Christmas, they began to come in numbers, families in wagons, individuals on horseback, until there were about 300 in the yard. We served them a dinner of mutton stew, corn, rolls and coffee. The women sat on one side of the yard, the men on the other. Then they gathered closer together while the Christmas message was given by one of the Ganado doctors, interpreted by a high school graduate. Slowly, then, they formed into a line for their gifts. Each child was given toys, something to wear and candy, and each grown person received clothing. The look of gratitude repaid the missionaries for their work,

In the days remaining I did something different each day, such as helping a new librarian organize the library; typing for a missionary who was translating the New Testament into the Navaho language; and one day I worked in the gift shop. At the end of the day I was given two Navajo dolls. Later I used them so often for table decorations for world friendship banquets that I DECIDED: IF I EVER TRAVEL I WILL COLLECT DOLLS.

When I was ready to return there was an intense snow storm and I could not use my return ticket. I had to borrow enough money to go to the California border and Boulder Dam before I returned. I rode all night on the bus, had the cheapest breakfast I could find, and took a taxi to the school, leaving the driver waiting until I could go to the office and borrow enough money to pay him.

◆   ◆   ◆

The book, "Grapes of Wrath," inspired the Quakers to have a work camp near Shafter, California, in the summer of 1939. There were eleven campers, and John Way, Director. The camp consisted of tents, dilapidated cars, and a building which housed the privies and running water for washing clothes and people. We borrowed some tents, had an old shed for cooking, a tin one for holding all our stuff, including a typewriter, and we slept outside. Though we were away from the city, the fresh air which I have always associated with the country did not exist. We lived just a little way from the Shafter sewer system which was being overworked (it is cheaper to feed potatoes to hogs than to people) and every evening the extra gas was let out. On the empty lots all around were piles of oranges which were poisoned and rotting, to keep the prices up and the people out.

The men brought in a building from another town, and it was used as a community center. We helped them develop a recreational program, and some church services in which we tried to interpret our thinking—that knowing God's love leads out to helping each other.

One of the outstanding labor leaders visited us frequently. We had many conversations with him about labor policies in the wineries and other industries in the area. We visited one winery on a Sunday afternoon, and were embarrassed when our guide opened the door of a workers' room without knocking or in any way warning them. It was an indication of the way workers were treated.

At times we went into larger towns to talk to people about the migrants. Two doctors in Shafter told us that they had been dismissed from the American Medical Association because they took migrants as patients even if they could not pay. They said that a disease could start anywhere and threaten the community.

Especially on Sunday afternoon people in good cars would go by the camp to stare at the tents and the people who happened to be outside. It was called "slumming." It was very uncomfortable for all of us, as we felt we and our neighbors were being treated like monkeys.

Some of us went to churches in Shafter and found some of them not friendly. The Baptists were sure we were Communists. But the Methodists asked us to speak from the pulpit!

I wrote the following, summarizing my feelings:

> I saw God's eyes today, hurt and sad.
> Why sad, I asked, as I looked toward the crimson sky.
> Then I turned my eyes from beauty and saw the homes nearby,
> Not brick nor frame but tents I saw, and children ill clad.
>
> The men, well tanned and scorched by the sun, and lean,
> The women sweeping the tents while longing for houses with floors,
> The children, hungry, going in and out of the burlap doors—
> The migrants are His, though many may call "unclean."
>
> Oh, God, may my eyes sting with Thy tears.

When the camp was over I spent some time with Beulah in Pasadena, then on to San Francisco to attend the American Library Association meeting. I took people around Chinatown as if lived there. The World's Fair was also there, which proved fascinating.

I then went to Seattle for a short time, the first since I had left four years before. I took care of the things I had stored with Mrs. Shelton, and visited with my high school and church friends. I went to Leavenworth to see Uncle Charlie and Aunt Birdie, my father's brother and his sister who had always been good to me. They were living in a little home on a farm, which had been given to them by old friends. I marveled at Charlie, although he was blind, he was putting shingles on the outside of the little house. He had learned to do work by feel. I went back to Salt Lake City by bus.

◆   ◆   ◆

During the Christmas time of 1939 I was with the Methodists again. A deaconess in a strip mining town had started a play with the youth, and had become ill. Nelle Wright asked me to substitute for her. It was another time to see home missionary work up close and to experience the life in the towns of our students.

Inasmuch as my library degree was an undergraduate one, I thought I would like to get a Master's degree in it, and decided to spend the summer of 1940 in Columbia University. I went to New York by bus, stopping to see the Niagara

Falls. I lived in an interracial house in Greenwich Village, a cooperative, sponsored by New York University. Everybody took part in the work of keeping the house clean under the direction of the manager who was a young black student. We had a large back yard, and sometimes on hot days we ate out there. The neighbors threw things at us because we were inter-racial.

When I discussed the outline I had made for a special study for Library School, the Dean would not accept it as it was mixing two disciplines. I took two courses in Library Administration, but I did not find them different from what I had previously at the University.

One of the men in the house was about ten years younger than I and we became good friends. Recreation was cheap—five cents on the ferry to Staten Island, passing the Statue of Liberty. A group of us often went to the concert hall, paying 50 cents for standing room only, hearing classical music.

Even though I did not know what I would do the following summer, I made arrangements for work in the library of the Library School for the next summer.

After school was out I traveled in New England, staying in Youth Hostels. I often walked alone from one Hostel to another, then joined the group that would gather there. Once I was the only one to arrive at one in a small town in New Hampshire. The people who sponsored it did not allow me to stay there, but took me into their own house. We picked wild blackberries and enjoyed each other. I stayed a day longer than I had intended.

Another time a group that was in the Hostel decided to climb Mt. Washington, where Harvard has a recreation center at the top. I walked with a Jewish man and for the first time realized that not all Jews are religious, but some are secular. He talked of going to Israel in the future to help the new country which was about to be formed. This opened up a whole new vista of international understanding for me.

◆   ◆   ◆

By the fall of 1940 war had begun in Europe, and we were being drawn into it. I was too vocal in the community, speaking and debating with groups wanting to get us into war. The Communist label got attached to me. At the end of the year the College President told me he could not have a pacifist nor a Communist on the faculty. We were ready to leave, with no time to look for other work. So the years of Westminster were over without knowing what the future would hold.

WHERE NOW, LORD?

NEW YORK

Having made arrangements for work in the library of the Library School at Columbia University, I decided to go to New York to take courses in Union Theological Seminary. Our Biology Professor drove me and a woman who had been in the group with Check Ramsey, stopping in cheap motels along the way. We had fun traveling together.

I lived in the Stanley Jones Ashram in Harlem, more currently called a commune. The leader, Jay Holmes Smith, had worked with Stanley Jones in India before Independence. Because he had been very much opposed to the colonialism of the English government, he and his wife were sent home by the Methodist Mission Board. We studied various injustices in the world, India, Puerto Rico and others.

The food was terrible. The manager who planned the menus gave us soy bean mixtures all summer. He was a vegetarian who thought we should be, too. One week he was away, and I had charge of the food. Even within the budget I served coffee in the mornings and had roast beef and other meat during the week. The group loved it.

The men had a street cleared from traffic for a playground for the neighborhood children. They played games with them, teaching them to play without fighting. We women did what cooking was to be done, washed the clothes, and kept the rooms clean in spite of the many bed bugs. We did not talk from the time we went to bed until after our morning worship, which was held in a nearby tiny park.

Many people visited us, some to give talks. One woman, a professor in one of the women's colleges, talked about simple living, stressing the need for beauty.

We tried to find some beauty, but that was difficult. That idea has followed me; sometimes it has been possible, sometimes not.

I enjoyed the friendship of a man I met through the Fellowship of Reconciliation. We went to a number of places together, most notably to visit Father Divine. He was a black leader who claimed to be God which turned many people off. However, he did a great deal for the blacks who were extremely poor. He asked for money from those who had it, and loaned it to men or women who could begin a little business, barber shops, shoe repair shops, etc. If they were in debt they could not belong. If people were hungry they were invited to dinner. There was a large table with a white tablecloth and lots of silver dishes and tableware. The end of the table was reserved for Father Divine and the amount of silver was amazing. For some this was a way of letting the people eat in the way he thought rich people ate. Others saw it as diverting the money from the poor to himself. Father did not come during the two hours we waited. Did he ever appear?

In between these activities I took two courses at Union Theological Seminary and worked, often at night. Coming back on the train and stopping in Harlem was scary, but I did not pay attention to the men who gathered there, and they did not bother me. Perhaps they knew I was with the group working with their children.

Also through the FOR I met a man who was from Denver, and we also went together somewhat. He agreed with the FOR that he would pay my salary for a year if I would work with the FOR in Denver. Where to, Lord? Fall of 1941, Denver!

DENVER

I rode by car with several people going to the National FOR meeting in Minneapolis, then afterward to St. Louis. As they were going further south, I took the bus to Denver.

There was an active FOR group in Denver, mostly a family of a renowned Baptist minister. Others were seeking ways to bring about peace, including an anarchist. They arranged a place for me to live with a woman who owned her home in a poor section of the city. To be a neighbor to all those around her meant going with them to the police, appearing in court for them, and many other important services.

She introduced me to two young men who lived next door, and were struggling with the idea of cooperating in war. They had been drafted but had not known about the conscientious objector status. We went with them to their trials, and I was surprised at the hostility between the judge and the lawyer. Both men were sent to conscientious objector camps, and one of them died soon after in a fire. I lost track of the other, but after the war he became the Executive of the War Resisters League.

In the FOR group was Miriam Peterson who was working for the Denver Council of Churches. I certainly admired the woman I was living with, but nevertheless found it difficult. Miriam and I rented an apartment together.

For the first few months I spoke in churches, colleges, youth camps, and wherever anyone could arrange. I planned a gathering of all FOR members and those who were sympathetic. John Swomley, the National Executive, came out as the leader. About 80 people came. My two young men friends were thrilled as they had felt very alone.

The friend I lived with first asked me to go to the Quaker Church with her on World Communion Sunday, as she did not like to take Communion with liturgy. It was fascinating to me, as they felt no need for physical symbols. I began attending that church and a friendship with Luverne developed rapidly. He was working on a Master's in Economics as he had been a high school teacher in Iowa. He often met me at the bus or train when I returned from a trip.

Pressures to enter the war were increasing rapidly, but President Roosevelt assured us he was trying to stay out. After Hitler bombed Poland, England declared they were "Fighting for the Principle of Self-determination of Governments;" Germany, for the "Defense of the Fatherland;" France for "Peace," sending their men out "Tenderly for This Sacred Cause." Men going out tenderly to war??

Then came the Japanese assault on December 7, and everything changed. We entered the war with Japan, and in a few days Germany declared war on us. This became another "war to end all wars." Openings for talks closed up, except as people could gather a few in their homes. I traveled throughout Colorado, Wyoming, Montana, Idaho, visiting families of conscientious objectors. Most of them felt completely alone, and the communities could not understand the position their children had taken. I traveled some distance to see one family who did not dare to admit they knew who I was.

Miriam and I did not have money enough to have a telephone, so I had to use a pay phone in the hall. Sometimes I saw people pass me with frowns. One day a man came to my door and wanted to talk about some kind of insurance. Miriam was not there, and for some reason I let him in. We began to talk about the war and he sought my opinion. I told him that I thought there is nothing Christian about war. How can you love your enemy and kill him at the same time? And so on. He did not argue, but listened, then looked at my books. He then said, "Your view is founded entirely on Christian principles?" "Definitely, yes." He left, never mentioning the reason he had come. I thought, is he from the FBI? Much later I discovered the Denver section checked up on many people. A Christian basis for opposition to war was acceptable with the government as that had been worked out for the conscientious objectors.

It was difficult for young pacifists to struggle with war, and Luverne and I shared many experiences. In the spring he was called back to Iowa for registration, and was sent to a conscientious objectors camp in northern Montana. We wrote frequently.

By early 1942 I realized I was spending more money traveling than I was receiving as salary. The Denver Council of Churches needed some extra work in the office, and some help with summer camps. This gave me more income, and I could still work with the FOR. I went to two camps in the summer. One was the Stanley Jones Ashram, with Stanley Jones of India, as the leader. We had worship in a building that was like a barn. Remembering the need for beauty in such a situation, I gathered together some others, and we made paper colored windows, found a cross, brought in wild flowers, and made it look like a place of worship. The camp liked it. Stanley Jones was inspiring.

The other camp was Camp Furthest Out, run by Glen Clark. There was an emphasis on personal spirituality, but with no social outreach. We could forget about the war, and the inequalities of the economic situation. Granted—this was a beautiful spot in God's mountains, this was His beauty, but I could not forget

His migrants. Before the camp was over Dr. Clark told me "You must become selfless as I am." Become selfless maybe, but like he was? That I could not swallow.

The second Christmas Miriam and I were together she did not go back to Minneapolis, and we decided to have our own "family" Christmas. We invited all the single women we knew who were living in Denver, among them Nelle Wright whom I knew in Salt Lake City. We had breakfast in our apartment, opened our presents, then about 1:00 P.M., we went out for Christmas dinner. That was a delightful Christmas for all of us.

In the fall of 1942 I had no FOR subsidy and became a full time Christian Education Director in the Calvary Baptist Church in Denver. After I had agreed they added the church secretary's work, which was to be temporary. I was also to help with the minister's calling. I found this difficult as there was not much hospitality, especially in the apartment houses. Much more delightful was the calling in the homes of all the youth on the list, whether they attended or not. Often I was working at night with meetings of leaders or youth. The pastor called the office every morning just at 9:00 AM. to see if I was there. I found I was often working twelve hours a day, with no specified day off.

One Sunday an Oriental man, Japanese-American I thought, came to church. The woman sitting next to him moved. I saw it and tried to see him afterward, but he left so quickly I did not have the opportunity. Whenever I mentioned this to others they would say "They're just Japs." I would respond "They are God's people to me."

In spite of the hours of work, I found time to still be with the FOR. One day I met Bayard Rustin from the New York office, who was scheduled to sing on the radio the next morning. I took him to a restaurant where I knew they had Mexican waitresses and the owner was from Europe. I thought they might not object to a black person. We were served, but only after waiting some time and having a discussion with the owner. Everybody in the restaurant left in anger. From then on the FOR had luncheons there trying to help the owner know that we understood the loss of business he had.

This incident drew together a group of whites and blacks that decided to try to open the restaurants in town to black trade. We went from restaurant to restaurant waiting perhaps an hour until we were all served. After some months of this, with encouragement from the YWCA, the owners decided to treat the blacks the same as everyone else.

I had to work the evening the group went to the movie. As the blacks had to sit in the balcony, all the group went with them. The blacks were allowed to stay but all the whites were arrested and put in jail over-night. They all felt it was a real educational experience.

A renowned black woman soloist came to bring a concert, and afterward we had a reception for her in the Brown Hotel, the outstanding hotel in town. Both blacks and whites were there in formal attire. The people at the desk were cold and polite but the elevator men were not. One black business man was sent to the freight elevator. The irony of the tuxedo in the freight elevator made him laugh. This reception caused quite a stir in the newspapers. In these ways we hoped to open the way for blacks to become first-class citizens at least in Denver, about twenty years before the sit-ins.

In the late spring I asked the Board to hire a secretary so that I could have more time for the Christian Education, as that had been the plan. For some reason I never could understand I got into trouble with the minister and the Administration Board. About two months later they hired an Associate Pastor, effectively telling me my days were numbered. I quit as secretary, but stayed on for the Vacation Church School which I had planned.

The Vacation School was a real success. I had good leadership and did some training. I taught the Junior Class, an active group of about twelve. I took them down town to see the museum, and we studied the replica of the city as the first settlers came. One of them discovered "there's no church!" Together we researched and discovered that the first church was Methodist, with its first services under a tree. The class decided to act this out, and without ever writing any of it, they presented the play for the closing program. Their parents were thrilled, and truly sorry to learn that I was leaving. Where now, Lord?

TO WISCONSIN, with stops along the way

Beulah Hart Simms invited me to come to a suburb of Chicago to visit her. I realized Montana could be on the way. I visited Luverne at the conscientious-objectors camp over a weekend. We enjoyed the opportunity to be together again. I took the train on to Chicago to be with Beulah, her husband, and their two-year-old boy. I looked for work in a church but there was not much available. In order not to wear out my welcome, I went to stay with FOR friends who had a large apartment, and everyone paid the rent daily, depending on how many were there. I found temporary work with the Methodist Publishing House in the shipping department, putting prices in books. There was a very long table which was so wide I could not reach the middle. It was very dirty with accumulated years (I was sure) of dust. I asked if I could clean it and I was told to go ahead. The next day I showed up in slacks, and climbed on the table, cleaning the center and then every book on it. It took me all day. I was surprised at the attention this got from other people in the building. At the end of the day the Executive came and looked at it, and laughed, telling my boss that it was time he hired a woman!

Meanwhile I looked for a Christian Education job and found one as a Youth Worker at the First United Methodist Church in Neenah, Wisconsin. The Publishing House wanted me to stay on, but I told the boss that I wanted to send in the orders, not send them out. He seemed really sorry to have me leave.

NEENAH

Neenah, Wisconsin, was a town of about 25,000, small in my experience. A paper mill hired many of the people. There was a large Presbyterian Church, with the little United Methodist on one corner of the same block. The two churches never did anything together. I could not afford to buy a car, but as it was flat country I bought a bicycle. The pastor, Rev. Riggs, said I did not have to become a Methodist, but in view of past experiences, I was ready.

Rosalie and I shared an apartment until her boy friend returned from the service, and they were married. It was a small but beautiful service in our apartment. Rosalie and I kept in touch for many years until her death.

My work with the youth was rewarding although we did not grow significantly. I taught the Sunday School Class and helped the youth with the evening meetings. I was able to find leadership for each of the committees we organized. This brought the group really alive. I concentrated on working with individuals who needed self-esteem, for I recognized its importance from my own earlier experience. I dug out the old high-school annuals for jokes, as they were so old these youth had never heard them.

As there were many young college-age youth working in the factories I started a college-age group. They carried on without much help, except for resources and encouragement. The pastor greatly appreciated this.

By the spring of the next year I decided we should have a Vacation Church School, although it was a bit outside youth work. The church had never had one, but the teachers were enthusiastic. The pastor was skeptical, telling some that he did not think it would work. Imagine his surprise when he visited after we were well started to find all the rooms full of children, all working on projects, thoroughly involved.

The youth group had an evening service for the church about once a month. Sometimes they presented a play they had worked out, or little messages. One time they asked me to present the message and they would do the rest. After that Rev. Riggs told me he thought I should take a church on my own. I answered that women do not do that. He brushed that aside, and in a short while had persuaded the Bishop and me (after considerable prayer) that I should take a church. There were two positions open, one in the Southern District, one in the Central District, both in the West Wisconsin Conference. I went to both to preach and chose the one in Central District because it had two churches instead of four. I noticed that if a man had been looking he would have been sent, without trying out.

THE MINISTRY

KENDALL AND WILTON, WISCONSIN

Luverne and I had already drifted apart, and I realized that I would really be an "old maid." This bothered me because it seemed everybody thought you had to be married to be normal, yet I did not feel abnormal. Soon after I arrived in Kendall I realized that one can serve God whether one is married or unmarried.

The first Sunday of January, 1945, I preached my first sermon, at Wilton, then at Kendall. It was exciting for me, if not for anyone else. I had arrived the week before in Kendall by train. It had been made clear to me that Wilton had a parsonage; however it was rented, and as the church wanted the rental money I was to live in Kendall. The towns were about ten miles apart, with Kendall serving a community of 400 in town and about 1500 dairy farmers. The Wilton area was smaller.

The only place available for me to live was upstairs in the home of Mr. and Mrs. Zimmerman. He owned the Hardware Store. They and their two girls were strong Wisconsin Synod Lutherans, which helped when she defended me in the community, and when I needed to understand that church.

The Church in Kendall was Federated Methodist and Baptist. The former pastor had been a retired Methodist from another town who came only on Sundays to preach. Since he had been asking to be relieved, the church expected a change. Their agreement to have a woman was half-hearted, I found. The yearly salary was $1500 plus $100 for rent. Having been a Baptist most of my life and only recently a Methodist, I found I sometimes could help interpret one to the other.

Bill Webber had registered as a Conscientious Objector and had been sent to a camp. I kept my ears open for comments. A few people thought it was terrible, blaming his mother. Most of the people had been very fond of him as he was a strong leader among the youth and they did not resent his being in the camp instead of the military service. The youth thought people had a right to their own opinions. They quoted the Bible pro and con. Bill's stand helped me to open discussions. This was nearing the end of the long drawn-out World War II, and at least some were ready to hear a few peace sermons.

My first funeral took place about three weeks after I arrived. I had heard that Mr. Revel was ill with cancer of the liver and I went to call. The family appreciated it greatly, but others frowned. He was an alcoholic (which I had guessed). None of the family ever came to church (were they welcome?) When he died I went to the home, and I also went on the day of the funeral. Because it was snowing heavily they asked me to come with them to the church in the country to make sure they had a minister. The community was "colored" (black and white). Fortunately the minister they had asked was there. He preached a pretty good sermon. The music was terrible. The songs were mournful, sung by a man and woman, both off-key, with nasal voices, almost monotones. Everybody sobbed loudly, especially the wife and children. One song was :"Ring the Bell Softly, There is Crepe on the Door." Another: "Daddy's gone to heaven." At the grave, Mrs. Revel broke down. Mr. Smeter, the undertaker, asked me to take her back to the car. On the way home, there was a complete change of attitude, with singing and laughter. Later I asked Smitty, as we called him, if that was typical of the funerals he had. He laughed and said he had never seen another one like it.

Smitty told me about another experience he had just before this. One of the women in the church had a leg amputated because of diabetes. She was in great pain with the nerves cut. Mrs. Liersch demanded that Smitty dig up the leg and straighten it out in the box so that her leg would stop aching. He did it to please her, laughing as he did.

About this time I wrote a postcard to a friend telling her the town was "backwoodsy enough to be interesting." About two years later Mrs. Zimmerman quoted that back to me. I had no idea the postmaster read the mail!

My first wedding was that of Gerald and Ruth Ostrand, friends from Neenah. Due to Ruth's aunt's objection, because of Gerry's cleft lip, they had waited twenty years. They brought a couple as witnesses, and came to Kendall. I found flowers and made arrangements for a dinner at the hotel in Tomah. Their gratefulness continued throughout their lives. Perhaps these early experiences helped the church to accept me for the few weddings and funerals that we had.

As the area was too hilly to use the bicycle I had to buy a car. There were very few available, especially second hand ones, which was all I could afford. I found a Nash, and Mr. Liersch taught me to drive it. I had to have it repaired often, referring to it as my Nash Lemon.

I found the preaching to be a creative experience. At the very beginning I had so much wound up inside of me that I wanted to share, and I did just that. After about six weeks, I found I was dry. From that time on the Bible was the source of inspiration, using many Bible helps and related materials.

There were a dozen or more active youth. They offered prayers naturally. One year they studied the Psalms, other times they used either Methodist or Baptist materials. They created and presented a number of dramatic worship services which were appreciated by the entire community. They were very family oriented, and during the summers they held their meetings outside on their farms, with parents as well as older children. After we had worked together awhile I heard that a national youth leader was to speak in Sparta, the county seat. We filled four cars and drove to the District Youth Rally. The youth leaders, Rev. and Mrs. George Bell, were astonished. They had never heard of the town, let alone the youth group. Before long I was asked to be the Sub-district Youth Leader, and later the same for the District.

I taught the youth some folk dances. Mrs. Webber told me this was sinful. We argued for three hours because I refused to say "dancing is of the devil." The youth were enjoying it, and we simply continued.

As this church had never had a Vacation Church School, I organized one. The Sunday School teachers were very willing to try it. Having always worked where we had facilities, having none was new to me. For the teachers it meant doing with what we had. We reached many children in the area who did not come to Sunday School. The first Vacation Church School was so successful that we had one each year.

Thanksgiving came along. I thought someone might invite me for dinner, but no one from the church did. That morning Mrs. Zimmerman, discovering that I would be alone, invited me to her sister's home. I was criticized for going to a Lutheran home. I asked, "Did you prefer that I stay alone?" There was no answer. I discovered that families are strong in the country, and sometimes so much so that another person is out of place, especially, perhaps, a woman minister. Rev. and Mrs. Bell invited me to their home for Christmas, and I went there for the holidays for a number of years.

In those days there were party telephone lines. When the telephone rang you could be sure several people were listening in. One afternoon when I was calling in a home and the phone rang, the woman had her daughter listen so that she would not lose any of the news. She was the person with the nastiest gossip in town. At one time a number of us went to a testimonial meeting in a neighboring church and she talked emotionally of being saved. I wondered, saved from what? Not her tongue, for sure. I came in for a lot of that, of course.

A family moved into town who wanted to join the church as Methodists. They had been attending a Christian Church, but had never joined it. They wanted baptism by immersion, because that is what the former church had done. Three of the Baptist youth were also ready to join. They had never seen an immersion, and did not want that. As we met in the Baptist Church there was a Baptistry but it had not been used for so long that it leaked. We borrowed a stock tank from the local Hardware Store. Thus it was that we immersed seven Methodists and sprinkled three Baptists that evening.

At another time we were having a special evening service, and to help make the Baptists feel they were not being neglected, I asked a Baptist minister to come to preach. After a long sermon he led an altar call which I thought would never end. Two of the youth came forward and knelt at the altar. A number of the people were critical because I had asked him. Years later I went to preach in the church of one of those youth, Rev. Clarence Wildes. He told me it was that night when he had given his life to Christ and answered the call to the ministry. I could think of many times more comfortable for the Holy Spirit to work.

The Conference was looking for a camp ground for the Central District and I was asked to be on that committee. We traveled to a number of places before we settled on Pine Lake. We began with tents and had one building for the dining room and all other activities. A few of our youth went. While we were there the war ended. We were surprised to find that these youth had known only the depression or war in their entire lives. Our youth wanted me to ask the black student, who was one of the counselors, to come to Kendall. He was well accepted by the church, the youth leading the way.

While I was working in Chicago I had spent some time helping out in the office of the FOR. There I met Perry Saito, a Japanese American man who was not required to go to a concentration camp because he was in college. He finished college, then went to Garrett Theological Institute. One summer I asked him to bring his family and come to speak in our church. One of the families invited him to come to a neighborhood picnic held at their home. The two little Saito children were in a wagon with two of the children of the neighbors when a mother grabbed her two out of the wagon. The hostess was much embarrassed, as I was also. Perry always made a joke of such experiences.

During my last year I tried to clean up the Methodist building to make it into a youth center for the community. My youth helped a great deal, but in the end they were the only ones who could use it as the Lutherans were not allowed to join in. I knew they believed we could not pray together, but I had not realized that we could not play together. I wondered how the Lutheran pastor felt when he saw his people coming to the Baptist Church for the evening services, or go up the hill to the Sunrise Services.

One Easter a number of non-churched people came. They, like my regulars, had become almost accustomed to having a woman for a minister. I was so intent on having every thing go just right, especially the sermon, that I forgot the offering! Was the treasurer mad at me! This was the time she had expected to get the extra offering to pay the bills. I asked her and others why they did not lift up an envelope to get my attention. It was my responsibility, not theirs.

The out-point at Wilton never did accept me fully. One of the leaders told others that he listened to two women all week and he did not want to listen to another one on Sunday. When I visited in his home I realized that his wife and mother-in-law did nag him all the time. I felt sorry for him, but did not appreciate his rejection of me. I was able to live in Wilton for a month in the home of a couple who went on vacation. I thought this would help in becoming a part of the community, but it seemed to make no difference.

There was only one wedding, that of a returned service man and his long time girl friend. They went to Mauston to the former minister to be married. One woman became ill, and I spent hours at her bed-side in the hospital. Her husband remained distant, but I worked with the daughter as much as I could. When she died, a minister from Tomah was brought in, and I was not informed of the day of the funeral.

The small youth group met regularly. They were high school freshmen when I arrived, so I was with them during those growing years. They were smart and developed leadership abilities. Each of them in later years let me know that those years meant a great deal to them.

The Vacation Church School was new, but I was able to persuade enough teachers to help. We did some Bible drama, and took the Junior group to the home bound. For many there were tears, for they often felt forgotten in that church.

One family did accept me. If we had an evening meeting they did not let me return to Kendall, but had me stay with them instead.

The treasurer had a strange way of reporting the money. The year never ended at the same time, making it difficult to know exactly where we stood. Some thought him dishonest and after the second year a new treasurer was elected. When I did see the books, I thought I discovered some money missing. In order to have the new man start off right I had the books audited. The company never did give any figures, only that there was not enough money to tear the church apart. However, the former treasurer was so hurt that he left the church. I wondered if I had done the right thing but there was no going back.

A man who was a self proclaimed preacher and his family moved into town. He said loudly that the church did not have a preacher. "God cannot work through a woman" he said. He wanted to use the building, then the membership rolls, then the treasury. The money seemed to be the most important thing, for that is when the Board really pulled back, yet not supporting me either, not wanting to hurt his feelings. When I called in their home they wanted me to give a testimony. I gave one stressing God's care and love. They were disgusted because I did not stand up to give it. There were five or six in the room and I was unaware that the posture was important. All this caused quite a strain, and one day I was putting my coat in the closet when I heard a voice, clear as a bell "Keep your church steady." "With your help I will," I said. And we did. The man who followed me lived in the Wilton parsonage, and had no problem with him.

I did not talk about any of the Wilton affairs to anyone in Kendall, but sometimes Mrs. Zimmerman would hear things through the Lutheran gossip channels. She was always very supportive, and angry with them when she heard that they were not responding as she thought they should. Their daughter, Elaine, was married when Bud Cook came home from the Service and I helped serve at the reception in the garden. The Zimmermans and later the Cooks became a second family for me through the years.

The strains began to show on my health, and I asked to be moved, not being sure that this was possible for a woman. At Conference I was moved to the town of Arkansaw, also in Central District, further north.

ARKANSAW AND EAST CHAPEL, WISCONSIN

When I arrived at the parsonage in Arkansaw, July, 1948, I was met by the chairman of the parsonage committee and her husband. I discovered there was no furniture, and as I had been living in furnished rooms, I had none. There was a piano, a refrigerator, and a gas stove as well as an old kitchen range, and a coal furnace. The committee gathered a few things and I bought some second hand. As winter came early I hated to build a fire every morning, so I bought a second hand coal feeder, and also a hot water heater. The chairman thought this was luxury as she did not have running cold water. My salary at Arkansaw was $2000 per year.

East Chapel was a very small church, a break-off from the church in another town. There were about half a dozen families, and many children. By the time I left one family had ten children, and I had baptized the last four.

The people in both these churches were more responsive than the Kendall and Wilton folks had been. In Arkansaw two factions had nearly split the church with the former pastor fighting with all of them. They really did not want a woman minister, but they realized that with all their bickering they had little choice. Fred Holden, the Lay Leader, had had a year at Garrett Theological Institute, and had persuaded the others that this woman was O.K. When I realized the situation I built in a third group of leaders. The other two groups had to cooperate, or be left out. All of them proved to be loyal to the church, no matter who the pastor was.

The ministers in the towns on each side did not like the idea of a woman minister in their area. The Durand minister talked to many of my people against having a woman as pastor. Loyal as they were, they thought of all the reasons they should have one. The other came to visit, quoting scripture. Fred sent him off his farm, telling him to stay out of our parish, and to mind his own business. At the end of the Conference year both of them moved, and the ones who took their places were anxious to work together. We were all together for five years, and worked out an unofficial team ministry, helping each other at many points. One of the most successful projects was the six-week training school for lay leadership held in Durand each year.

Early in the first year I found a second hand small copier, using stencils. I made bulletins for the Sunday worship services, and also a monthly news sheet. As no one had done this before, both churches were delighted.

The District Superintendent of the Northern District had said, when I was applying, that he would not take a woman minister in his District. He was the person in charge of the fund raising for the Pension Fund which was being extended. My predecessor had refused to let the church pay anything on it. I insisted that we were honorable people and that we paid our bills. In a short while we sent the money little by little until our asking was paid. I learned later that the District Superintendent was teased by his colleagues because the pastor who was supporting his project was the woman he had refused.

As at Kendall, I enjoyed the preaching. The preparation for the sermons took about 15 to 20 hours each week, and was intellectually stimulating. Putting the ideas into my own words, and into a way the people might remember, was a challenging task. Fortunately for me the Interpreters Bible was being published during this time, and I found it invaluable, not only for the sermons, but also for the evening Bible study group.

We developed an active youth group which preferred to meet on Monday evenings. We had good meetings and developed evening worship services for the church. I visited in all their homes, both when they were home and when they were not, to understand their situations. The District Youth, too, took time. For a year one of our girls became the President. Planning several District rallies each year was good experience for the youth and for me.

Afternoons were spent calling. At first I called on all the members, then I realized there were other non-Catholics in the community. I began to go into each valley, knock on every door, looking for the Protestants. I am sure the local priest never knew how many Catholics asked me in for coffee. I bought a camera that could use slide film, and took pictures of the Protestant farms. Then I would ask one of the Methodists to have a party and invite their neighbors. I would show the slides of their farms and of them, which was a great surprise. They had never realized that the church was interested in them and in their work. There was no immediate increase in attendance, but in later years as some of these farmers retired and moved to town they attended the church, and one became the church treasurer. I simply sowed the seed and God gave the increase. I called it my "pre-evangelism".

I had thought that all slums were in the inner city but as I called I found some rural slums that astonished me. Some of the houses were shacks, extremely dirty, with vegetable peelings thick on the floor. I called more often in these homes, hoping to reach some of the young people. I am not sure I ever did, but many of the mothers wanted their children baptized, as no one from the church had paid any attention to them before.

Calling in the two little hospitals in the towns nearby was rewarding. One experience of pastoral work stands out. Phyllis was a girl of 17. She had not come to Sunday School or church, nor did her parents, but I had contacted them in my calling, and Phyllis had come to the Vacation Church School. She was diagnosed with bone cancer. I managed to get to the hospital every day no matter what else was happening. I tried to help her develop a faith which should have been growing all those years. She became quite dependent on me, and sometimes as she got worse I stayed overnight in her hospital room, substituting for her mother who could not get away from the other children and the farm work. Phyllis' funeral was the most difficult one I ever had.

Almost as soon as I arrived I started talking about a Vacation Church School for that fall. I found the teachers hesitant yet willing to try it. We scheduled it just before school started. We were all surprised at the huge turn-out. The teenagers helped with the little ones, and I had a class for them in the evening. There was no hesitation after that first year.

With many things happening that had not been there before, the church was coming alive. The opposition to a woman minister began to dissolve. Even the first Christmas it showed. It was the habit of the women's group to give the pastor a Christmas present. Imagine my surprise when they brought me a very feminine slip. They happily explained it was the first time they could give the pastor something a woman could wear!

The women's group, though small because so many women were working on the farms, was an active group, helping people in the community. I went to the men's group which met in the evening, reminding them that when they had a man he went to the women's group. At first they weren't sure about this, but when they could teach me to throw darts they began to realize it could be fun.

I have not yet mentioned Wisconsin weather. The winters were terribly cold for me. One winter at Arkansaw we had a week end of 50° below. I used a ton of coal. Another winter we had six weeks of subzero weather. I went out on the porch without a coat, for it felt warm—it had warmed up to zero. Fortunately for me the man who ran the snow plow lived across the street, so I could usually get out of the yard. Walter tried to help me keep warm. He sent me money to buy a fur coat, an electric blanket, and an electric coffee maker. All meetings during the week were held in the parsonage so as not to heat the church.

Summers were hotter than I was accustomed to. It was my habit to wear a white dress in the pulpit to make me look cool. One Sunday the women at East Chapel put a corsage of red roses on my white dress. When I got to Arkansaw even the men noticed. From that time on I had a corsage for every Sunday morning. The woman across the street took charge of them. As people had flowers they brought them to her. She made the corsage, I ironed the ribbons and returned them to her. During the winter one of the women made artificial ones. The affection this symbolized was wonderful.

About 1948 the young men began to come back from the Service, many of them to marry their home town sweethearts. They seemed to glory in the fact that a woman pastor was something different, and they did not have to get into the old routine quite so fast. I made my first attempts at pastoral counseling.

One day I fell on some cement steps and landed in the hospital for three weeks, including my birthday. My congregation brought me a whole basket of fruit and many cards. The time was long because I was released twice to take care of funerals. The concern shown was gratifying.

The National Youth Association offered to send out youth to churches to do physical work as well as work with the youth of the local church. I applied and had five wonderful young people for a week. Our group loved them. We built an outdoor fireplace so that they could have hot dogs, etc. after their summer meetings. It happened to be a time when strawberries were ripe. Families had invited us all for lunches and dinners and all had strawberries every meal. They were delicious! Since I had known about poison ivy on the Pacific Coast, and it had never bothered me, I assumed I was immune. Thus I agreed to be the one to burn it. I was not immune and I spent the remainder of the summer getting rid of it.

Red Wing, Minnesota, had a radio station which had a half hour worship service each morning. After I had been at Arkansaw awhile I was invited to take part about once in two months. I went on Monday, gave the message live, then taped it for the rest of the week. At home I would listen, and sometimes be mortified. Once I seemed to be talking about "Gaw". Afterward I went about the house saying "Goddd". I began to put the ends on all the words. Also I learned not to drop my voice at the end of a sentence. This listening to myself on the radio was better than any course in public speaking I had ever had. For one thing, it was real—it wasn't on a tape you could change at will.

Although Arkansaw was 125 miles from the Pine Lake Camp a number of our youth went to the Junior High and Senior High Camps. I would drive one group, usually the Junior Highs, and stay as a counselor. Sometimes I was a counselor for the Senior High Camp as well. One tent of six girls, one tent of six boys, and their counselors were together for study and action projects. For two years I directed the Junior High Camp. In preparation for this I was required to go to camp training for a week each year. These included nature study, folk games, and a preview of the national material. They were very helpful. It was a lot of work getting counselors and training them in the spring, but they all worked together beautifully. At camp everybody was busy and tired enough to rest when it was time. We had one problem we counselors could not seem to solve. One of the youth came up with a suggestion we were sure would not work but we tried it. It was perfect! It was this type of youth as well as adult leadership that made the whole camp experience worthwhile.

Both the Conference Director of Christian Education, Rev. Fred Smith, and his Associate, Fern Scribner, became very good friends, and I worked with them on a number of Conference projects. I got involved in Conference Youth work as well as continuing that in Central District. Training Adult Workers with Youth and Vacation Church School Teachers, helping to start the Young Adult Camp and continuing with it, and other projects, took me away from the local church for a short time now and then. However, none of the local work was cut short. At one of the Quarterly Conferences one of my parishioners objected to my being away so much. The District Superintendent answered him: "Well, would you rather have someone who is not capable?" There was complete silence. They had had enough of those.

The ministers were organized into sub-districts, and ours met each month for lunch. This was a great fellowship for me, even though I was the only woman. Also we organized an ecumenical group in the same area, including the wives. One was the minister of the Church of the Brethren. I had long wanted to attend one of their services, and after consulting with his people, he invited me. An entire dinner was served, during which everything that was done was for someone else. After dinner they washed one another's feet. I was impressed by the symbolism of the entire service.

While still at Kendall the Conference told us Approved Supplies (lay ministers) that we would have to take the Conference Course of study. As the others were men it would lead them to become members of the Conference. As women ministers could not become members, I did not take it very seriously. I knew nothing of rural sociology so decided to go to Garrett Theological Institute in Evanston, Illinois, during a summer session for a course in Rural Church Administration offered by "Rocky" Smith. I had been preaching for a year and a half and thought it was time I learned how. Thus I took a course in preaching from Dr. Irwin. Both courses were excellent. Dr. Irwin talked me into transferring my two years of Seminary credits toward the Bachelor of Divinity Degree the men received. "Rocky" Smith agreed. This was a whole new idea to me, but I decided they might be right when I found my class sermon printed in the Garrett Tower. I attended the summers of 1946 and 1947. As I moved in July of 1948 to Arkansaw I left the required regular session until the winter quarter of 1949. I left on

Sunday afternoons and returned the following Friday. During that quarter I took all the beginning health, psychological, and final preaching examinations.

It happened that Walter was having difficulty with a leg injury, and was attending an engineering college in Milwaukee, Wisconsin where the Cooks had settled. Their home became our rendezvous. We met on Sunday late afternoon, and Monday morning he left for his class and I went to my class in Evanston which began in the afternoon. After listening to my stories about the Nash Lemon he bought me a used Plymouth.

When I took the physical exam, the skin test for T.B. was made in my right arm. It was so painful I could not take notes for two weeks. After several exams the doctor found a very small spot on my lung. As it was almost the end of the semester I finished the courses, then took the x-rays and tests home to my own doctor. He simply prescribed an hour of rest each day. As everybody was afraid of T.B., I did not tell the congregation about all this.

We took a comprehensive examination instead of writing a thesis for the Bachelor of Divinity Degree. The professors would then suggest a course or two to strengthen the weak points. I was determined that I wanted to take Clinical Pastoral Education (CPE) in a hospital. In spring quarter I studied all the courses I had at Berkeley and at Garrett, and passed the exam with no requirements of further courses. In the winter quarter of 1950 I took the CPE at Mantino, Illinois, a mental hospital. This was a tremendous help to me in understanding not only the people of my congregation but in understanding myself.

I graduated from Garrett in June, 1950, with a Bachelor of Divinity Degree, with Distinction. I was the only woman in the class that year. The men became members of their various Conferences. However, being a woman, I was still an "Approved Supply". It bothered me when the woman who became my Conference Delegate could vote, but I, a full time minister, with the same training as the men, could not.

That year at the West Wisconsin Conference I was ordained as a "Local Elder", the preliminary ordination as Deacon having been done two years before. Neither of them really meant very much. When the appointments were read I heard that I was moved to another church. I was shocked, as was my Lay Delegate. The past two years had been spent getting the people to work together, and sometimes succeeding, and now I was to be moved. When I asked the District Superintendent about it he said a man had asked for my church, and as he was a member of Conference he had priority. When I got home the Administration Board of the church was meeting. They were very angry and Fred Holden called the District Superintendent who said he could do nothing about it without the approval of the Bishop who was on his way to Africa. You could almost see the sparks fly out of that telephone as Fred told him they would not let me go. The Bishop was reached, and I stayed. That brought the church together as nothing else could have done. When I talked with the man to whose church I had been assigned his Board had said: "What the hell will we do with a woman?" He had met with them until 11:00 P.M. trying to persuade them.

Twice I went to the Rural Life Conferences, one held in Minneapolis and one in the Detroit area, directed by Rev. Harold Huff, formerly one of the Sub-District ministers. These were helpful in sharing with one another the problems and solutions of the rural church. At one of these I met Fred Owen whom I had known at Berkeley. He had become a United Methodist minister, also.

The Board had specified that I had two weeks of vacation. Most of these I spent with Miriam Peterson with whom I had lived in Denver. Several years we enjoyed the Baptist Center on Green Lake, Wisconsin. We would swim, work in the craft shop, and attend the lectures and Bible studies. At other times we would take short trips.

Objections to women as ministers would come at unexpected times. I did not argue but held on to Galations 3:28, "There is no longer Jew or Greek, there is no longer slave or free, there is no longer male or female; for all of you are one in Christ Jesus." Here are the three classifications of the society of the time, and all barriers between them are erased by Jesus. Many women thought that it was the men who kept us from having their clergy rights, yet I found some of them very supportive, especially Fred Smith and Winslow Wilson. Sometimes it would be a woman who would say: "Would you want a woman Bishop?" Why not?

When I read Phillip's translation of I Corinthians 11:5 "When you preach, keep your hat on" I jumped right out of my chair. I looked it up in the King James version, and it read: "When you pray or prophesy keep your head covered." Keeping the head covered indicated it was a public meeting, even though it might be held in a home. To prophesy—that means to speak out loud and on a certain subject. To prophesy is such a religious term that we don't even think what it means. Women spoke in church!

After six years at Arkansaw I accepted the offer to work on the Conference staff, and moved to Eau Claire, Wisconsin.

The first wedding I officiated

Vacation church school teachers and youth helpers

Sherry Dale Herbst

With Minnie Pickering's father; Eula Johnson, Minnie Pickering , and her mother

At the Arkansaw church

CONFERENCE CHRISTIAN EDUCATION

WEST WISCONSIN CONFERENCE

In 1954 when Mrs. Marian Miller, who had been the Associate to the Executive Secretary of the Conference Board of Christian Education, was asked to become the Executive, she requested that I be her Associate. I accepted with the salary of $3500 per year, almost double my former one. I was not a Poor Kid any more!

Marian Zimmer, who was the Children's Worker for the Lake St. United Methodist Church, and I had a two bedroom flat above a grocery store in Eau Claire. I was gone much of the time, traveling to the churches of Northern Wisconsin, training church school teachers and youth workers. Also I was responsible for the Conference Youth Council. I was a counselor for several of the camps at Pine Lake. Marian Miller and I worked together well.

When I moved to Eau Claire I bought a new Ford as the old Plymouth did not hold up to the extensive traveling. I had a months vacation, and it was spring before I could find time to take it. A friend, Myrtle, from Arkansaw, and I drove out west as she wanted to see her sister in Bellingham. On the way we stopped at Glacier and Yellowstone Parks and Grand Coulee Dam. I took her to Bellingham, then went to Seattle to Phyllis Hoogan's home. I spent time with her and Agnes, Judy and Ethel. I went to the Queen Anne Church to visit with Dr. Richardson. In Shelton I visited with Francis and family. Myrtle and I were both happy with our trip.

Bishop Northcutt was not supportive of Mrs. Miller. Some of the ministers were critical because she spent a great deal of time in the Madison office and did not get out to the local churches. The pressures became so strong that she left at the end of the year. She was a widow with three children, and was buying a house. The man who took her place was paid a thousand dollars a year more in salary, plus a house. Consequently there was not enough money left for me to work full-time. I agreed to work-part time for just one year and take a small church part-time. The new Executive was not told this and was chagrined when he discovered it. I continued to travel, but he took over the Conference Youth. The Bishop said one man could do the work of two women.

At the Conference of that year, 1955, I was called in to see the Cabinet for the part-time appointment. The Bishop left the room. The District Superintendent told me that I was to take a small church outside of Eau Claire for the summer, and I would be appointed to a larger one in the fall when the minister went south. When, during the summer, I discovered he was not moving, I talked to the new District Superintendent who knew nothing about the arrangement. The Bishop told him I had not met with the Cabinet. Of course I had not met with him because he had walked out.

That summer I enjoyed my little church which was half-way between Eau Claire and Chippewa Falls. I thought it was important to keep it open because the population between these cities was growing and would become large enough to support it in the days to come. I was Director of the Junior High Camp at Whispering Pines, a beautiful new camp in the northern part of the State. Late in the summer Marian Zimmer moved to a church in Chicago. Soon after that I was called to be a part time Director of Christian Education at the Lake St. Church. The new educational unit was nearing completion, and this gave me the opportunity to finish some of the work I thought Marian had neglected. The church is across from the Junior High School which did not start school on Wednesday mornings until 10:00 A.M. to give the students an opportunity to attend Week Day Church Schools if they wished. For many parents of other churches it was easy to bring them at the regular time and have them attend our church school. This, plus the large Sunday School and the youth group needing help, took more than half time, but I enjoyed it.

It seemed that at the next General Conference, which was to be in April of 1956, the issue of women becoming members of the Conferences might win. Bishop Northcutt told me that he would not have a woman member in his Conference. I attended a National Christian Education meeting and met with the Executive Secretary of the Detroit Conference Board of Christian Education. With the support of his Associate, my friend Fern Scribner, he hired me quickly and agreed that I would move in the spring. Nobody specified when it was spring, so when it was convenient from the point of view of the Eau Claire church, I moved to Marquette, Michigan, in April 1956, as a Field Worker for the Marquette District.

DETROIT CONFERENCE

The few apartments were filled, and I found rooms in a home. Within a few days the District Superintendent and I were driving young people to Port Huron for a Conference youth training session. I did not expect to find ice on the road that late in the spring but my car slid and turned over. No one was injured, and the District Superintendent took the youth on to the camp. Although the car was totaled I received a good amount for it and bought a new Ford.

The General Conference met in Minneapolis soon after. I went for a few days but was not there when they discussed the question of women being members of Conference. It passed, and women were to be admitted as full members on the same basis as the men. I almost felt sorry for Bishop Northcutt who was presiding, knowing how he must have hated it.

At the meeting of the Detroit Annual Conference in June, 1956, I applied for membership. The Board of Ministerial Training talked with me, then sent me out. They argued for an hour, sometimes loudly. Finally one of them emerged and asked me if I had had the physical exam. I had not done so. He said, with anger in his voice, "I am not going to let them keep you out on a technicality." He made arrangements with a doctor to give me an examination that evening. As there were no more technicalities left the Board voted to admit me as a Deacon, which meant two years of probation. Until that year blacks belonged to an Annual Conference in the Central Jurisdiction, but now they could join another. That was a record setting Conference, as one woman and two blacks were admitted. Bishop Reed was very proud. I was admitted in full connection as an Elder in 1958. In that class was a young man from India, and the main speaker was his father. The men were ordained, but I had been ordained eight years earlier as a lay minister. For me, this was a change of status. Officially it stopped discrimination against women as ministers, but actually local churches often objected.

With a supportive Bishop, an Executive Secretary who was great to work with, and District Superintendents who had respect for women, the six years of traveling in the Upper Peninsula of Michigan were good years. We extended the Education committee to include the Missions and Evangelism committees as they were doing little by themselves. Since the Upper Peninsula is a narrow strip between Lake Superior and Lake Michigan, I found it was quite windy even in good weather. But it was beautiful. Some leaves turned gold, and some deep red, all with various shades of green mixed in. There was always one day when all was more beautiful than others. Winter came early, often in late September or October. Snow followed soon and we did not see the grass again until March or April. We had red flags on our car radio aerials so we could see each other over the snow piles on the corners. The snow plow would come each night, piling lumps of hardened snow on the edge of the driveway. As there was not room for all the cars in the one garage, mine was always out. Thus I would start an hour early, shoveling snow, and sweeping off the car before I could venture further. In spite of that I traveled a good deal.

The District Superintendent had his own way of doing things, and I did not feel free to call him on the phone and ask him questions about the District. I would go to his house for an evening to play scrabble, and inevitably we would talk shop. I could then ask him the questions I wanted to know and could answer his. After two years we had a new District Superintendent. Immediately he called me to help him with the management details for the Michigamme camp which had not been done. This set the stage for our work together. It was easy for us to call each other to discuss our work.

Some of the pastors asked me to preach when I came to visit. Then I would meet with the teachers and youth workers. Some of the men who were lay ministers could not serve Communion. They were also the ones who did not want an educational worker interfering in their church school affairs. I would be sent to those churches to serve Communion, then I could talk to the teachers while I was there. Sometimes the church school superintendent would call her teachers together for an evening meeting, and I would stay overnight with her, although that had not been planned ahead. This proved to be an effective way to get to some of the smaller churches.

The most effective program I had for the larger Sunday Schools was when I went to a church for two or three days, meeting with the teachers of each department, going over their literature with them. Invariably they would think of many things they could do with it, which had not occurred to either of us before. This took much preparation on my part, but I found it was worth it and the churches appreciated it.

The District Superintendent asked me to go to a town called Paradise in the eastern part of the Peninsula to see about a Sunday School. I found a group of both men and women anxious to begin a Methodist Sunday School, as the only one in town was too conservative for them. Each one decided what part of the work they would do. The little school grew, reaching many of the children in the town. In a short while they organized a church. It was delightful to visit them from time to time, worship in their new church, and later to see their parsonage.

Youth work, was, of course, a large part of my work. I worked with the adult workers with youth, and also with the district youth officers. We planned rallies and sometimes dramatic worship services. Each year I took some of them to the Conference training camp at the Port Huron Camp, about 550 miles, staying overnight along the way. I looked forward to these trips as much as the youth did. Also I was Conference Junior High Director, which meant some traveling down state for training programs.

Most of the summers were spent at Michigamme Camp, having helped the Deans and youth plan the programs earlier in the year. Each study group consisted of six boys and six girls, and their counselors. I sought counselors that combined college students with mature adults. We had a good craft program besides the usual swimming and ball games.

It did not take long for the Director of Christian Education of the Marquette Presbyterian Church and me to get together. If I was in town we ate Sunday dinner together at one of the restaurants. As she was the only Presbyterian education worker in that district, she had some responsibility toward it, too. Thus we had some joint church school training projects, especially for crafts and music which it was difficult for one denomination to do alone.

Each District of the Conference had its educational worker. We met with the Executive in Detroit each month. The 500 mile drive was tiring in the Ford, so I bought a Pontiac, which was the most inexpensive heavy car. In the winter I took the train which ran from Marquette to Chicago, and then I transferred to Detroit. When I could drive it and the Mackinaw bridge was not yet built, I could take a nap on the ferry, for I had already driven 200 miles. Sometimes I just watched the bridge being built or marveled at the way the ferry cut through the ice. When we used the bridge I found a place to stop for an hour's rest along the way.

Because of the experience of Christian Education in rural churches, I was asked to lead a section of a laboratory school for church school teachers which was held in a rural church. In a laboratory school teachers learn as they teach the children. In the small rural church we had what we called "organized chaos." It was noisy, but with everybody involved no one paid any attention to what the other groups were doing. It lasted two weeks, though some stayed only one. A young Lutheran minister and his wife came to this section. As an obedient wife, she let him do all the talking, but I suspected she had a lot to share. When it was being decided which class they would be in, I insisted that they break up, learn all they could, then share with each other afterward. The man did not like this at all, he wanted to be with his wife. After a week he agreed with me, and said it would change not only his teaching, but his whole ministry. He would make sure she would have an opportunity to express herself. I hoped it would work out that way.

One year we were studying the Native Americans. We had two women from the Blackfoot Indians as teachers. One of the teachers in the Junior Department insisted that we have a teepee. Our friends from the Reservation had never seen one, so did not know how to build one. When we could not dissuade her, we called in the Boy Scouts to build it. The teacher never did see the humor in it. The experience in these schools encouraged me to run short, weekend schools in the Marquette District.

Usually vacations were taken at Christmas time, as people were too busy to welcome an educational worker. Also it was deer-hunting season. The District tripled its population at that time, as people came from Detroit and other parts of the state. The women were busy getting the cottages ready and taking care of the hunters. I would catch up on correspondence and paper work, then take my month's vacation. After the first District Superintendent retired and moved to Florida I went to see them. I took a bus trip to Miami and other places. I was impressed by the Everglades especially. I was very cold most of the time. I hovered over any small heater I could find. Those who lived there thought it was warm and had the windows open all the time. I realized that in Michigan you may be cold outside, but your house was warm. In Florida it may have been warm outside, but to me the houses were cold.

MEXICO VACATION

One year I went to Mexico. I flew to Mexico City and met the tour group. We were in four touring cars, five people and the driver in each one. While we were in Mexico City I had time to visit the Methodist Church and visit with the Bishop and some of the missionaries. As we toured the city I was especially impressed by the University. One day we were invited to a home for luncheon. It was delightful, except that I was expected to drink champagne. I tried some of it to be polite, but thought it tasted like vinegar. That was my first and last of that. Also we went to a courtyard where they were enacting the posada, the drama of Mary and Joseph going to the Inn and being turned away, singing all the way. Finally they were let in. They all gathered for the breaking of the pinata. Men were controlling the rope up above, and would raise it and lower it as they wished. When I was blindfolded they let me break it. All the children came running, almost knocking me over, to get the candy.

The bull fight seemed horrible to me, but certainly not to the audience as a whole. At Our Lady of Guadalupe I saw people, mostly women, crawling on their knees for a long distance to go to the Chapel. I wondered, does God really care what our posture is when we pray. One town we visited had a large sign which said, "No Bibles Allowed." The guide said they had been having trouble with Protestants coming in. One evening we went to the beautiful dance program.

Janitzio was a very primitive town. Our guide had told us to bring candy for the children who were expecting it and ready with aprons to fill. The smell of urine on the street indicated there were no facilities. As I stood looking at the lake below, a young boy came and talked to me in very good English. He was a student in the U.N. school across the lake. He wanted to know if I was from California. When I told him Michigan, he got excited as this was the name of his province. He had not known there was a Michigan in the U.S. and it gave us a special bond.

At Acapulco I thought I would not take the tour to the bars, until one of the drivers who did not drink told me that the floor shows were worth it. At each one he told me what the non-alcoholic drink was. The shows were delightful, including the diver who dove from a high rock into the ocean below. I had seen this in pictures, and it was really exciting to see it actually done.

After the tour I went by bus to Tampico on the Gulf Coast. When we stopped for lunch flies were everywhere, but I found some bread in a screened cupboard and had a Coke. This was my first time to find a hole in the floor for a toilet. I was not much impressed by Tampico, and flew the next day to Monterey where there is a good deal of Protestant activity. I visited some missionaries and had a good time there.

◆   ◆   ◆

Several years I went to Philadelphia to visit my friend Miriam Peterson who was working for the Baptist Headquarters there. While she was in the office I roamed about the city, seeing the tourist sights. Especially I wanted to see the Liberty Bell, as I had been told that when I was two or three years old it came to Seattle, and someone sat me on it. When she wasn't working we talked and shopped.

I went to the suburb of Springfield to see my uncle, Ed Leighton, Mother's brother. This had been a second home for Walter. Jennie was very fond of him, and took him in with her own young adults, our cousins Marion and Edward. All except Jennie, were agnostics or atheists. I had good-natured arguments with Ed, who blamed God for all the wars. There were no Christmas decorations as these were considered pagan. I brought hostess gifts, not Christmas presents. One year, after Ed died, Jennie, Marion, and I were the only ones there. I went to the midnight service of the Methodist Church which Jennie attended, and bought a poinsettia. The next morning she was surprised, and explained that Ed thought anything to do with Christmas was pagan. Mother had told me that was her mother's idea, but the first year after she was married she had a Christmas tree. Then Marion told her mother that she did that, too, as she had always wanted a tree. Jennie was shocked and said that she would have liked to celebrate it more, but she knew that her word did not count much against her husband's. This was the first time since she was married that she had any Christmas.

THE WORLD COUNCIL OF CHRISTIAN EDUCATION

The experience during those six years that turned my life upside down was the trip to Tokyo for the World Council of Christian Education in 1958, after I had been in the Detroit Conference just two years. I flew to Seattle, spent a few days with my friends, and Cecelia, as Francis had died the year before, and joined a Methodist tour group. We stopped at Juneau and Anchorage on the way.

The Conference consisted of about two thousand active church workers from countries all around the world. The plenary sessions were held in a large auditorium, with all the Americans, Europeans and some of the Africans sitting about a third of the way back. The front had small chairs for the Japanese and other Asians. Lectures were in English, with some translations as needed.

We were divided into small groups, remaining in the same one throughout the Conference. Ours was chaired by a man from Ghana. I was fascinated by the ideas and ways in which the people expressed themselves. We were in Japan a little more than ten years after World War II had ended, yet I heard no lingering hatred for the Japanese. It was inspiring just to be there.

On Sunday, Betty Tennant, a missionary friend, took me to the small church where she had previously worked. After the usual greetings and hugs following the service we were walking to the train station when we saw a couple of blocks all decorated with crepe paper with many designs. Betty explained that it was the "Star Festival" in memory of two stars that fell in love but the gods would not let them be together. As we walked slowly, looking at the decorations along the street, we met an American couple coming from the opposite direction. We stopped to talk, and Betty explained the meaning to them. Suddenly we realized that we were surrounded by Japanese men, all with their cameras taking our pictures. It was a queer feeling, for usually we were the ones taking their pictures. This time it was turned around.

One afternoon Betty stopped at a wood working shop and told me these people were Christians. I bought a Madonna to hang on the wall. At dinner time I showed it to my group and in the morning we filled two taxis taking us to the store. Some bought several hundred dollars worth of beautifully carved pieces, having them shipped home. In later correspondence Betty said they thanked her profusely for making it possible, for it had been equal to a usual year's sales. Betty also told me the best shopping place for dolls and other things for gifts.

One afternoon the whole Conference was taken to one of the lovely parks in the city. I found myself walking alone along the shore of the lake. Instead of looking at the beauty or the people my mind was on the future. I thought of those

Christian leaders in my group; the star festival which became a symbol for me of the need for Christ; the wood carvers and their difficulty in making a living. The idea began to take shape, and then the DECISION: IF IT IS POSSIBLE I WILL SOMEDAY GO TO ONE OF THESE COUNTRIES AND WORK WITH SOME OF THESE WONDERFUL CHRISTIAN LEADERS.

The day after the Conference the tour group went to a resort at the foot of Mt. Fuji, but I stayed in Tokyo for a peace meeting. This had been organized by Kagawa, an outstanding Christian leader. He was a peace activist, and was horrified at Japan's militarization and war, and felt he had not done enough to stop it. Before I left for the Conference a Methodist peace group in Michigan had given me a message to read, which I read in the early afternoon. During the tea time I sat at a card table by myself, and who should come and sit there but Kagawa! I was thrilled. I don't remember any of the conversation, just that he was wonderful.

I took the bullet train to Osaka. As it was a very clear day I had a beautiful view of Mt. Fuji. I took a taxi to the hotel and when the rest of the tour came they were jealous, for they had not had a good experience at the resort, and had not been able to see Mt. Fuji. Most of the group went back home, but my schedule said Hiroshima.

I joined another Methodist group which I had arranged to meet in Osaka, and went on to Hiroshima. After the sight seeing in town of the Peace Park and the Museum the President of the Methodist College entertained us with a dinner. I sat across from two men, perhaps in their early forties, who told me that they had just returned from spending six months in Michigan with Ford, learning how to make automobiles. They were asked, what will you call your company? They spoke of several possibilities, including Toyota. The speaker for the evening was the former President of the College who told us he had been out of town the day of the bomb. As soon as he heard about it he returned home to find the school destroyed, his wife and many of his faculty boiled in the river, and most of his students either burned to death or badly injured. We had a personal look at the results of the bomb.

China was not open to tourists, as our country was afraid of Communism. In Taiwan when I visited the museum a young American woman who was working in Taipei showed me how to know good jade, and told me to buy it in Hong

Kong. I contacted one of the missionaries who took me to the Woman Society of Christian Service meeting at the summer camp. She quickly gave me a small bowl and filled it with food which was in the center of the table. Everyone else ate out of the one large bowl. There I met Gladys Aylward, called the "London Sparrow", who took children out of north China to safety. Her work was being made into a movie, The Inn of the Sixth Happiness. She was trying to sue the movie company because she did not want Ingrid Bergman playing her part. However it was so well done that I, for one, was glad she had not been successful.

This missionary contacted another and told her I would be there the next day. This one took me to a school for children, as there was no public school there. She sent me by taxi, after arguing with the driver for the price, to another missionary who was also expecting me. She showed me another school and a hospital. I was beginning to feel guilty because I was staying in such a beautiful hotel and others were living so simply. She said: "If you have it, enjoy it. If you don't have it, don't worry." I've been reminded of that advice now and then.

The shopping in Hong Kong was curtailed by the fact that if you bought anything you had to pay a dollar and sign a statement that it had not been made in mainland China. All I bought was a jade ring and earrings, and had a wool suit tailored. In Manila I met with Marian Walker who took me to visit Harris Memorial College, a school for Deaconesses. Singapore was the place one could buy Chinese things without restrictions. I bought a lamp and some figurines. Bangkok was so exotic I decided it was worth the entire extended trip. The many temples with architecture so different from anywhere else that I found them fascinating. One that attracted me was the Temple of the New Dawn. It is covered with broken china which broke in a storm on its way from China. I met my cousins, George and Rosalie Kline, for the first time. They took me to dinner and a gorgeous Thai dance. George was working for a construction company, building roads.

◆   ◆   ◆

Back home, I showed slides of my trip to the churches in the Marquette District working with the Missions Committee. Four years later I realized that it was time to move to another place. It was getting harder to find new things to present to the churches, and Harold Bremer, the Executive, was getting more difficult to work with. I wrote to the Board of Global Ministries. After a few examinations I was accepted with the work to end in June. It was some months before I knew I would be going to the Philippines.

The spring schedule in Marquette was hectic. In May I spent two weeks in an intensive group dynamics workshop. Immediately after I flew to Atlantic City for the Women's Society of Christian Service Assembly held every four years. About ten thousand women were there, and when it came time for the Communion Service, a whole group of men were brought in to serve it. I was sitting with about a dozen women pastors, and we wished that we had been asked to be included. Then I went back home for a camp counselor training session which was largely my responsibility. I then had just ten days for taking care of odds and ends and packing. Fortunately, Myrtle came from Arkansaw to help me pack. I still had to have a physical examination for the Board, and I landed in the hospital for a few days. Finally I shipped what I would take with me to the Board warehouse and saying good bye to friends in the Upper Peninsula, I drove to Albion for Annual Conference.

The Master of Divinity at Garrett.

With Bishop Reed Receiving full Clery rights 1956

THE PHILIPPINES

FIRST IMPRESSIONS

After saying goodbye to friends and colleagues at the Annual Conference in June 1962, I went immediately to Greencastle, Indiana, for a New and Furloughed Missionaries Conference. This was inspirational and being able to talk with missionaries was a big help. I discovered that older people such as I, at age 50, were needed as well as those just out of college or Seminary. As I was on a three-year term under the Women's Division, I went to the shorter seven-week training at Drew University rather than the one-year training at Stony Point. Had I or the Board any idea that the term might stretch out to almost fifteen years, it might have been a different decision. A number of denominations cooperated in this missionary training. The first section was a study of the area we were to be working in; for me it was the Philippines. Its history, geography, anthropology, and language were all new to me. The second section was the study of linguistics (preparation for learning a foreign language). The third was a study of the church in the world, including how to deal with Communism and other issues. Through all of this was stressed the place of the Gospel.

The freighter I was to take to Manila came to New York and my baggage I had shipped to the warehouse was put on it. I met up with it in Los Angeles. In between I flew to Seattle and stayed with Phyllis Hoogan. I was anxious to spend some time at the World's Fair as I remembered how much the 1909 fair had meant to Mother. Each day I went to it with different friends, thus being able to visit and see the Fair at the same time. I loved the view from the top of the Space Needle. When I visited the Philippine Exhibition I met the Methodist Christian Education Executive for the Philippines with whom I would be working. This was an excellent contact even before reaching Manila.

Los Angeles was the next stop, with a day spent with my aunt, Ollie, Mother's sister. I proudly drove her white Cadillac to Knotts Berry Farm for a wonderful chicken dinner. I talked to my cousin, Claudia, on the phone.

As I boarded the freighter I found that there were two other passengers, both United Methodist missionaries, one going to Hong Kong, the other, Adair Myer, a Deaconess going to Manila for one year. The trip was very slow, seventeen days without stopping anywhere. The accommodations were luxurious, with air conditioned rooms and lounge, and eating at the Captain's table. The bar was quickly closed and a large bowl of delicious fruit was on the table each evening. We talked and read and swam in the pool and got excited seeing the flying fish. Often the Captain would let us on the bridge. We had heard vaguely that we were supposed to buy the Captain a drink the last night but we forgot about it. Many years later I heard from someone who had been to an Elderhostel that a man who had been a Chief Engineer was telling the story about three missionaries that didn't even buy the Captain a drink! I nearly shouted for I was one of those! He is still laughing about it!

As we approached Manila we changed course to avoid the worst of a typhoon. I awoke at night hearing the engine pounding very slowly. We seemed to be tossing here and there. I wondered if we would sink. In the morning the Chief Engineer was not at breakfast as he had been up all night keeping the ship afloat. The passage we entered was more shallow than they expected which took constant vigilance. We reached Manila thanks to much hard work on the part of the crew.

The group of missionaries who met Adair and me included Marion Walker whom I had met on my previous trip. When one of them heard that my name was Marion he said "Not another one!" I soon discovered that there were two others as well. When we arrived at the Social Center where we would be living, we found the Filipinos to be delightful—not at all the cool, calm exterior stereotype we had of Orientals. These were outgoing and friendly. We loved them immediately.

Manila itself was a busy city of about three million, with another three million in the suburbs, all a combination of old and modern. Modern busses, recent model cars, hundreds of "jeepneys" (jeeps left from World War II) which hold ten people and were used as busses, the horse drawn carriages, and the bicycles with a cab side for two, all mixed together in the traffic.

The Social Center where Adair and I lived the first year is one of our chief Methodist projects. There is a dormitory for about one hundred women students who attend one of the four large privately-owned Universities in the area. A beautiful little chapel with bamboo seats and bamboo altar and cross provide a fitting chapel setting for the dormitory girls at 6:00 A.M. and for services on Sunday. Madelyn Klepper was the person in charge. She left soon for a year in the States, and upon her return stayed there until she retired. Then it was taken over by a Filipina who did much more personal work in the poor areas surrounding the Center.

The Harris Memorial College trains Deaconesses. They were on a very busy corner of Taft Avenue where there was much traffic made worse by the constant honking for the vehicle in front to get out of the way. There was a large building for classes and a dormitory, and a house where the women missionaries lived. In the back was a building for the Filipina housekeepers. Later it moved to a suburb, with new buildings built by the United Methodist Women. One of the missionaries sent money for a building after she retired. The former buildings are still owned by Harris, but the large one has been changed to house small businesses.

The Philippine Christian College is on Taft Avenue, with the traffic noise, however back a little ways from the street. This is an excellent small college for the Protestant students. It is run by the Methodist Church and the United Church of Christ, which includes all the other main-line Protestants (UCCP). Several sections moved outside of Manila to the Seminary campus giving them more room for increased enrollment in the city. When the missionaries left they were replaced by well-trained Filipino professors.

Mary Johnston Hospital is another fine project. It is a modern hospital, staffed entirely by Filipinos. Founded by a missionary who placed it in the midst of the slums, it has at least a third of the patients who cannot pay for its services. Nurses are trained in an adjoining building. The Philippines trains so many doctors and nurses that they come to the United States to work. There has been a move in recent years to give them advantages if they go to the rural areas where they are badly needed.

After Adair and I had been in Manila about two weeks, one of the missionaries decided we should go out to the Provinces. One of the missionaries took us in his jeep until we reached a parsonage family, and he asked them to keep us for a couple of days before sending us back to Manila. What an introduction that was! They did not know we were coming and they had to house and feed two new missionaries. The Pastor and his wife were gracious, as if it were no problem to take us in. There was a Deaconess living with them, and two children and a "helper," as the maid is called. I thought the fish soup was good until I reached to the bottom of the bowl and began to spoon up the scales. That did something to my appetite, but I kept a straight face. At night the two of us slept on the one bed in the house, with no mattress, just a mat made of grass on the wood base. There was a mosquito netting which protected a couple of mosquitoes until morning. About four o'clock both Adair and I woke up, thinking we would get up but discovered that all of the women in the household were sleeping on the floor of the same room. We would have had to walk over them to get to the comfort room, as the bathroom is called. We decided we did not need to get up. The Deaconess entertained us for two days introducing us to many aspects of life in a small town. With instructions from our host we found our way back to Manila. We took a bus which had to stop on one side of the bridge which had been washed out by the typhoon. There was a narrow temporary bridge large enough for jeeps and walking. On the other side was a bus waiting to take us to Manila. That experience so early in my time there was immeasurable in making me independent for future traveling.

A few months later one of the missionaries took me to the town where Marion Walker worked. She had found a house to start a school for children in the mountain area. There was an artesian well where the people not only drew water, but also urinated. Doctors from Mary Johnson went every two weeks by bus to heal them and also teach them cleanliness. They made latrines and realized they never did succeed fully, for the people used them only when the doctors were there. The men constructed a little church, and the day I was there some of them were carving a beautiful door. Their reaction to a church that cared about their whole life was beyond expectations. After she retired Marion went back to that town and stayed, with the girls she loved taking care of her until she died.

I had a strange experience when I went to the bank to deposit my first check. At the missionary training the amount of salary we would receive was very carefully avoided because it was based on the cost of living in the various fields. I looked at my check and suddenly became aware that it was fifty dollars more than the one I had been receiving in the Detroit Conference, but this one was my pay for three months! Of course I realized that housing and an old jeep were furnished. Would I be a Poor Kid again? If so, I could manage it this time.

My first year was spent in Language School. Usually those on a short term did not study the language but for some reason I was sent to it. I studied Tagalog, the language used in the Manila area. There are about 75 dialects, but almost every one knows one of three trade languages: Tagalog, Ilicano in the north, and Cebuano in the south. Tagalog is the best known, and a kind of Filipino language has been developed based on it. Whether every one uses it, I am not sure, but it was used in the Manila area.

Learning a new language was difficult for me, perhaps because I was older. Prefixes and suffixes are added to a root word, so very quickly you have to put it all together. I found religious terms especially difficult, yet needed. Besides the school I tried various things: attending a Tagalog Sunday School Class, Tagalog movies (very violent), T.V. shows (also violent), radio programs, comic books and readers for elementary school children. I entered into conversations with the girls at the Center and with people at the Central Market, near the Center. One lady who sold bedding especially enjoyed helping me learn what phrases mean and how to bargain.

Some experiences made me wonder about the need to learn. Two experiences especially contributed to that. One was with a youth group who were speaking Tagalog, while I struggled to understand them. Suddenly they began to speak in English, not for my benefit, they said, but to be able to better express what they were trying to say. Another time I was out on a side road which I thought was far from a town. I went to a little shop and in Tagalog asked for what I wanted. The clerk replied, "Say it in English, please."

Immediately after Christmas the first year, I drove my old Jeep station wagon with five other missionaries to Baguio, known as the "Summer Capital." As the road is good only in parts, and the mountain climb is quite steep at the end, to an altitude of about 2000 feet, I really wished for the Pontiac. We attended a Conference on Philippine Culture for both Catholic and Protestant missionaries. This was so helpful that I went almost every year. Our Board owned a cabin where we could stay free. Near it was an Episcopal School and weaving center where we went to watch the women sit on a pillow on the floor and weave. I bought many gifts there through the years, and some for myself.

The first year, though, three of us went on into the mountains by bus. An Episcopal missionary whom we met at the Conference invited us to visit his town. We stayed with delightful missionaries. The Igorot women wear colorful skirts, with a sash tied in back, and blouses, all made of hand-woven cotton. The men wear simply a "G-string" or loin cloth. We saw many with shirts as this is "cold weather," but no pants. We went to see some burial caves where non-Christians bury their dead. The very short coffins at the mouth of the cave housed the dead person completely doubled over. That was to save room, our host said.

About the time Language School was over, Adair returned to the States and Madelyn was back at the Center. I moved to San Fernando, Pampango, a town about 30 miles north of Manila, to live at Edna Thomas Hall. My work was with the Middle Philippines Annual Conference, consisting of six provinces. I spent a month on each District, working closely with the District Deaconess. The larger churches have Deaconesses who have been well trained in Christian Education at Harris. My emphasis was to help the smaller churches with their Sunday Schools and Youth Fellowships, taking the District Deaconess with me. In some cases we could have a group together for training; in others, the churches were too scattered. The problems were much like those in the Upper Peninsula—little money, nothing to work with, and a minimum of leadership.

One Province stretched out on one road along the China Sea plus some mountains on the other side. There was the city with the Navy Base and its 1700 prostitutes to "service" them, as the Navy put it. There were many children on the streets with strange combinations of hair and eyes. They were ignored by the church. There was one large church; the others all small. I went along the road, visiting each church on a Sunday morning, and I was told later that I was the only missionary who had visited the church at the end of the road.

At Edna Thomas Hall we continued the month-long training school for Church School teachers begun by my predecessors. In all the churches it was the high school students who were the teachers, as no adult thought it was essential. The dormitory upstairs was large enough to house the 75 students and the downstairs had tables enough for feeding them. My helper and another woman did all the cooking on our stove heated by small pieces of wood and straw. One disconcerting factor was that someone came in the day before the teachers arrived and cut down all the bananas in our yard which were just ripe enough to eat, and which we were counting on for supplementary food. The teachers were disappointed, but they accepted it far better than I did (though inwardly).

We had three classes. For the third year we introduced a Laboratory School. There were so many different dialects that most of the teachers would not be able to speak the language of the children at the Hall. We moved the Laboratory School 15 miles away so the teachers and children could understand one another. The children near the Hall were in the first two classes. Finding Deaconesses who could teach both the students and the teachers at the same time was difficult. One, Afri, did an excellent job. In spite of its many problems I thought the whole school went well.

Those first few years were difficult, traveling much of the time, staying in homes. When I tried to wash up at night after a day of perspiration, there was usually no water. On one trip I had one basin of water in four days. No one told me that every morning one took a bath by pouring a can of water over oneself. This was found in a little room off the porch, called the "bathroom". It was difficult to sleep on the floor, but usually there were two pillows, and I used one as a mattress for the upper part of my body. It worked quite well if I didn't move around too much. I never learned to keep mosquitoes out of the net; I usually woke up with one or two. The houses were on stilts, because when the rains came the whole yard was full of water. The toilet was a hole in the floor, with the animals underneath. I was awkward at squatting. No one told me, either, that if there were a number of people in the house the women get up early, before the men. The men go out to the bushes. The floors are split bamboo. The first time I went into one I did not take my shoes off before I climbed the ladder and my small high heels caught the floor with every step.

Only once in awhile did I eat a meal with the family. Sometimes the man of the house and I ate together, then the wife and children would eat what was left which was the traditional way. Or sometimes the hostess would put me in a room with a table, and bring my food to me. I ate by myself then. The family would be eating in the kitchen. I could eat with just the large spoon, and I had learned to eat with my fingers but I did not know how to bridge the gap. I often left a small package of coffee behind, as direct hostess gifts were not acceptable. On one trip two Deaconesses and I had taken a half day's trip by bus over the mountains to a little town to train teachers for a Vacation Church School. We bought food for the minister's family as well as for ourselves, but we never ate with them. I was not sure if it was a sense of social distance, or if they were afraid I would criticize them. However, most of the ministers ate as one family and I ate with them.

Rice was eaten three times a day. They ate a great deal of fish, much of it dried. If it was served whole, the head was left on. It was hard for Americans to see this, but I was told it was the most delicious part of the fish. Much of the food was served lukewarm. "Cold" food meant left over. I often would put the soup on my rice, as I did not like the salty fish sauce they used on it. There were various soups, like the fish soup we discovered on our first time out of Manila. There was a soup with greens and whole large shrimp, shell and all. Or one with a little meat and greens which tastes almost soured, but then you decided it had vinegar in it. They ate a very tiny shrimp, which they put into their mouths whole, shell, eyes and all, chewed it and spit out the shell. The people we knew could afford very little meat, perhaps a fourth of a pound for a family of 8. In Manila we lived close to Central Market, and when I saw the meat dropped in the gutter, then hung up to be sold, or all the flies, I early learned where the American meat market was.

Christmas was always a fascinating time. Early in December carolers were everywhere, ragged, little children, going from door to door and singing Merry Christmas—for money. Everywhere one went adults as well as children ask for Merry Christmas. If you had to stop for a police check, the policeman would say "Merry Christmas?" I thought I could never use those words again in the American sense.

The decorations were beautiful. Every house had a large star made of crepe paper and cellophane. Even the most unattractive street became beautiful. Christmas trees were coffee trees with all the leaves taken off and painted white. Formerly we could get capis shells free and we made ornaments. One could do almost anything with them, punch holes, glue, decorate with whatever was available. Later they were used commercially and we could no longer get them.

Both Catholic and Protestant churches had services for nine days. The Catholic churches also had much activity with sales in the church yard and just outside it, along the road, were temporary sheds for gambling.

The youth had their "Christmas Institutes," which correspond to our summer camps, immediately after Christmas. The first year I went as a counselor. It was typical of conferences, with the dining room roof made of grasses put up just for that time, with rough tables and benches; the cooking was done on a few rocks outside. I was surprised at the ability of the cooks to use such meager equipment for 75 youth and leaders. There were some fine ministers who inspired us all.

One night we went up to the top of a high hill and after considerable discussion we had a worship service. In the midst of it we noticed it was getting dark and realized there was an eclipse of the moon. Dark! Not a light of any kind anywhere. We couldn't see each other so we reached for the hands nearest us, hoping we didn't leave anyone out. We were almost breathless. As we began to have a little light again, we sang softly, marveling in a new way about God's creation.

Easter had its own activities. The Catholics went to church on Good Friday as well as Easter morning. The Protestants gathered in Manila for a service in the park at 6:30 A.M. with about 10,000 attending. There was no increase in attendance at the morning services as we have in the U.S. Being a Protestant meant more than once-a-year attendance.

The first year we went to see the "flagellantes", as we were told we would never want to go to see them later, which was true. For penance men were in the street, beating themselves on the back until the blood ran. Sometimes they would call on a friend to help them; he would beat them until they fell to the ground. We wanted to call out to them Paul's message that salvation is by faith.

The procession I found so fascinating that I went a number of times was the "Black Nazarene". The church at the Quiapo corner burned in the 1700s, and the only thing that was saved was the statue of Jesus, which was completely black. This was a celebration remembering that day. It was held the Monday of Holy Week for four hours. All streets in the Quiapo area were blocked off. The statue of a black Jesus was carried out of this church drawn by several hundred men pulling it by ropes. On the base of the statue were one or two men protecting it. All of the men wore towels around their necks, which those closest to the statue would hand to one of the men who would touch the statue with it and hand it back. Sometimes one would try to climb on the base and be beaten down. They would fight to get closer to the statue. Sometimes as I just stood watching, a well-dressed man would talk to me and tell me that if their towel could touch the statue it would bring them good luck and good health for the next year. Then followed the statue of Mary, other religious statues, then lots of advertising ones. There were thousands of people in the streets watching.

The last time I went I took a friend and we walked down a street thinking that we would be able to see it better. Two men came to us and told us that the procession was going to come down that street and to follow them. We did until a young woman opened a gate and said "Come in, you will get killed." We followed her upstairs to a family who made room for us at the window. Just then we saw the statue turning the corner and coming where we had been. There was no room for anyone else in the whole block. We had a wonderful view from above, watching the men protect the statue, often kicking someone off who was trying to get on the base, now and then a fight ensued as someone tried to move up in the line. We were grateful for the hospitality of that family.

Living near Central Market gave me a fascination for all of the markets. I found out many things about the people, their crafts, the embroidery, the handwoven materials and the wood carving, the Christmas stars in Manila, and many other things. It was a wonderful place to watch the people while shopping. I went to the market in every town, and, if possible, in every country I visited.

Typhoon Dading gave us a close call. Most of our trees were uprooted, as were the neighbors'. Roofs were being blown off the neighbors' houses and they came to us for shelter. All we could offer them were the tables downstairs because the floor was covered with water. I made lots of coffee and took it to them. That was all I had. Then I disconnected the gas tank. Three of the teachers I had been working with were at the apartment. Two of them had been sleeping outside on the porch, but became so frightened they came inside. After awhile one of them decided she wanted to go back to the porch to get her clothes which were hanging in my closet. As she was slowly winding up her long hair I held the door open for her. Suddenly a tree from the next yard crashed onto our porch, coming right toward the door. The porch was torn off the house and pushed fifteen feet into the yard. We were breathless. In only a few minutes we would have been on the porch. What would have happened to us? Part of our roofing was torn off with water pouring into the dormitory sections of the building. By morning the only dry spot was my little living room. Almost everything was pushed into that room. The girls left for their homes and in a few days I was assigned to substitute for Dr. Ocompo, teaching Christian Education at the Union Theological Seminary in Das Marinas, Cavite.

UNION THEOLOGICAL SEMINARY

Dr. Pat Ocompo, Professor of Christian Education, was on a lecture tour in the U.S. under the Womens' Society of Christian Service. I taught the courses she had projected. While I was there Dr. Georgia Harkness and her friend Verna Miller stopped there on a world tour. Dr. Harkness had taught one summer session when it was still on Taft Avenue and she was anxious to see the new campus. I invited the faculty for lunch with them. She had been my advisor thirteen years before at Garrett. The bowl of fresh salad vegetables somehow seemed to stay at her end of the table for she said they were the first ones she had on the entire trip. Needless to say we had a grand time filling in the intervening years.

When Dr. Ocompo returned she wanted to stay in Manila, as her home was there and also an opening for her at the Christian College. Expecting this, the Bishop and Dr. Guansing, President of the Seminary, asked me to return to the Seminary to teach Christian Education. I readily agreed, and began in December, 1964.

This was a beautiful campus about 20 miles outside Manila and in its second year outside of the city. It was half-way up a hill, breezier than Manila, and thus much cooler. The buildings were one story, made of cement block. Not all the buildings had been built at that time. The faculty houses were large enough for a family. As there were both American and Philippino faculty, the houses were intermingled. About 200 mango trees gave the campus shade.

The Seminary was begun in 1907 by the Methodist and Presbyterian Churches. Since that time the entire United Church of Christ supported it. There were about 90 students, a few from other countries of Asia, Africa and Europe, sponsored by the World Council of Churches.

Four degrees were offered. For those who had completed two years of college the primary one was the Bachelor of Theology; a smaller number were in the Bachelor of Christian Education, and the Bachelor of Sacred Music. For those who had four years of college the Bachelor of Divinity was awarded. This program grew fast and out-stripped the others and changed later to the Master of Divinity.

Faculty of Union Theological Seminary in Manila 1972

Accompaning Kindergartners to park in Manila.

A Christian education class

The Library

The Chapel

Soon after I arrived I was told, not by the President, but by a faculty member who had been on furlough, that a Christian Education Professor from California was coming to teach the second semester. Of course he had thought Dr. Ocompo would be there, not me. He would be embarrassed to tell her not to come, so I agreed. I wrote to the woman suggesting she teach what she wanted to, and I would teach other courses. This worked out well. I had not thought about teaching a course on group work, and she gave me some good ideas. In some things I was amused. She took the girls to the market to buy different colored seeds for some crafts. To the market for seeds??? These girls would have found them on bushes and flowers. I was glad I had worked with the girls in the barrios before I went to teach, as it gave me insights I might not have had otherwise.

It was hard for me to realize that missionaries on furlough would ask Americans to come when we already had Filipinos doing the work. Besides the Christian Education woman being asked, a librarian came also, even though a Filipino librarian was on the staff. Jeannette Newhall had just retired as Librarian from the Boston University School of Theology. She joined me in a nice house. A new library was under way and Jeannette spent all of her time that year planning and working with the builders. The Filipino librarian worked in the Library. The next year the Filipina left, making some excuse to the general public. It was good Jeannette was there for the building, although that was not the intention of the missionary. It seemed that these men thought the Filipinos were inferior. Perhaps it was colonialism left among some missionaries.

I loved to take visitors to the top of the hill to Lake Taal, admiring the view of the lake and the island with its volcano. People were often a bit frightened when we told them that it was an active volcano. "But, never mind," we would say, "there is no danger. It has not erupted for more than 50 years." Little did I realize that one day I would be standing in that same spot watching that same volcano spout black volcanic rock and white steam, an exciting, magnificent sight. I was awakened by the thunder and lightning which I thought was the strangest storm I had ever known. Early in the morning we saw a cloud which resembled the pictures of those caused by the bomb. If the wind had been in the opposite direction our campus would have been covered. The entire school went to see the spectacle. As we watched we realized that hundreds were trapped and hundreds more were drowned by a tidal wave as they fled in small boats. Within a short while cars were on the way again, this time with clothes, food and money for the victims. Truly Taal was awesome and beautiful and horrible all at once.

I found the teaching of Christian Education challenging. It was quite different to teach a whole semester than it was in the short term workshops I had been doing. I enjoyed having one or two subjects rather than jumping from one subject to another. I enjoyed the students and learned a great deal from them. I was one of the few without a Doctor's Degree, and began to work on one, taking classes at Philippine Woman's College which was accredited at Columbia University. A major problem I found was that the reading was all American material, and I tried to translate it into Filipino culture. I found a few of the students also trying this and we shared ideas with each other. I learned that one had to have two complete terms (that is, eight years) left in service if the Board would pay for the Doctor's Degree. If I finished it at all, it would be when I retired. I decided it was impractical. I studied all I could for the course in Developmental Psychology, especially trying to find all the Filipino materials available. I taught that course to all the first-year students, no matter what the degree. The papers they wrote for me at mid-term in which I asked them about their own childhood and youth were extremely helpful.

During Jeannette's second year I worked with her in the library now and then. I helped with some of the cataloguing which was new to me, for we used the system of Union Theological Seminary in New York. We were having difficulty cat-aloguing books about the Philippines. It happened that Jeannette knew the cataloguer for that Seminary and asked her to come and help us. Ruth Eisenhart came then, for her month's vacation, living with us and working on the catalogu-ing system.

Ruth and Jeannette left before school was out and went to various Asian Sem-inaries, helping the librarians. Before my three-year term was over the Seminary asked me to return after a year's furlough and I was enjoying it so much I agreed. This took considerable paperwork between the Seminary and the Board of Glo-bal Ministries, and all agreed that I would become a full time missionary. I stayed until after graduation to begin the furlough.

THE FIRST FURLOUGH, 1966

I met Ruth and Jeannette at the Missionary Guest House in Bangkok, Thailand. Former faculty and students of Boston University School of Theology seemed to be everywhere, and Jeannette could call on them for information and sight-see-ing. In Thailand a former Boston University faculty member had been in Bangkok many years. As she took us to the temples other guides would some-times come close and listen. She admitted that she had written the guide books and they all knew her special knowledge. We went to a dance program, which was so different and so beautiful that it is hard to describe. Every movement of the head, fingers or feet mean something in their culture. The doll I bought expresses it slightly.

We went to Calcutta, India. We found we were staying in the best hotel, and we felt guilty. As we were registering, Jeannette saw a Quaker leader she knew and talked with him about it. He reassured us, as the only other option was in the slums, and he thought it would be unwise for him or for us to be there as tourists. I was impressed by the men who carried our luggage on their heads. We stayed only one day, then we went on to New Delhi.

We discovered the International YWCA was excellent, inexpensive housing. We went by very crowded train to see the Taj Mahal. One has to see it to know its beauty. We went to the Red Fort, from which you can see the Taj at a differ-ent angle, still gorgeous. We went to all the temples, but it was Gandhi's burial place that inspired us. Its simplicity matched that of his life.

When we stopped in Beirut, Lebanon, to change planes for Cairo, there was a change of schedule and we did not leave until evening. People were scattered to the various hotels and we missionaries plus those from Burma were put in the Phoenician Hotel with its Oriental splendor. We bathed, rested, walked around the town and walked to the American School. I bought a doll in the gift shop. Those free meals were absolutely delicious. When, years later, there was a civil war and I saw a picture of that hotel being burned I was devastated.

In Cairo Jeannette's student took us to the Sphinx and the pyramids. I was glad we went by car, not by camel. I went to the bottom of one of the pyramids and found nothing there, as it had been robbed through the years. We spent the several days remaining in the wonderful museum, learning about the people and their history.

We flew to Ammon, Jordan, then to East Jerusalem. We stayed in a beautiful guest house of St. George Episcopal Church. All the rooms opened out to a garden full of flowers. It is a Palestinian Church and had guides ready to take us on tours. Most outstanding was Qumran where the village of the Essenes was being reconstructed. I went into the Red Sea, sitting in it and talking with others. Our Palestinian guide took us into the Dome of the Rock, as beautiful inside as it is outside.

One evening I went with a Canon of the Church, meeting at an Eastern Orthodox Church, one of the two rooms which might have been the place of the Last Super. We walked along the Via Delorosa to the building where Peter was supposed to have denied Jesus. We walked up the Kidron Valley, stopping for Scripture and prayer all the way. At the Mount of Olives we spent some time in prayer. We returned quietly to the starting point. For me this was the high point of the whole trip to Israel, and I was sorry the others had missed it.

We crossed into Jerusalem and went to the usual sights. One day as we were walking up a street we heard shouting below us. With others we sought shelter in a doorway, while these men came up the street, shouting full voice. We asked what they were saying, and we were told "We'll drive you to the sea!" These were Palestinians telling the Jews that they were not wanted, and threatening violence. The people we talked to told us of violent incidents in many places. For a people who believe in "an eye for an eye and a tooth for a tooth," we worried about what might happen in the future.

We took a tour out of Tel Aviv to Tiberias where we stayed overnight, with 120° weather along the way. In Capernium and Nazareth we remembered our Scriptures. In a Kibbutz almost at the Lebanon border we encountered lots of propaganda for Israel. Along the way we saw villages for Bedoins and were told how well off they are which we questioned.

Back to Tel Aviv and on to Athens: The Acropolis came first, of course. With the directions we wandered about trying to figure it all out. In the market I bought a little Greek Orthodox Priest. We went on to Corinth, and as we stood where Paul preached we quoted to each other bits of his letters. Ruth left us in Athens as she had to get back to work in New York. She had been a wonderful companion.

In Rome we stayed in a guest house run by nuns from Belgium. They admitted Protestants only, as they said there were many places for Catholics to stay, but very few for Protestants. One was an historian who took those of us staying there on tours of the city. We visited the places where the tours go. It was the catacombs where it was great to have a guide who had studied their history. She pointed out a place where archeologists are finding an old Roman temple from before Christian days. She also took us to the Papal Gardens. There was no commercial tour but she was allowed to take visitors on Wednesdays. We were fortunate to be there on the right day. The gardens were formal and beautiful. As it was summer and the Pope was away, she took us into his apartment, and we looked out the window where he gave his blessings. We blessed the whole world. One morning early we walked to the Vatican and looked around for ourselves. In all the chapels priests were saying Mass, most with very few worshippers. Most amusing to us was the young priest who was feverishly looking for a place to say Mass. Later in the day we joined others in an organized tour and marveled at the Sistine Chapel.

Both Jeannette and I had read a biography of Michelangelo, so in Florence we made his work our focus. We went to all his sculptures. I loved the "David." As I went around it and looked at the carving of all those muscles, especially on the back, and the detail of the facial expression, I thought it was magnificent. In the market I bought a small replica of it.

In Paris we were on the left side of the river. As we walked over I was impressed by the art work along the sides of the river, but also the chalk work on the bridge itself. I hated to walk on it, but it did not matter to the artists who kept right on painting. This was the bridge closest to Notre Dame which thrilled us. We also found La Chappelle, a small cathedral which had the most beautiful stained glass windows I had ever seen. It was hard to find as it was inside a police compound. Fortunately Jeannette had received a card from one of her former faculty members telling us where to find it.

In London Jeannette spent most of her time with the editor of a book she had written for Libraries of Theological Seminaries. I wandered to all the usual places. In the Museum I was especially disturbed by the carvings belonging to the Parthenon. They seemed so out of place in London, as did the Rosetta Stone. I wondered why London does not return them.

When we arrived in New York, Jeannette went home to Boston, and I went to Ann Arbor for Annual Conference. Then I spent a little time in the Upper Peninsula with friends.

At the request of the Board of Global Ministries, I flew to Louisville, Kentucky where the Board was meeting. Now that the Seminary wanted me to return, and it was not a Women's Division Project, I was being transferred to the General Board and also commissioned as a full-time missionary. This was a stirring moment for me, corresponding to the acceptance into the Conference. It also involves such things as pension and health insurance. From there I went to New York for Summer Session.

At Union Theological Seminary I took three courses: one in Administration of Theological Libraries, for I had been warned that on my return I would be in charge of the library. The second was in Children's Work. As I had been teaching a course in this, I thought taking one would give me ideas. Instead I found the teacher taught the same material, but I was very critical of the way she did it and I was bored. The third was in Pastoral Psychology. This built on my previous training and was very helpful. I was dismayed one day when the professor of the Children's Work class cut me off when I was giving a report, and bringing some insights from the psychology class. She said "We don't know about that." To me it was elementary in the other class. I had heard about a lack of communication between disciplines, but this one I ran into head-on.

After Summer Session I wandered a bit, visiting friends. While speaking to a youth group in Washington, D.C., I met a woman who lived four blocks from the Capitol. She invited me to stay with her and her roommate. They took some money for meals, but none for the room. I spent several days there while I visited the Smithsonian Institute.

When it was time for fall semester to start at Columbia University, I returned to New York and had the same apartment at Union that I had in the summer. Again I took three classes, from three of the Colleges. One was at Columbia from Margaret Mead, "Anthropology". This was fascinating, and just having a class from her was wonderful. Although her work had been done some years before, she had kept up with the times and was not out of date. A class at Union Seminary was "The Gospel and Asian Revolution" from M.M. Thomas. He was an Indian professor who had visited our campus. I found it fascinating, also. At Teacher's College I took a beginning art class, but I learned nothing. I handed my work in ahead of time, but the professor did not have her criticisms of it ready until the next semester, when I was gone. I never did get credit for the class, even though I wrote about it. I thought that strange for Teachers College.

During the semester I spent a good deal of time in the Union Library looking at periodicals, cataloguing, and general administration. I wrote out my questions and one afternoon Ruth Eisenhart spent time with me explaining all that I was asking about. This was worth another class. She gave me her ticket to the opera "Aida" at the Lincoln Center. The seat was in the back row of the balcony but I was thrilled.

Actually I felt a bit left out of things, with excitement in the Philippines because one of their own had been chosen World Queen. As one news correspondent said: "The Philippines is in the limelight and it feels good." For a small country that was usually in the limelight only if something bad happened, I was feeling good with it.

The semester was over at the end of January, and in the midst of a snow storm I left for Michigan. Soon I was speaking in churches in both Michigan and Wisconsin. I spent a few days with the Cooks in Milwaukee, and with friends in the Upper Peninsula. I flew to San Francisco to get the passenger ship back to Manila.

The trip was more interesting than the one by freighter for there were many more people to get acquainted with—Japanese, Chinese, Filipinos as well as Americans. A Japanese woman and I spent much time together, though attempting to talk had problems. On Sunday morning many of us on second-class wanted to go to church, which meant going to the first-class section. We were lined up single file with people watching us as we went in. Did they think we were criminals? Or was this a carry-over from the race fears of another day, when Asians were in second-class or lower, and the "good people" only in first class? We weren't sure but it was an interesting experience.

◆   ◆   ◆

THE LIBRARY

The work load was heavy that next year, for I was doing as much teaching as before, and the library was added to it. With a cataloguer, a circulation librarian and a typist we got along quite well. However, while I was gone the professor who took care of the library met up with some difficulty, and I had quite a bit of worry getting it straightened out. Also there were many mistakes from the former librarian that Jeannette had not finished correcting. Then there was much to do in ordering and especially bringing the ordering of periodicals up to date, as these had been neglected. Several student assistants were added to the library staff, making it possible to keep it open longer hours, including week-ends and holidays. The faculty as well as the students appreciated the freedom this gave them. It was fun getting back into the library work again and I was glad for the opportunity to renew my knowledge and skills.

After a few years and I was getting along quite well with both the teaching and the library, the Board of Trustees asked us to revise the whole curriculum. This took many evenings. They were doing a little too much dictating, I thought, especially in my department. But we worked it out.

This helped me to realize that it was difficult to feel one's way into another culture. Just as I thought I had made some progress, something jarred me to the realization that I was still an outsider. In missionary training we often talked about "identification with the people." But I began to wonder what that meant. This is often thought of in economic terms, especially by those on the outside.

Should we live crowded in Manila, where privacy is not a value for anyone? Two of our American families tried it for awhile but returned very apologetic. They could hear all their neighbors, and the neighbors could hear every thing that happened in their apartment. Our faculty families lived in good houses and Filipino and Americans lived as neighbors. More important than this was the fact that the missionary worked under Filipino leadership, with the people, not for them. It was amazing what a difference those two prepositions made. Sometimes people still thought in terms of the old paternalistic days. The resulting tensions caused a good deal of soul-searching and a deeper understanding of what it meant to be the helper and the helped.

1970 was an unusual year. During Summer Session I worked in the library and taught homiletics (how to preach). I divided the students into groups and had them preach in their native language and be criticized by the class. Their evaluations were encouraging.

SINGAPORE, 1970

One week after school started I left for Singapore to attend a month-long Study Institute in Christian Education for professors of Theological Seminaries in South East Asia. There were thirty five delegates, coming from Indonesia, Singapore, Saba, Hong Kong, Thailand, Japan, Korea, Taiwan, India, the Philippines and the United States. The leader was Dr. Randolph Crump Miller, a professor from Pacific School of Religion, in Berkeley. Dr. Loder, a professor from Princeton came as the theologian. He and Dr. Miller worked together and with us beautifully. Each of us had written a paper before we came and these were read and discussed. The cross cultural discussions were stimulating. Often we went from morning to evening in the meetings, with the only time off between 1:30 P.M. and 4:00 P.M. Jane Arp and I found each other quickly, although each of us roomed with one of the other women. Sometimes we slept in the afternoon, more often we went shopping. The few free evenings were usually filled with concerts.

One evening the delegate from Singapore took us to the "Night Market", much like a two story mall, that opened at 5:00 P.M. and was open all evening. Among other things we helped the woman from Saba buy the material for her wedding dress. It was great fun.

One evening we took a walking tour of the Chinese area of the city. This was advertised as "walking non stop 3 hours". We really did walk for three hours. We went past very crowded housing, where ten people might live in a very small room. We passed very nice homes with modern cars. Many people were eating, some from the men who cooked it on the street while they waited, others in nice dining rooms. A man had a group around him, reading to men who could not read. We went along the street where the "Concrete Nannies" lived, women who worked by the day, lived very simply, and sent their money back to relatives in China. I bought a doll to remind me of them. The part that amazed me was the making of paper models for funerals. I quote from a section of the tour description:

"Paper model makers are prepared to supply everything of the best so that the living may help ease the torments of the last journey. There are paper effigies of servants to accompany the dead as well as replicas of all material things on this earth: money, houses, cars, ocean liners and jet planes. (I was especially delighted with the modern kitchen, gas stove, refrigerator, dining table with beautiful dishes). A large square red box which contains all these things is sealed and the name of the deceased inscribed on it, so that when it is burned at the graveside he can claim it in his next world…All must be done to enable the soul to adapt to its new environment in Hell. Here it meets a highly complex system of rewards, punishments, and financial obligations. Ransom must be paid to Hell's rulers to procure rebirth in a prosperous life, 'squeeze' money must be given to judges, tips to hungry ghosts and certificates must be held to enable the passage through any barrier." The guide told us that customs are changing fast and all these things may go. I wondered how much of this had been influenced by American consumerism.

Weekends were for sight-seeing, sometimes the total group together, sometimes Jane Arp and I went on an extra tour. She and I squirmed as we watched the snake handler bring the snake around his neck. Another of these was a little ways out of Singapore to a Lutheran Church near a large factory and the residences of the workers. This church was truly ecumenical. It had classes in cooking, sewing, shop work. etc. for the workers, as well as the usual Church and Church School classes. One of the interesting things to me was a large cross outside, separate from the church, and in front of it a small pool. This was for the Baptists to use as a baptistry, for they did not have a church building. Although Singapore has often been held up as a model country, "very clean", I thought it very oppressive. I thought so even more when about a year later I heard that all the work for the people had closed and they could have worship services only in the church.

BALI

After this Conference I went to Bali. Most Americans at that time took expensive boat trips and stayed in the American hotels on the coast, or a little later they flew in to the town of Denpasar and stayed in the beautiful hotels there. I did neither. A student of ours, Balinese, was pastor of the tiny Presbyterian church in Denpasar and made my arrangements, but was out of town for a meeting. In order to make a living for his family he owned a travel agency and had a manager and an assistant. There were three modes of transportation: old taxi, three wheeled car, and riding on the back seat of a motorcycle. Sometimes I used one, sometimes the other. I was in a nice, but not luxurious, hotel in the city. I could walk around, watch the people going to the temple carrying fruits on their heads, and shopping was easy. I was amused at the life sized gods with aprons on, at almost every street corner. Was this Adam and Eve mixed with Buddhism? Or some Buddhist teaching we don't hear about?

The dances were exotic. The message is always the same: there is a conflict between good and evil, and the good always wins. The monkey dance was unique. It was at night, and about 150 men encircled a flare which was the only light. They kept up a constant chant, imitating monkeys. At times they all moved in unison, sometimes only one section did. It was a background for the two main characters representing good and evil. Other dances involved beautiful girls also in exotic costumes.

The guide took me to see the work the people were doing, the stone carving and weaving. In the market were beautiful baskets. When the guide found that I was interested in the life of the ordinary people he decided to take me to a Buddhist wedding. There was one Caucasian couple and all the rest were Balinese. First there was food, lots of it. Then there was a tooth grinding ceremony. They think that teeth are more beautiful if they have spaces in between. If the young people had not had it done by the time they are married they do it then. There were five young people; the bride, the groom, and three others. The men working on the teeth were directly in front of the person, so one could not see how it was done. A group of men sat nearby, groaning. The younger guide said that although they give you something to ease the pain it hurts a great deal. He told me it is very expensive, for the technician and assistant must be Brahman, or high caste. After this was over the Buddhist priest performed a fascinating wedding ceremony outdoors with the participants seated on the ground, one on each side of him. There was much offering to the gods. Only after it was over did the bride and groom stand together.

The next day the guide took me on a truck which 17 Indonesian teachers had rented to go to Pura Basakin, one of the most famous temples in Bali. It was a long rough trip, about three hours each way. The American always had clout, and I sat on the front seat the entire way. Every so often the person sitting next to me would change so that they could practice their English. The temple was very old, on the side of a mountain, and had three pillars. We walked around and spent awhile there, but I was not aware that any of the teachers were worshipping. During the conversations I asked the teachers about the rice terraces, which were just like those in the Philippines, but smaller. They told me, as had the Filipinos, that 2000 years ago the Chinese had taught them how to raise the rice on the mountain side.

From Bali I made a couple of overnight stops and went on to Kuala Lumpur in West Malaysia. Here I had made arrangements to stay with a missionary. It was a Sunday, and as she was a pastor she was too busy to do any thing with me. I left my purse in the apartment, and with it the card giving me the name of the apartment building. I took a taxi to the Mosque, one of the most beautiful buildings I have ever seen. The archway of pillars surrounding the courtyard was very elaborate. I stood there spellbound. I went on to the museum which I found very interesting. As I went out to the street, I realized it was one-way, and I did not know the way back. I took a taxi and tried to tell him my predicament. The large building he pointed out did not look like the one I had been in. Finally he took me to his office. The boss knew English and sent me to the Methodist Church. Sure enough, that large building was the one. I was looking at the back of it, but when I got to the front I recognized it. The boss had told him to go easy on the charge, but I gave him a tip for all his trouble. This was my first time to be lost in a country where I did not know the language. It was a very desperate feeling.

◆   ◆   ◆

When I returned to the Philippines I discovered an increased growth in nationalism, speeded up in part by the Vietnam War. Feeling that the West was invading the East, the opposition to the American military bases on Filipino soil grew dramatically. As tensions between East and West grew, missionaries found themselves becoming symbols of the old European status quo. How does one become a symbol of Christ, instead?

A new addition to the campus in 1971 was a section of the Philippine Christian College, which had its campus in the city of Manila. An agricultural college and some other courses were transferred. A building had been built for classrooms which helped the Seminary as they had a need for them also. This brought many more students on the campus.

FIESTAS

Besides the teaching and other campus activities, there were the fiestas in the various communities. Each town has its Saint, and once a year the whole town celebrates the Saint's day. The gambling begins about a week ahead in little huts set up along the road. The day itself is honored by feasting. We went from friend's house to friend's house, or to some we didn't know, to eat. Mary, who worked in our office, often wanted me to go so that she could have a ride. One of our favorite fiestas was the one in Silang, the town nearby. Most of our faculty went to that one. We started at the doctor's home where we had all the traditional food, especially "lechon." A three-month-old-pig had been roasted over an open fire for hours, resulting in a delicious pork roast. As the Filipinos liked the fat and the skin, there was plenty of lean meat left for us. The head of the pig was the centerpiece for the table. Then we went from home to home eating as little as we could. Mary always reminded me: "Watch your stomach!" We searched for their delicious "leche flan," better than our custard. One day I walked down the street and saw a coffee pot in the window, and oh, how I wanted a cup of coffee after all that rich food. I walked in, introduced myself, and asked for coffee. The hostess wanted me to eat but I explained that I could not eat another bite, that I would just like to have some coffee. She had the most beautiful table decoration I had seen. I found that she taught Home Economics in a college in Manila. One year I was in the U.S. on furlough, and the next year when I stopped for coffee, she scolded me for not being there the year before. I had no idea there was a roll call.

One year Mary and I were invited to the home of one of the college girls. It was in a small barrio not far away. We went to her home, and the girl was not there. It seemed to not be important for the one who invited the guest to be at home; it was just important that she be fed. Her mother was a lovely hostess. Then we went to her father's other family a few blocks away. We knew that some men who lived in Mindanao, an island in the south, would simply leave his family, go to work in Manila, and have another family there. However, I had never heard of two families so near each other. A few years later when the man was suddenly killed and Mary and I went to the funeral, it was the first wife who was there, not the second one. Also it was known that he had been supporting a woman by whom he had five children. She lived near us and occasionally worked on our campus. We took her home from the funeral to relieve the wife of embarrassment.

Another fascinating event was All Saints'Day. Each year a few of us would go to the Chinese Cemetery, where each family had a plot. Many of the tombs are a whole building, many of them ornate. The mourners were happy to have us come in and visit. All evening people were feasting. Late in the evening food was provided for the spirits at midnight. We did not wait for that. The men played mahjong as they waited to eat the food the spirits didn't eat.

THE 1971 FURLOUGH

Our furlough options had changed so that we had a choice of taking a three-month furlough after we had been there three years, or a four-month furlough after four years. The one year of being away was gone except for special circumstances. Many of us did not like to have someone else take over our work for such a long time. Inasmuch as I had the opportunity to go to the Conference in Singapore the year before, I chose the four-month plan for 1971.

Having discovered that I could stop in Korea on my way to Seattle without extra expense, I did this. I stayed in a guest house which was used by military wives as well as others. It was here that the newspaper reported that the Governor of my Province had been arrested for importing gold bars illegally. This was denied in the Philippines.

It snowed the morning I arrived. The change from 85° to 33° in one day made me shiver almost continuously. My friend from the Institute, Sun Ae Chow, was President of the Presbyterian Women's Organization in Seoul. She took me sight-seeing in town and we spent some time at the Palace Grounds. We visited Ewha College, a large and well-known Methodist College. The Theological Seminary was small compared to ours and was heated by a small stove in the center. Horrors, I thought! She and a missionary and I went to a restaurant where we sat on pillows on the floor, Korean style. Later we went to her home and met her husband. The first room was in American style, as that is what her teen-age children wanted. The second room was Korean, with the heat under the floor and concentrated at one end. I sat on the warm end with my legs back, and roasted. At one point I tried to stretch out my legs but the missionary quickly told me to put them back again. In spite of being a bit uncomfortable at times, I was grateful for her hospitality.

It was clear when I arrived at Sea-Tac, and I was thrilled to see Mt. Rainier, for me THE MOUNTAIN. As Walter was living in Olympia I spent about three weeks in the Northwest, visiting friends and showing slides and discovering "instant family". I spent Easter with the Cook family in Milwaukee. Then there was a month of intensive speaking in churches, mostly in Wisconsin. The schedule seemed to double as I went along, so that sometimes I spoke five times in three towns. Usually my "day off" was spent traveling from one area to another. Then I went on to New York to visit the various offices, and catch up with my supervisor. I spent two days in Boston to visit Jeannette and went on to Europe.

After a stop in Amsterdam with the usual sight-seeing, including the depressing Anne Frank home, I went on to Berlin. Judy Kruger's daughter, Susan, was teaching English there in order to learn German, as she intended to teach it. About 10:00 P.M. Susan and some of her young friends picked me up. We went to the main street but a demonstration was going on so we left and went to a wine cellar—June Tiefer Keller. There we drank "Berlinawassa", a sweet drink with a little beer in it. I had told her I did not like beer, but she said this was different. So I drank it. Actually it did not taste like beer, and I decided that a small amount of alcohol would not kill me. Really, I did not care for it but did not say that as Susan and her friends were such good scouts, and were so delighted that I would go with them. It was about midnight when I returned to the hotel.

As Susan was teaching I took a commercial tour of East Berlin in the morning. We went through the famous Checkpoint Charlie. We heard a loud bell ringing, and we asked what that was. Neither the guard nor the driver had heard it! Did it mean someone had been found under one of those cars they were searching? There was no way of knowing. The wall was really a tragic thing. 10,000 soldiers guarded the wall, keeping East Berliners in and almost every one else out. Life seemed to move more slowly there, with much less traffic and fewer people on the street. It was terribly depressing to see the buildings ruined by the war, but encouraging to see the new buildings going up to replace them. We heard lots of propaganda for the Socialist state. Food was at reasonable prices. Housing was being remodeled, and rents were not high. I thought, if only we could have those things plus freedom!

As Thursday was a holiday, Susan took me to East Berlin by train. We went through the Fredericksburg checkpoint, and it took nearly two hours to go through all the red tape. I took pictures of the changing of the Guard. In a window we saw fur coats which cost about $1,000. I asked Susan how could people in a socialist country afford that as all the propaganda had indicated that people were economically equal. She laughed and said the government people have plenty, its just that the wealth changed hands. As we left the whole roll of film was blanked out, except they had not quite got to the guard part. They tried. It was good to have a friend to show me around.

At Cologne I was glad to see the Cathedral again, then took a boat to Mainz, getting a good look at the old castles all along the way. In Mainz I visited the Gutenberg Museum where the printing press was invented and the first book published was the Bible. Frankfurt and Heidelburg were visited. The U.S. had 25,000 men stationed in Heidelburg, fifteen years after World War II. Why, I wondered?

At Nuremberg Dr. and Mrs. Wilhelm Anderson, who had spent a sabbatical with us at Union, met me at the train. This city was the seat of the Nazis and was badly destroyed. We went to the old castle which was being restored. In the square was an old beautiful church which had been Catholic, but at the time of Luther became Protestant. A market place was in the square, selling fruits and vegetables. After visiting with one of their daughters who was in school, we went to their home in Neuendettelsau, a little town where he was rector of the Lutheran Theological Seminary. He explained that Bavaria is Lutheran because it depended on the ruler of the Province whether it would be Catholic or would follow Luther. They took me to Rothenburg, a very popular tourist spot. It is a walled town, more than 1000 years old. During the war they surrendered quickly so were not destroyed. We seemed to walk right into the middle ages, except for all the tourist cars. The old church (now Protestant) was built from 1373 onwards. As we walked down the street some buildings had old time signs hanging out, and a few young people in old time costumes, made it all picturesque.

After having stopped in Munich I went on to Innsbruck. As it was cloudy I could get only a glimpse of the Alps. The beautiful Cathedral was built in 1700, over the earliest church built by Christians in the Roman army. On Sunday I went there for the service. There was a half-hour concert at the beginning with orchestra, organ, and excellent choir. The music all through the service was beautiful. There were no seats, people stood or sat where they could. I sat on a kneeling rail during the homily. This was the first church I had seen in Europe which was full.

In the afternoon it was still cold. I dressed warmly and walked up the hill to the old castle, the Schloss Amras, built in 1471. No one had lived in it since Archduke Francis Ferdinand and his wife, Sophia, were assassinated. This started World War I. There was a guided tour explaining all the uses for the armor. The section that made me cringe was the children's armor. Did the children, also, go to war? I thought this was new! I almost wished that today's child warriors that we hear about in Africa could have armor. Or did they have it because their father did? I wished I had asked the guide. Also in the castle was a huge collection of clocks and other intricate objects that had been collected for several hundreds of years.

After another stop and some complicated train trips, I arrived in Bossey, Switzerland. This was the Retreat Center of the World Council of Churches and was my main European destination. It was a two-week Bible session. I had a single room, with a wash basin. Three of us were in a section by ourselves and shared a bathroom. This was much better than I had hoped for. When I went for tea at 4:00 P.M,. many of the delegates who were coming from 60 countries were arriving. It sounded like the Tower of Babel. We had orientation for two hours and discovered that most of them knew enough English to communicate quite well.

We studied the Bible in our Ministry. The first two days we were introduced to Jewish thinking, and on Friday evening we went to the Jewish Synagogue. We women sat with the Jewish women in the balcony and the men joined in the worship. The women did not worship at all, they just watched the men. We thought either they liked being segregated, or they were using the situation to their own advantage.

On one of the Sundays we had an early Communion Service. The Eastern Orthodox and Eastern Catholic did not take part as it was against their rules.

Some of us thought that in such a group as this Communion should unite us, not divide us. But it was not so. I was glad we had had an afternoon worship service in the little chapel, led by the Greek Archbishop, which included all of us.

We had various approaches to the Bible presented, first the problems of translation. Having tried to learn a new language there was not much new for me there but it was a good review. Then we studied Mark 5:1-20. This is the passage where the demons leave the man and go into the swine and then into the lake. We had a literary-structural analysis; then a historical critical analysis, and finally a "faith" analysis. The leader for this section took the demons literally: Jesus believed in them, therefore they existed. They actually did go into the swine and were drowned. One man from Central America argued that Jesus did the wrong thing for he ruined the entire livelihood of the man. The leader was not pleased. Many of us tended to agree with the objector. I did not find out why a man was raising pigs if the Jews did not eat pork. We met in small groups to study this passage for today. Rev. Krebs, from Australia, and I wrote a meditation using today's business practices as a basis.

The day we had the reports from the small groups they were given with little discussion. Ours was very well received by the group. The final day we had an evaluation, then a final worship service which we had all planned.

When I arrived in Vienna the hotels were full, so I took a room on the fourth floor of an apartment. I was surprised that the taxi driver took my bag all the way up the stairs. Rev. Krebs and his wife had come to a health club on the Danube, not far from Vienna. Our little group had given me money to take him a bottle of wine for a gift. My landlady told me that her boy friend would take me. He was French and knew no English, so she translated all day. On the way I smelled something wrong with the car. I told her but she did not translate it for him. We found Rev. Krebs and his wife in the midst of intensive health activities, but we were able to have a good visit. They were delighted that I had come. After we stopped to have the clutch repaired, we went to a small village to buy new wine. I discovered this was why he had agreed to take me. The car was filled with new wine. The woman invited us into the kitchen and offered wine. I took a sip to be polite, but thought it was terrible. There was also rye bread and very thick raw bacon. Some of it was lean, so I ate that. It was not really too bad but fortunately the dog was under the table begging for all he could get. I paid my landlady about as much as the bus would have cost but this type of trip was more interesting.

The next day I walked around town and bought a ticket for a bus tour along the river. I told the man I really would like to go to the opera but I was sure I would not be able to get a ticket. He said it was not a popular one, that if I could get a ticket he would refund my money for the ticket I had bought from him. Sure enough I did get a ticket for the opera and he refunded my money. That evening I went to hear Palestrina by Hans Pfitzner. It was slow moving, but the subject had to do with church music, and the conflict between the old and the new in the 1600's. The music all the way through was beautiful. It took four and a half hours. Walter bought the recording for me the following Christmas.

The next morning I went to see the Crown Jewels in the Hapsburg Palace, walked around town a little more then went to the airport for a 2:00 P.M. plane, which was changed until 7:40 P.M. An American girl whose plane had also been changed and I became acquainted, especially when we discovered that she would be coming to the Philippines the next year. When I arrived in Prague, Czechoslovakia, I was too late for the reservation which had been made for me. The clerk telephoned until he found a room in a little Czech hotel. It was without private facilities, but very clean. It was also cheap, and popular with Czech people. It had a good dining room and there was a man there who spoke English.

On Sunday I went to see Rev. William Schneeburger, the Methodist District Superintendent for Czechoslovakia, who had been recommended by several of the friends at the Seminary. Early in the morning I took the bus to Jablona nau Nisau. The person sitting next to me suddenly changed with a person who spoke English. She asked me lots of questions then told every one else on the bus. Others would give her questions to ask. It was confusing for an American to be from the Philippines, and that took some explaining. Everyone was concerned about me, as American women do not travel on local buses alone. When I got to the stop I saw this tall man in a black suit and said: "That is my friend." Everybody relaxed.

Rev. Schneeburger took me to his home; we had coffee and coffee cake, then went to church. He preached a dynamic sermon, even though I could not understand it. He had been serving this good-sized church (for Protestants) for 5 years, and this was his last sermon. The people hated to see him go and I didn't wonder. He is also President of the Czech Council of Churches.

After dinner we went for a walk and talked where it would be difficult to be heard. He told me that many of the political leaders were discouraged because they believed that they really had a new society, socialism, where incomes were more nearly equalized, and with FREEDOM. However the Communists had taken over the country, and it had become Russian Communism and without freedom. Previously they had built a statue of Stalin because they appreciated the Russians saving them from the Nazis, but they have torn down the statue. As to the work, the churches were small as the entire country was Roman Catholic. When he thought there were spies in the church he tried to present the Gospel more clearly as he thought this was a missionary opportunity. The man was sent, and it could be his only time to hear the Gospel. He did not preach politics as he felt that was not his job. The church was more successful with the youth than the Communist Party was, so they were putting on the pressure, and the next year the youth camps might be closed. It was a law of socialism that without graft nothing will happen. He explained: if you wanted your car repaired there were few people to do it, so in order to have him work on your car you gave the man something for himself. The doctor had many patients and was paid by the government. How do you become a person and get the care you need? Give him something "under the table." In theory all were equal but this was not true. In practice everyone was looking out for himself. This desire for material things was really universal. Ministers were paid by the State on the 1949 basis and prices had gone up 100% since that. There was no hope of more for them. The South Indiana Conference gave them $5000 to buy a house to use as a church. The people bought all the furnishings and are doing the remodeling. Prices of food were low, rent was low, standard of living was low, salaries were low. A manager of a factory had to be a party member first, then the manager of the factory. Those who did not have ability joined the party and got the good jobs. The town made costume jewelry and charged three or four times the cost of making it. All the surplus goes to the State. They said no taxes, but in reality the taxes were excessive.

With all this information about the workings of Communism, I headed for Moscow. On the plane it was simply incomprehensible that anyone would not drink wine, or would drink two cups of tea. Arriving in Moscow I discovered that Intourist had me well cared for with a deluxe arrangement at the Hotel Metropol, famous, old, and luxurious. I met my guide at 1:00 P.M. and she took me on a tour of the city, with a great song for the socialist type of government. She left me promptly at 6:00 P.M.

In the evening I went to the Ballet, "Swan Lake." I was told to go through the garden to get there. I had an excellent seat for about $4. I loved it. When it was over the garden was closed and I could not go back the way I came. I followed a group of people, then discovered that was not the way to the hotel. I walked along, certain that if I could find a straight road to the right, I would get to the hotel, but I did not find any. Finally I realized I was lost. I saw a telephone, and realized I could not even read the numbers, let alone the words. I had walked several blocks before I found a policeman. He knew German, and with my few words of German we communicated. He told me to take the bus number 2 which came fairly soon. I got on the back of the bus and I was supposed to put my money in the slot, but I could not read the numbers. How much? I went to the front, told the motorman which hotel; he nodded, then I tried to get him to take what money he needed, with sign language telling him that I had not put it in back. He said "Sit". I tried again, and he said "Sit". So I sat. He took me right to the front of the hotel, took no money, and beamed. To be lost and alone at ten o'clock at night in a city overseas is horrifying. Many people had told me that I would never be without a guide, because Russia wanted you to see only what they wanted you to see. I have used my experience to show it was not true. I was without a guide and desperately wishing for one!

The next day my guide took me to some of the churches which were museums. I thought it a bit strange—the atheistic socialist government showing off the art of the churches and the glory of the Czars. She did mention once how terrible it was to have so many riches when there are so many poor. I requested that we go to the Evangelical Church (Baptist), which we did. Rev. Orlov told us that they have six services a week with about 1000 people, many of them young. All services are two hours long, with three sermons. He looked intently at my guide and said he had seen her before, but she denied it. Then he told her she had been there two years before with a children's choir from the States. She had to admit it was true.

That evening I went with a group to the opera to see La Traviata. It was beautiful. Again a good seat for $3. The next day the guide took me to the Economic Exposition. I thought the buildings were quite elaborate. There was lots of propaganda about the socialist system being better than capitalism. In between all this she talked about the pastor remembering her. She asked many questions about the church and Christianity. What a wonderful opportunity for witness this was. Meanwhile I was also thinking about Communism. Everybody works for the government; no one can be fired. They don't seem to care whether the work is well done or not, like the slow service in the restaurants, the maids sitting around doing nothing although the rooms are not cleaned. I was astonished to see a man throw some wood out the window from the fifth floor of this luxurious hotel instead of taking it down the freight elevator. I wanted to go see what was below, but decided not to. Foreigners are not supposed to give tips, they are served without them.

Meanwhile I had a new concept of bourgois. American Communists talk of it as upper middle class. The term here and there is used loosely. I had thought a beautiful building could be that, but the Exposition was ornate. Also I had thought of ballet and opera as in that class. The guide was shocked at this idea. They are for the people, and the people go, often directly from work and in ordinary clothes. There are 500 theater companies, 250 of them folk theaters. The government is planning to increase consumer goods by 45%, so that is not bourgois, either. Just riches, I guess, like the Czars.

The first plane on the way back to Manila was old, very noisy, small and slow. I remembered all the talk about how far Russia is ahead of the U.S. and I wished for a little more economic development on their part. The plane had many Russian men who were studying hard. We stopped at Karachi and I bought a Pakistani doll. Somewhere an Indian man got on and came and talked with me quite a bit. At times he would sit with one of the Russians. He told me that the reason they were all studying so intensely was that they were technicians going to Hanoi. As this was in the midst of the Viet Nam war, I decided to say nothing. When we got to Calcutta, (about 5:00 A.M.), the Indian's nephew came to the plane and told him to get off immediately as there was a general strike and it was dangerous outside. The Indian man told me to get off and get the next plane to Manila. I didn't know what happened to the Russians, if they were stuck there or if they went on to Hanoi. Nothing seemed to move anywhere. I learned later that a man from Bangladesh had been elected President of what was then Pakistan-Bangladesh. The Pakistani people rejected him. Bangladesh then separated from Pakistan. The Calcutta people were of the same tribe as the Bangladesh, and that is why they were striking with them.

About 8:30 A.M. I got a plane to Bangkok. I had planned my trip so that I could have a day to shop there. A woman staying at the Guest House went with me to the week-end market to see the gorgeous orchids. Then she invited herself to go shopping with me. I made sure she would just follow along with what I wanted to do. She wanted to look for shoes so we did, and I bought some sandals, too. I bought some material I had seen previously, and a star sapphire ring. The next day I left for Manila, with delayed planes, probably because of the continued delay in Calcutta.

◆   ◆   ◆

I arrived in Manila just in time for the beginning of the semester and the inauguration of the new President, Dr. Emerito Nacpil. A brilliant man, for some years he had been a theology professor. The ceremony was held in the quadrangle of the library building. The students had braided coconut leaves to form a native roofing. The whole campus was decorated. A dinner, including the native "lechon," was served to the special guests. It was a joyous affair.

A nice thing happened to me a few months after I got back from the furlough. I had been driving the oldest Jeep that belonged to the missionaries under the Women's Division and the repairs were pretty constant. The man who was the liaison between us and the Board had a good deal on a few new cars. It did not take me long to get to Manila and come back with a new German Taurus. It was great.

Imelda Marcos had a concert hall built on the waterfront. Concerts became available. Some of us went to hear "Carmen", and a Russian Dance Troupe. Also I began swimming at the YWCA pool in Manila. This is the only clean out-door pool in the city. We had one closer to the campus but our students would not let me use it, as they said it was not clean. So once a week was all I could manage.

My second-year class was large enough to begin a laboratory school for the Christian Education majors. I had a difficult time finding personnel, but with the help of one of the faculty wives and Afri, a Deaconess who had helped me before, we got along well. I was able to continue this each year with various helpers. My students appreciated it, but I do not think the idea spread as I had hoped.

Another new thing for the campus was the decoration of the campus. In this I involved both the Christian Education and the second-year Bachelor of Theology students. The type of leadership they were accustomed to was very dictatorial, both in the home and in society. I wanted to give them an opportunity, not only to study the different types of leadership, but also to experience them. I majored on group work, where the group made the decisions. After a few trials I discovered that decorating the campus was ideal. At Christmas time they made life-size figures of the Holy Family. We used paper-mache and dressed them with crepe paper. The students decided on a manger. They wove the grasses and made one, putting the figures inside. We had just finished it when we woke the next morning to a pouring rain. As soon as we could we all went out to see it, and the grass manger was absolutely water-proof! How those students could do that was beyond me. I tried to help them to think how to use that group decision process as pastors.

Because I had done a good deal of sewing in the past, I was fascinated by the way the dressmakers could simply take one's measurements and make a dress to fit. One of the stores offered such a six-weeks course on Saturdays. I went to it thinking I would enjoy it after I retired.

Some American visitors made us aware of our differences in thinking about the nature of the overseas church. For years we have been critical of political colonialism, but only recently have we begun to see through the eyes of our Filipino friends that our church structure is somewhat colonialist. Autonomy is much discussed, for the local church would like to make decisions and it would increase their responsibility in the church. However, when autonomy came to a vote of the Central Conference it was voted down. When one sees these things from the point of view of those who have been under colonial governments, one can understand the desire for independence in the church, even though financial independence may be far off.

FERDINAND MARCOS

September 1972 will long be remembered as the time that Ferdinand Marcos declared Martial Law. He had been elected the year before in a fairly calm election, although the person running against him never conceded. Formerly the elections had been dominated by "goons and guns". Often the two opposing parties would seek to kill each other off. There were many war lords with private armies. The lobby of the Intercontinental Hotel was the scene of a murder where the body-guards of one contestant killed the opposing one as he entered the Hotel. Politics was a dangerous business.

During Marcos' first term he did a few good things. The one I most appreciated was the cleaning of the huge piles of garbage on the sides of the roads. The
Maosts were making a lot of noise. We learned later that the Presidential oppo-
nent and some of his rich right-wing friends had sent some rebel minded-youth
leaders to China to learn guerrilla warfare. It was thought that they could overthrow the government but would not have enough leadership to run it, and then
the right-wingers could take over. We wondered what kind of a government we
would have had if they had succeeded.

All Universities and Graduate Schools were closed. We did not know why, but
our Seminary was one of the last ones to open. None of our students or faculty
were questioned at that time. We had two students who did not want to be inter-
rogated in one of the Manila schools and they came to us not really expecting to
become ministers. To their surprise they discovered that their revolutionary ideas
were in the Bible and they became excellent students and pastors. It was later that
we discovered that immediately after the declaration Marcos' men had gone to
the University of the Philippines and arrested a number of students. As the newspapers printed what Marcos wanted us to know, we were unaware of this. When
the young people were released they told of the horrible tortures that they
endured.

Marcos called it the "New Society". In the beginning the Ilicanos, that is,
those who lived in the northern part of the country, and spoke Ilicano as Marcos
did, were bound by the cultural pattern to support him. Even our Bishop Grena-
dosin, whom we all thought was super, now became a supporter, watching the
activities of his neighbors in one or two blocks where he lived. One of our professors said that they are so accustomed to an autocratic type of leadership that when
they do not have it they do not do what they ought. He said "martial law is not
what we want, but it is what we need." We Americans found it hard to sympa-
thize with those who felt this way.

We saw the New Society building "national discipline" (obedience to the
State); the abolition of private armies (in one turnover of armaments one man
turned in several armalites and more than 700 rifles); no more political influence
of the rich (unless friends of Marcos); rule by decree; the abolition of Congress;
and the cancellation of the right to oppose the government. All of this was happening at the time that Nixon's scandal was being publicized. The democracy in
the U.S. did not look vary good at that moment, either.

It was when one of our students was imprisoned because they thought he was producing literature, that the pressure came home to us. Then the Executive Secretary of the National Council of Churches, Le Verne Mercado, was imprisoned because he should have known that an employee of his opposed Marcos. This brought cables locally and from all over the world. Suddenly he became a V.I.P. Imelda, Marcos' wife, had asked Rev. Mercado to give the opening prayer at the dedication of the new concert hall. He was released in the morning and gave the prayer in the evening. With this experience he was able to get our student and a number of others released. Another mistake that Marcos' army did was the arrest of two priests and a group of students during a retreat. Those who carried out the raid robbed the nuns' rooms where the retreat was being held. This angered the Catholic Church. Marcos was so embarrassed that he sent money to the nuns, who immediately gave it to the poor in the slums. These things put both the Protestant and the Catholic Church in a very critical mood.

Marcos had sham elections. Our students told us that when they went home to vote, Marcos' men would come to the town the night before and tell them that their vote was 99% for Marcos, and their votes against him were not counted. On a later furlough I heard President Reagan introduce Marcos as a democratic leader. I called the hot line and said that if we have a President who does not know the difference between dictatorship and democracy we were in a bad way.

The Viet Nam War was becoming a worse disaster than we had at first realized. Rev. Richard Deats of our faculty sent out a letter to all the missionaries of all the groups he could find in the Philippines, asking them to return a paper with a signature if they would join in opposing the war. Out of 700 missionaries, only 25 signed. How can you carry on the work of Christ if you have war, we wondered? That few did not stop us. From the late 60's on we had sit-ins in front of the American Embassy, often with speeches, always with posters and leaflets to hand out. If we were not careful the communist group would come and be very aggressive in handing out their literature, but as time went on and they grew stronger they held their own demonstrations.

When Pope John XXIII called together his Conference in Rome in 1973, Emerito Nacpil, at that time our Professor of Theology, was one of the Protestant observers. A few years later the Bishop who had been the host for the Protestants came to Manila and contacted our Emmie. We invited the Bishop and also the faculty of the Catholic Seminary, which was near, to come for dinner. The next January, during the week of Church Unity, they invited us for dinner. From that time on, either one of us invited the other. We even exchanged faculty as speakers occasionally. This was a rich fellowship. When Pope Paul IV came to Manila I joined the million people sitting on the ground but did not try to take Communion. His homily was good, and I was interested in watching the people around me. I saw some of the Catholic Seminary faculty, and they greeted me warmly.

With the increase of nationalism, one of the cries we heard was "Misionary Go Home." Our President, Emmie Nacpil was among them. Richard Deats took this seriously and found a job with the Fellowship of Reconciliation in New York. When Emmie found out that Dr. Deats was leaving he and others of the Filipino faculty went to Deats' home and begged him to stay, but he had this excellent job and left. At this time I began to say "I will go any time you say." Always, it was "Don't you go." There seemed to be no relationship in their thinking between the "Go Home" and the personal relationship.

Usually every year we had a faculty member from one of the Theological Seminaries in the States come and teach during their sabbatical. One year Dr. John Swomley, with whom I had worked during World War II, brought his family and spent the year with us. One day a visitor from the U.S. Air Force Base told me that the army had raided our campus. That was news to me. I looked at the books that Dr. Swomley had on his reserve shelf (he was teaching non-violence). Also I looked under the desk where Mao's books were kept and all were still there. When I asked Emmie later he said the army men had been there and wanted to search all the rooms because they were sure that one of the students was producing literature against Marcos. Emmie did not allow them to go to the rooms but instead he went and searched them. He came back with everything he could find, a paper here or there which could easily have been secured in Manila, and no indication of publishing or copying. They were satisfied and left. We knew whom they were suspecting, and he was later imprisoned on that suspicion even though they could find no evidence.

Introducing Marjie Swomley to the various shopping areas areas was fun. One day I took Marjie and her daughter Joan to the Quiapo market, one of the largest in Manila. Instead of taking them through the front area, where there were a lot of little unimportant things I took them to a side entrance where the beautiful embroideries were. As we entered, one of the men said something in Tagalog and all the other vendors laughed with him and at us. I knew from the reaction that it had been something nasty instead of the usual "long nose". I said to him in Taga-log, "I understand". I really had paid no attention to what he had said but thought he should know better. He blushed, and everybody started laughing at him instead of at us, and he got so embarrassed that he left. Marjie and Joan seemed quite unaware of what was happening and I did not tell them. It remains one of my amusing market experiences.

Some of my friends in the U.S. thought I had begun to "live" because I had gone to some concerts, the dress making class, etc. However, I never thought of my "living" as being recreation with the work being less than "living." I thought about some of the times I have been "living:" the joys of Seminary graduation, knowing that the man who graduated Summa Cum Laude and received a prize for the best work in the Bible Department, would be going on to Library School in Manila to be trained to join the faculty and take my place in the Library. The man who graduated Magna Cum Laude had been very close for I was one of the sponsors at his wedding. In the Philippines that makes me a "ninang" which was equivalent to being a member of the family. It was seeing the willingness of a fine young man to wait another year before coming to Seminary because there were not enough scholarships to go around; seeing a shy, poker-faced teen-age girl come alive with vitality as she participated in a religious rock opera done by our little youth choir. There was a special reward when I worked with students who had just begun to think through the confusion of native beliefs and Christian the-ology, until they gained a new strength of faith which became their own. I cele-brated an Easter birthday, the second time in my life. I had an open house for all the faculty, students and staff on campus (school was out), with two conditions: no presents, and no asking my age which was always verse two of the birthday song.

There was more "living" when I entertained guests like Jurgen Moltmann, who was an outstanding German theologian. Our faculty attended the consecra-tion of a Catholic Bishop, a man who had been head of the Catholic Seminary near us, and who had been a very good friend. We were thrilled when he invited us forward to take Mass with him. I was happy to welcome my new house-mate, Miss Mabel Metze, who was under the Disciples National Board. She had been teaching in Manila and now would be teaching with us for a year before she retired. It was a special thrill to watch the cross be put on top of the new round chapel, built at least half by many gifts sent to the Seminary in my name. There had been much "living."

FURLOUGH 1974

When school was out at the end of March in 1974, I left for a three-month furlough. I went directly to Olympia and spent three weeks with Walter and the family and friends. A month was spent speaking in churches in Wisconsin and Northern Michigan, with the days in between spent with the Cooks in Milwaukee. I then went to Lake Junalaska, North Carolina, where the United Methodist Church had its archives. I learned about taking care of archives, for I had been collecting sermons and other materials from the early pastors in the Philippines. No one else had done this and it seemed to me that this early historical material should not be lost.

The final month of the furlough was spent traveling in Scandinavia with the hotels and trips arranged by SAS. I will pick up just a few of the experiences. I flew to Bergen, Norway. The woman sitting next to me talked all night, telling me about her experiences as the wife of a man from Iran. When they went to Iran she was not allowed out of her house without him, and she had no friends. She said nobody of her family believed her, but I did for I had heard other stories like that. So she talked on and on, to the exasperation of the other people around us. In the morning I was met at the hotel by Gurie Herigstad, a cousin of Judy Krugers. She took me around all day and in the afternoon we had coffee (which, typically, was a whole lunch) at her mother's. I dropped off to sleep in the midst of this. They put me to bed and I slept for a couple of hours. In the evening her brother and his wife took me to dinner and a dance program. Such hospitality for a friend of a cousin!

The two day trip by boat and bus through the fjords and mountains to Oslo was beautiful. Along the way we had "cold board," which had 87 varieties of delicious food. From Oslo I went to Copenhagen, with the most interesting part of the trip being the home and museum of Hans Christian Anderson. From there to Stockholm, where the Summer Palace with its collection of Chinese artifacts surprised me. I did not expect to see such a room full of China in Stockholm. Also I saw the crown jewels. The king is not crowned, which seems unusual. Yet it seemed to fit in Sweden. In Helsinki I walked around the town, and took a two-day trip to the lake section in order to get a visa to Russia, which took two days. This filled the time, and was quite a beautiful trip.

I opted for the bus to Leningrad instead of the boat, for I thought I wanted to see the countryside. Actually I did not see much, for there were not many towns, and just small trees. After all the destruction of World War II, they had not had much time to grow. There were 11 folks on this tour, all very friendly, especially a German couple. The Hotel Leningrad looked like an Intercontinental and was deluxe. However, the elevators were very jerky, and it was really not clean, like Scandinavia. They seemed to try for a show but it was difficult. The "Hermitage" was one of the most luxurious palaces I had ever seen. It had a great deal of art work, a beautiful stairway, and 30 gorgeous chandeliers in one room.

The summer palace was fascinating. The interior had not been rebuilt since the war, but the gardens were delightful. There were 150 water fountains with gilded bronze figures. About 50 were in one grand staircase. Peter I who built it was a practical joker. There were trick fountains where if one sat on the bench to watch, the spray came up and got one wet. These were lots of fun. The grass was green, but really needed cutting. It was so difficult to keep up a good show for tourists.

I went shopping by myself in the store, like a mall, that was a block long. I bought a shawl with a long fringe. The sales girl just stood there and I approached her with my purchase, that is, when I could get close enough. She wrote a receipt, and then I went into another line to pay, then into another line to get my package. It took about half an hour. I could not find the store for tourists only.

We found people cordial and helpful in spite of the Cold War. I had been walking quite a ways so decided to go back to the hotel by bus. I took a No. 10, but going the wrong way. I asked the young men sitting in back, in slow English, if this bus would take me to the hotel. One of the men got off with me, took me to a trolley stop, asked the directions, then waited to see that I got on the right bus going the right direction. Would we do that?

While in Leningrad we went to the opera "Eugene Onegin", words by Pushkin, music by Tchaikovsky. I loved it and bought the record before I left. We also went to a Russian Dance.

After going back to Helsinki and Stockholm, I took a bus to Oslo. Although it looked like a back road to me, as there was almost no traffic, the map showed it as the main road. For me and the other librarian on this trip the exciting thing was the stop at the home of Selma Lagerlof. It is called Marbacka and is near Karlstad. Both of us had read books by her and being able to go inside her home and see it furnished as it had been when she lived there was a special treat. Most of the rest of the group were bored.

Another interesting thing on that road was when we saw a community dancing around a May Pole, for they were celebrating Midsummer Day. We persuaded the driver to stop and they invited us to take part. We just watched joining those who were sitting on the grass. We wished we could remember how to dance around the May Pole so we could have joined in if only for a few minutes.

The most important thing in Oslo for me were the museums at Bigday. We saw the ship of Amundson and also the Kon Tiki in which one scientist sailed across the Pacific to prove that the Polynesians are related racially to the Incas of Peru. We wondered how such a little raft could go across the Pacific.

The tour to the North Cape was the best part of the entire trip for me. I went by plane part of the way, then was joined by others. We went by bus, ferry, and a small boat on the Arctic Ocean. In the far north we stopped to see the Lapp Camp. They had gifts in a tent, and the guide said they wanted us to think that they were poor and lived in tents. There were cabins at the foot of the hill. The dog shook hands with each one of us, then raced down the hill and sat on one of the porches to wait for his owner. It would have been hard to mistake his meaning. For one dinner we had reindeer meat, and for another whale meat. Both tasted somewhat like venison to me. It had been too cloudy to see the midnight sun until we got to Alta. There it was clear and only a few of us were awake at 12:00 midnight to see the sun go down and go up again without setting. I was glad to have been able to take this trip at the end of June for that was when this sight can be seen. From there I went back to Oslo and then to the Philippines

◆   ◆   ◆

The most exciting thing that happened on our campus that year of 1974-75 was the beginning of a Theological Education by Extension project. The idea was begun in Central America and had spread to many countries. With this program we made theological education available to the people who were serving churches but had not had the opportunity to have Seminary training, and, to some degree, for laymen also. Both the Methodists and UCCP had programs but neither were satisfactory. We opened up ten centers where students studied with supervisors who were graduates of the Seminary and the faculty went out three times each year. With the 140 students in the Extension project and the 110 in the residential program, we were training 250 ministers. We started preparing materials, which was a challenging task.

While I was in the States I heard some "Evangelicals" worrying about missionaries not being Christian and not spreading the Gospel. As I was sitting in Chapel and listening to meditations on the book of Acts, and hearing appeals for evangelism and for keeping Jesus Christ in the center of our message, I wondered what they were worrying about. Some missionaries from some of the other denominations were holding a conference for their Filipino leaders and they invited our faculty. No one wanted to go, so I said I would. The main speaker talked on at length about the need to save souls. Then he said this was a personal thing only and they did not have to deal with social issues. One of the men rose and said, "Before some of us were Christians we were animists. The evil spirits dictated every thing we did and how we did it. We were constantly trying to appease them. Are you saying that now we are Christians that we are Christian with just half of our lives?" Another man added "If we are not Christian in the market place we are not Christian at all." The missionary closed off his speech, surprised. I thought it was terrific.

Being a "ninang" for weddings was always fun, but to be the minister for one was especially prized. Egrie lived in Das Marinas, the town nearby, and came to sing in our little church choir. She came on the jeepney but it was not safe for her to return that way after dark. I drove her in my car but asked that one of the men go with me so I did not have to come back alone. It was not long before it was the same man, Sol Toquero, each week. When he graduated and they wanted to be married, they asked me to be the minister because they said that I was responsible. The wedding was at 6:00 A.M. A little after 5:00 A.M. I discovered that her mother was not coming. I drove to her home and persuaded her mother that as this wedding was in both Filipino and American style, and the mother of the bride is the most important person, after the wedding party, in the U.S., she came. Egrie wore a beautifully embroidered white dress. The reception at her home was delightful and many people were glad her mother had come to the wedding. They were a consecrated couple. I was especially happy 30 years later when he was elected Bishop, although two other students were also.

The second-year students I had during the last year were the most creative and ambitious that I had since I began teaching there. The campus decorations had been rather the usual sort of thing. This group dug out the life sized figures made by the previous class. With the strong increase in nationalism, they decided to dress them in Filipino clothes. I had used a white figured plastic table cloth as padding when I came and I had never used it again. They made a Barong Tagalog out of it. I wanted to cut it, but they said no. They folded it and dressed Joseph in it. It looked great. They used some other materials for Mary and for Jesus. They put them on the roof of the Chapel where everybody could see them. One of the men climbed up to the cross and put up a star they had made. The whole campus was thrilled with it. The second semester, instead of the laboratory school, they decided to plan and present a four-hour teaching seminar in one of the small churches nearby. Teachers came from a number of the small churches of several denominations. The students did an excellent job. They realized that these people had the same problems they had found, and they could share ideas. One day they worked on a game that taught church administration. They got so involved I could not get them stopped at the end of the hour. After about ten minutes of the next class time I went to Emmie Nacpil's class and apologized. He laughed because he had been hearing them, and was happy that a class could be that interested in what they were doing. So was I!

One evening I did not feel well and went to the home of the woman doctor who was the wife of a student. While there I became very ill and she was afraid I might become dehydrated. Her husband drove me in my car (as he had none) to the little hospital in Silang, the town up the hill. The Doctor gave me a shot and put me to bed, which proved to be the examining table, for the night. In the morning there was no breakfast and I asked the nurse if I might have a cup of coffee. Only later did I realize it was from her own supply. People constantly came in the room and stared at me. One of the students was to drive my car to come after me at 10:30 A.M. but by 8:30 A.M. I had all the staring I could stand. I asked the nurse if we could close the door or do something. Within a few minutes I was on my way home with the doctor's driver and car. As I left I looked into the rooms and realized that they did not have a bed they felt was suitable for me and also that families were bringing breakfast to the patients. I was learning what life was like for the common people.

One of the disturbing things about the political situation was that Marcos was making rules for the Muslim area in Mindanao Island. They were objecting but he did not listen. He sent the army and they fought back. That continued for all the time he was there, and even afterwards.

The opposition to Marcos increased as time went along, as did his dictatorship. The youth and adults who opposed him became the New People's Army (NPA). They were in the hills. They would go to the mayor and tell him his town would have to support them and give them "tong"(money), or he would be killed. The people needed food and the government did nothing for them, and the NPA would promise to help them, so they would shift their support to them. Both the army and the NPA were cruel, and it was said that they would know which one killed a person because of the way the body was dismembered. The leader of the group went into exile in Belgium and gave orders from there because Marcos wanted him killed. An interesting side issue became evident. If a group tried to increase the wellbeing of the countryside they became enemies of the NPA, for if the poor people became contented the NPA could not have its revolution. This was the "conservatism of the radical."

In the search for those who opposed Marcos the army would move a whole community to a camp in which there was not enough food, or water, and no bathroom facilities, and leave them there for a couple of months. Many children and older people died. When the farmers were allowed to return they often found their houses bulldozed and their fields burned.

The worst mistake that Marcos made was when his men killed Aquino, his opposition. Aquino had just come back from the States and had studied Martin Luther King's non-violence. How this would have worked out at that time we do not know. Aquino became a martyr.

Imelda Marcos was having a field day. She became Executive of the Greater Manila Area. She did a few good things in the beginning. She persuaded people to grow some of their own vegetables instead of buying them all at the market. She seemed really interested in children, developing some homes for the street children (there are many of those). All the news published in Manila was that she was doing a terrific job. A magazine in the U.S. carried an article about her when she went to Mexico City, saying that she spent one million dollars in one day. That magazine was not allowed in the country so friends from the U.S. sent the article to us. This type of thing happened several times so in that way we were aware that Imelda was spending the taxpayers' money. Later a reporter saw only her shoes and did not see, or at least did not report, her thousand dresses and the huge vats of expensive French perfume.

Thus we found that a "benevolent dictator" does not remain benevolent and his power as a dictator grows stronger as the years go by. The Pilippinos were so patient!

FESTIVALS

One of the fascinating festivals was the ATI-ATIHAN. The Manila YWCA organized a group of 45 to go to Aklan on Iloilo Island for this festival in January of 1975. Imelda had brought the festival to Manila a few years earlier and I thought it was wild. So I wanted to see it in its home place. It commemorated the landing of a group of Malaysans seeking freedom from a tyrant ruler in Indonesia, centuries ago. We left at 6:00 A.M. by plane on Thursday and returned late Sunday afternoon. There were three of us Caucasians, one woman who was with her daughter-in-law from Thailand, and Ruth Feuer and myself. Ruth and I immediately became friends. Her husband worked with U.S. AID, and she decided not to wait for him to accompany her to the festivals. Thursday was rather quiet and we walked around the town and shopped. Friday morning our local host took us in jeeps for several kilometers to a spot he knew, then hiked several kilometers to a waterfall, then another kilometer to the ocean beach and we went swimming. Then we hiked a few more kilometers back to the jeeps. Friday afternoon Ruth and I were shopping and the drums began to beat, bang, bang, BANG, bang, bang, BANG. The clerks began to move their feet to the rhythm. People all along the street started walking to the rhythms of the drums. This kept up all afternoon. On Saturday one of the women painted our faces with lipstick and eyebrow pencil, for if that was not done our faces would be smeared with soot from the bottom of the kettle. Then our group joined the parade, carrying a large YWCA sign. Various tribes were in distinctive costumes, most of them made of capis shells, the round, flat shells. They were in different colors and types. The most striking tribes were the ones who had covered themselves with black soot, and wore white shells. Several hundred were in the parade with many others watching. We saw American tourists surprised when their faces got blackened. It seemed that the whole town kept with the rhythm of drums. I could keep it up for only an hour, then I went to our hotel to get my camera and take pictures. The next morning, Sunday, there was a huge open-air Mass and President and Mrs. Marcos were there. The various tribes marched before them in their unique costumes. We did not join them. The whole experience was free, happy and wild.

That experience got Ruth and me started going to various festivals. The MORIONES festival was from Maundy Thursday until Easter afternoon on the island of Marinduque. We asked Philippine Airlines to find us a place to stay. They reported that the hotel was full, meaning, of course, the hotel for Americans. We told them never mind, just find us a floor to sleep on. They did much better than that, for they housed us in a resort on the ocean beach run by a doctor's wife. They had a big house in town as well. We had a large room and our own private facilities, probably the owner's room. Of course the toilet did not flush but who cared about that? At least it was private, and a private shower. This was in contrast to the little motel type rooms every one else had, with shared facilities. The dining room faced the ocean, had only a roof, no sides, and the food was excellent. Each guest really had personal attention. When we weren't in town we were swimming or on the beach.

This is the story of Longinus, a Roman centurion who was blind in one eye and when he pierced the side of Jesus a drop of blood spilled on his eye and healed him. This is supposed to be scriptural although I could not find it. The costumes are those of Roman soldiers, made by the men themselves. Most of them are made of wood although more recently some are of paper-mache. To participate in the festival is to do penance. "They really suffer because if is so hot and the masks are so heavy," the children of our host told us. When the men were not marching and were just watching something else, they would push the masks up or to the side. It was a weird sight.

Saturday night to follow the tradition that guests were crowned, our hosts sat all of us, about eight, in chairs. They used a rice-ring for a crown, put flowers into it, sang to us, crowned us, then threw flowers and coins to us. Of course the children ran after the coins, but Ruth and I were able to retrieve two pesos each. Much food followed, including the lechon. There must have been fifty people, many of them relatives. Also some of the guests from the American hotel came, as they were not celebrating the Filipino way. Dancing lasted until late, but Ruth and I went to bed.

At 4:00 A.M. we were up, leaving at 4:30 A.M. to go with the young people of our host to town for Easter morning Mass. We did not attempt to participate in that. Afterward the entire congregation broke into two groups, one followed the statue of Mary wearing a black veil, and the other followed the statue of Jesus. One of the young people put candles in our hands; we lit them, then followed the Jesus section. At an appointed place the two statues met and were under a canopy. After a graceful dance, a young boy dressed as an angel was lowered from the top of the canopy. He sang, then he was quickly lowered further and he grabbed the mourning veil from Mary's head and he was quickly pulled up into the canopy. Mary did not need to mourn for Jesus had risen. All formed one procession going back to the church with dancing and music all the way. I began to wonder, have Protestants lost too much of the drama?

I looked for a doll that would resemble these costumes, but could find a head only. One of the sons of the host who was attending college in Manila, told me he knew someone who would make one for me. That sounded good to me. A few months later, after he had been home for another vacation, I received a call that there was a doll waiting for me in our Manila office. It was a beautifully carved piece, a man with the centurion costume, painted just as they wore them. The price was so small I wanted to double it, but I knew I could not do that. It has thrilled me, to have one of my dolls made just for me!

We knew one of the women guests was a V.I.P by the way she carried herself, knowing she was more important than the common people. She had with her two Vietnamese girls who, our hostess thought, were the daughters of the ruler of South Viet Nam in exile. This woman gave us a ride to the next town for the pageant later on Sunday morning. After about an hour of dancing by girls in lovely costumes, men coming on horseback, and more dancing, lights were turned on the stage and girls were dancing before Pilate. Then we saw Longinus, who knew his life was in danger because he had become a Christian. He ran behind some trees put there for the occasion. He was found and was brought before Pilate. He was condemned to death and was taken to a guillotine. His head came off, (paper-mache?) and the soldier held it high. It was a bit gruesome, but there was music and more dancing and everyone left happily.

At the airport we found that our reservations were still good, but that the V.I.P. woman had reservations on a later flight. She decided she wanted to go on the earlier flight. She persuaded a number of people to wait for the later flight so that she and her entourage could go on the earlier one. We were amazed that people would give in to someone just because they thought they were important. Later one of my students told me they would gladly do that.

A festival in Bulacan which celebrated the harvest was fun to watch. CARA-BAOS were said to genuflect before the church, but we did not see this as we were being hosted up the road. We had a good view of all the animals with all their decorations, running, as though in a race. At the end some were pulling carts of merry-makers.

The SPRING FESTIVAL, in a town much closer than the others, was colorful. Large paper flowers decorated every house, and shops were also decorated with the paper flowers, indicating what they sold. There seemed to be no parade, but many people were looking out their windows and greeting any tourists who came by. It was small and not exciting, but very beautiful.

Another was the FLUVIAL FESTIVAL in Bocaue, Bulacan. A large, four stories high, beautifully decorated boat carried the statue of the Christ Child down the river. There was loud music and the boat was crowded with people dancing or just watching whatever was going on. We were on a bridge, watching it come. There were many small boats along the side. As they passed each other they threw water on each other. The boat stopped close enough to the bridge so that all the tourists on it could throw money to the boys on the front of the boat. They quickly dove into the river to find the money. They had great fun, and the tourists shouted to them and cheered them on. All the while the music and dancing continued. It was a fascinating, happy time.

In 1976 I was 65 years old, and it was time for me to retire. As I was preparing to leave there were of course the final farewells. The International Committee of the YWCA gave me a luncheon, and the wife of the Ambassador from Indonesia gave me a gift. During the student-faculty party I was the Queen of Queens on the Night of Nights. The new librarian, well trained in library and theology, came to work just after Easter. Then three friends from Seattle, Phyllis Hoogan, Judy Kreger, and her cousin Helen Larm, came for a visit. We had a great time seeing the sights in Manila. However, riding in the car in the city frightened them as there were no rules, and we simply had to fight our way through the traffic. They delighted in riding the rapids at Pagsanhan. I took them on a regular bus to Baguio. We hired three boys to dash on to the bus and hold a seat for us. Then their friends pushed our baggage through the window. When we were able to get on without being crushed we slipped into our seats quickly so no one else could take them. They were mystified as they watched a goat being put under the seats and found they were walking on sacks of rice in the aisles. After sight-seeing and shopping in Baguio I decided they had enough of culture shock, and took them back to Manila in the air-conditioned tourist bus. It was wonderful to have them!

The next week I went to Central Luzon for Annual Conference. When the President of the College found that I was scheduled for one of the regular rooms in the college dorm basement she invited me to stay in her home, with a room on the second floor. I willingly accepted. Then typhoon Didang came. I took off my shoes and socks and walked across the road with the water almost up to my knees. We were all in the gymnasium for the Conference session when the lights went out. About 10:00 P.M. we were all expecting to stay there overnight when I discovered that the College President had sent a student to rescue me. He knew every rock in the area. We took off our shoes and waded almost knee-deep to her house. The whole Conference was stranded for days—but I was high, dry and well-fed. I felt for those I had left behind in the basement for everything was soaking wet. After about two days I had a ride back to Manila with a lawyer and his wife. As his driver knew how to drive after a typhoon, we got there safely. When I got to where I had left my car, it did not start. I took a bus home and picked it up later. 300 people at the Conference were stranded longer than I was, and 75,000 people lost their homes. I described this typhoon in detail because it affected me personally, but we had many storms. Once we had six typhoons in six weeks. It might have been one of those where the library floor was covered with water and my student assistants mopped it up before I knew about it. I will admit I was glad to leave the typhoons.

THE TRIP HOME, 1976

FAREWELL

At the airport a whole bus load from the Seminary was there to see me off. The travel agent was there and checked me through quickly; then I went outside to talk to people. Ruth Feuer and Dr. Ocompo (my predecessor) also came. Then I was checked by security, and there was no more visiting.

The Board gave me a six month furlough to travel, visit churches and get settled. I decided to spend two months of it traveling. The only way I could afford to do this was to stay in missionary guest houses as much as possible.

THAILAND

The first stop was Bangkok, landing there in the early evening. Having been there before, I stayed just overnight in the Missionary Guest House and flew in the morning to Chung Mai. A former student, Kamon, and the missionary friend I had known in Singapore, Jane Arp, were my hostesses.

Kamon took me shopping right away, and I bought two dolls, a man and a woman dancer. The latter is a good representative of the real dancers as her hands and feet are very expressive and her costume corresponds.

Jane took me to a large Buddhist Temple high on a hill, for the higher you are, the closer you are to heaven, she explained. We walked more than a hundred steps, with tribal people in their native costumes going and coming. On our return to the base we stopped at the gift shop where I bought Christmas ornaments—a bell, angel, tree and star. I was surprised to see them, as they looked like Christian symbols to me. Jane reminded me that vendors know what Americans buy, no matter where or when they sell.

In the evening Jane and a volunteer worker and I went to a "Cultural Center", a restaurant where we sat on the floor, but it was carpeted, and air conditioned, hardly typical Thai. The food was good; then the classical Thai dancing, where every movement of the feet, arms and head means something in their culture. Afterward we went outside for some tribal dancing, including some flame throwers. All was delightful.

One morning I went to a breakfast with missionaries. It was held at the Christian Hospital, and included teachers, nurses and doctors. It was good to hear about their work as we talked together. I appreciated the ecumenical aspect of the mission.

Sometimes Kamon, sometimes Jane, took me to the little cottage industries, usually a whole village making the same thing. Hand-woven silk, hand-painted umbrellas, silver pounded by hand, lacquer, all were fascinating. Kamon could ask, without prying, how much they were paid, and usually it was less than $1 per day.

One day as we left Jane's apartment and went through a large room, Jane introduced me to a woman playing the piano. She was teaching music at the college. When Dorothy Travaille moved into the Gardens Building 20 years later we discovered we had already met!

One of the doctors I had met at the hospital was on the plane going back to Bangkok. As one of the Doctors Without Borders, he introduced me to that organization. He had been in Africa and was visiting missionary friends. The meal was so spicy that I did not eat it, telling the doctor that my cast-iron stomach had rusted. He did eat it, looking at me as though I was weird. Fortunately there was some food left at the Guest House. In the morning I saw the doctor asking for a doctor, and looking like he needed one. I was glad I had not eaten the food on the plane.

I received a letter from Mr. Win Din who was my correspondent for Burma. He asked me to bring some medicine for an injection. At the pharmacy I discovered it would cost over $100, quite a bit for me to provide at the beginning of my trip. The pharmacist told me to call a Baptist missionary who quickly agreed to take care of it. Money for medicines in Burma came to him regularly and he sent someone every week with medical supplies as nothing was available there.

BURMA, or MYANMAR

Rev. Win Din, Director of Church World Service, and Rev. Aung Rhin, National Council of Churches Secretary, met me at the plane in Rangoon, and took me to the Strand Hotel. I went to the dining room for a cup of coffee and struck up a friendship with Mrs. Thorson, who had been on the plane to Chiang Mai as well as to Rangoon. She was from Denmark. We decided to meet for meals occasionally as we would both be there a week.

The next morning Rev. Din presented me with my schedule all made out for the week. I was astonished for I thought I was on vacation. His wife was with him, and we went sight-seeing, first to the Shewdagon Pagoda, the huge temple we had seen as we entered the city. Built in 500 B.C., the top was real gold, but the lower part was painted with gold leaf, and had to be redone every year. There were smaller temples nearby. In Burma, I was told, the Buddhism was mixed with animism. Devotees were pouring water on a small statue of the Buddha for good luck. If a person was born on Sunday, he poured it on a certain statue, if Monday, another one, etc.

We went to a reception hall on a lake, called Kawaweik, the name of a mythical bird. The hall looked like it was floating between two huge birds, although it was made of cement. It was new, very fancy, and very expensive to have receptions there. I asked about this kind of money being spent in a socialist country. Rev. Win said "It is 'Burmese Socialism', anything goes." We went out of the city to the Inya Lake Hotel for lunch. This was a new hotel, government run, and looked much like an Intercontinental Hotel. I thought it also was expensive. Then we went on to the World Peace Pagoda, built by a former Prime Minister to symbolize the need for peace in the world. Quietly, Rev. Din indicated the need Burma had for peace.

In the ensuing days I learned that to have "tea" with a group meant to give a speech. When I learned that the faculty members of the colleges could not leave the country to study in the United States or anywhere else, I realized how much they wanted anyone coming from a graduate school to share ideas with them. During the week I met with and gave talks to the Christian Education Committees of the National Council of Churches; the Methodists where I met two ordained women; the faculty of the Divinity School; and the Baptists, who were quite well organized, with a publication society for their own materials.

At one point I was afraid I would not have time to shop for a doll, so during a rest period allotted me, I took a taxi to a market and bought one.

One morning I waited half an hour for Rev. Din, then he took me to Seminary Hill. There all the students of the five Christian colleges were waiting for me to speak. They sang to me in Karen and Burmese. The men on each side of me told me what to say, different things but at the same time. I ignored them both and said whatever was on my heart and in my mind, using an interpreter. As there were a few hundred youth there I wondered why they did not have one ecumenical college. I did not ask, as I knew that denominationalism could be very strong in missions overseas instead of the ecumenical projects which I preferred.

One evening we went to the home of the sister of Mrs. Win Din for a delicious Burmese meal. The home was much like a Filipino one, with the same type of bamboo furniture. Mr. Tha Din was the last leader who was allowed to leave Burma to study overseas, and he went to Yale. In the discussion I asked about the salaries of workmen, and found that they are very low. As in China, this was called "simple living," not poverty.

I began to think differently about the big international cartels. I had thought of them as destructive to a country, but in a country that has kept them out there was little one could buy. I left two rolls of movie film, because a German Church sent a movie camera and projector, but they could not buy film. If a person had to have surgery he had to find his own antibiotics and dressings, and these were not available. Only government workers could buy a car, which cost U.S. $40,000. There was no foreign exchange. The country tried to be self-sufficient, but did not realize how interdependent they really were.

When I went to the airport to leave for Nepal, I naively declared my jewelry as required. I had to show it to the official and noticed an employee watching. I put the jewelry back in the case and in a bag, covered it with a plastic bag full of stockings, and locked the suitcase. The official sent it to the plane for Nepal.

NEPAL

Mrs. Thorson and I sat together on the plane to Kathmandu. When I opened the luggage for customs inspection the bag was unlocked and the zipper partly opened. I went to the office of the Union of Burma Airways immediately, and with two men watching I took everything out of the suitcase. A black pearl neck-lace and earrings, and jade earrings were missing. The manager said to write it out and take it to the office the next day. When I did I was told that there would be an investigation and that it would take time. I had one letter to that effect, but in spite of letters on my part I heard no more.

The Guest House in Katmandu was at the Headquarters of the United Mission to Nepal. This work in Nepal was begun when a United Methodist layman, a Dr. Fleming, secured permission to study birds in Nepal. His wife was a doctor, and she started healing people, then asked to begin a hospital. When that was granted several Methodist Church leaders from India met with Flemings and decided that this would be a Christian hospital, and that any work evolving from it would be ecumenical. From the beginning they worked with the government, starting schools and more hospitals. It was always a service-type work.

It was against the law to convert anyone to Christianity. The Summer Insti-tute of Linguistics had been converting some people and as a result had been ordered out of the country. Another group that had a good Christian Book Store had been ordered out also. The United Mission had a new five-year contract which could be broken by the government. Because of the hospitals and schools they ran, and their consistent work with the government, they expected it to con-tinue.

There was one Protestant Church, a part of the Mission, which I attended on Sunday morning. Rev. John Schaffer was pastor, a former executive of our United Methodist Mission Board. He was a nice man, but, I thought, a very poor preacher. He invited me to lunch later in the week, when we had a good time dis-cussing the Board and the work in Nepal.

With the help of Mrs. Thorson, who had pre-scheduled tours; Rev. Jonathan Lindall, a missionary who had been there twenty years; a few taxi rides and a bit of walking, I was able to see a number of interesting places. However, it was cloudy and sometimes rainy the entire time, so that I did not see the mountains.

The center of Katmandu looked ancient. All the buildings were of brick and they looked as though they could fall down at any moment. I took a taxi, and when I got out to walk a young boy of 14 or 15 came and walked with me, speak-ing excellent English, hoping I would hire him. When I discovered he knew the history I let him come with me as he was a better guide than the taxi driver had been. The Mahaboudha Temple was new, having been rebuilt after a 1935 earthquake. Each brick contained a figure of the Buddha. The Golden Buddha was discovered after the earthquake. For hundreds of years there had been a cement statue of the Buddha. The earthquake broke off enough of the covering to reveal a solid gold statue underneath. It was presumed that it had been covered to protect it from invaders, and the memory of it had been lost.

On one trip we visited the Hanuman Dhaka which was the old original castle. We walked up the nine flights of stairs and looked out over the city. We watched workmen rubbing wood carvings in order to be able to repair old parts of the Castle. At the home of the Living Goddess we saw a girl of seven or eight who popped up in the window when we paid. She never could play and she was always watched so she would not get hurt. She stayed as the goddess until puberty. She could not marry as there was a belief that if anyone married her he would die. To be chosen was a high honor.

Outside of the city we passed rice fields, many of them terraced. We went to an ancient town, on the top of a hill, built in the 13th century. It seemed very primitive. The streets smelled and the people did not look clean. The temple was called Bugh Bhairana to placate the tiger god, the god of destruction. When Prithwi Nurayan was conquering the valley in 1766 to unite the Kingdom, the town resisted and he cut off their ears and noses to make them surrender. The knives used were hanging in the temple.

At one town there was a small temple in the hills. On Tuesdays and Thursdays animals were sacrificed. We saw chickens and goats being sacrificed. This was gory. I wondered if people felt better because it was done, or if they thought the gods felt better. Were the Biblical sacrifices that horrible? I was glad that Christians and Jews did not continue that practice. We went to Pashupatinoth, a holy shrine of the Bagmati River which flowed into the Ganges. We stopped to watch a cremation which seemed more gruesome than the animal sacrifice.

As I flew to India the clouds cleared and I saw the mountains for the first time. Although I was not new to mountains these were a thrill, for I could see Mt. Everest and the other Himalayas.

INDIA

In Bombay I took a taxi to the Methodist Guest House, bargaining with the driver to cut the fare but he cut it by only 9 rupees from 39. That was not very good, I thought, for an experienced bargainer. The Guest House was one floor of a new building housing the Methodist Headquarters. The rooms were air conditioned, there was hot running water and a private bath, which was much appreciated. The manager was Mrs. Finney, a British woman, who served tea every afternoon.

On Sunday I went to church with the Finneys at Taylor Memorial Methodist Church. The pace was very slow, with a monotone delivery. When I took out the camera, the front assembly fell apart. Fortunately I had another camera with me, but it was much older. I was disappointed for I would want good pictures for the remainder of the trip.

I decided to take a walk just around the block from the Guest House so that I would not get lost. I walked between street dwellers, families living on the sidewalks, and in the gutters. A few had plastic for a sleeping cover. I thought I had seen poverty in Tondo, Manila, but it was not like this. I wanted to sit in the gutter and talk with them, person to person, as equals. I could not, as I did not know the language or the culture. I was surprised to see so many services being carried out on the sidewalk: barbers cutting hair, shaving, typing services and many others. I discovered that they are all untouchables, for no one else would touch the street people. Although officially the caste system had been made illegal it still existed. It happened that people were streaming out of a train station just then, and as I watched them, none of them looked at the street people.

At the Guest House I met Mrs. Caroline Simpson, who had just come. We walked together a short distance to the Oberoi Sheraton to shop. She would be staying eighteen months to finish her PhD in textiles at Baroda University. We went to the Prince of Wales Museum, and I quickly found that I could out-walk her. Finally she sat down while I continued. On the third floor I found a room full of old textiles, so I went back and got her. She was thrilled. She went back to the Guest House and I continued on. When I walked to the Taj Mahal Hotel I saw more families living on the street. The combination of luxury and extreme poverty bothered me. When I went through the Gate of India, a monument built in 1911, the area was full of street families. I wondered if they were allowed on certain sections of the city. Mrs. Fleming did not know the answer to any of my questions.

I had been directed to a section with many small shops. I had fun going in and out of them, deciding whether to buy this or that, finally buying a piece of mixed silk and polyester, for about $3 per meter. Then I walked some distance to the Cottage Industry Store. This was a large store where people who made things in their own homes brought them to be sold. I bought a doll, the nicest one I had seen, for about $3. Also I bought a peacock enamel on brass, very inexpensive.

After trying to find a bus to the Hanging Gardens, I gave up and took a taxi. It was called "hanging" because it was on top of a reservoir. The most outstanding thing for me was the way the bushes had been trimmed. I especially liked the one representing the man driving his two caribou. From there I had a beautiful view of the city.

The third night I had a roommate, a delightful Indian woman who was a leader in the Methodist Church, and had come into the city for a meeting. While she was visiting in the Philippines she had come to my home to visit her Indian friend, Premlata Lal, who stayed with me awhile. She remembered my dolls, but we did not remember each other. We had only a short while to visit that night, as she was busy in the morning, and I would be leaving.

When I left for Kenya I took a taxi to the Air India building and waited for the airport bus. It was old, slow, noisy and rough. When I checked in I was told my baggage was eighteen kilograms overweight! It had not been overweight before, and I did not buy that much. I suspected he had his foot on the scale, but if I confronted him I was afraid that might be against their culture and it might cause a big stir, as it would in the Philippines. I just argued a little. He charged me for only five kilograms, about $25, which I still felt was outrageous. He gave me a coupon for a full dinner at airline expense because the plane was two hours late. Actually we did have tea and dinner on the five hour flight, so I did not know why I had the free lunch. I had to admit it did help balance the feeling of being cheated.

KENYA

The Guest House of the Church of England in Nairobi was on a high hill just out of the main section of town. The center of town is a beautiful, modern city. I walked down to buy my ticket for the safari I had requested. Many of the tours were a week long. I bought a ticket for a three day safari at $50 per day with two overnights, realizing that would be long enough for me to be watching the animals.

Our Methodist missionary in Nairobi was Dr. Malcom McVeigh. When I went to his office we talked for some time about the work and politics there. He would be leaving shortly to work in the U.S. Methodist Headquarters, but a new couple would be coming to do evangelistic work on the coast.

We started on the tour the next morning. The other passengers were a man and his daughter who talked very privately all the way. I suspected that they thought they would have a private car. Neither the driver, Joseph, nor I, ever carried on a conversation with them. After the first evening when we were directed to the same table and they ignored me, I made it a point not to sit with them so they could be alone. We drove through the country of the proud Masai tribe, but the driver did not let us take pictures because, he said, the country did not allow it. They did not want them to make their living that way. However we stopped at an inn, and were allowed to take pictures there for about $1.25. The handicraft items were expensive,$10 for a very crudely carved witch doctor, $10 for a bead necklace, very wide as they wear them. I never did find a doll dressed as a Masai. Joseph said they are very primitive people. (Question in my mind, Did the country want to keep them that way?)

The first part of the road was good, then miles of washboard dirt, across the Athi Plains. We arrived for a late lunch at our first stop, the Amboseli Lodge. This was a very plush lodge, with automatic gas water heater, etc. Did I worry about being colonialist? The driver tried to convince me that it gives people work, and the "natives" of the region are too primitive to know the difference. I remembered my missionaries' advice "if you have it, enjoy it" which I decided to do.

In the afternoon we gathered to go on a photographing tour. It was tremendous—giraffes, zebras, elephants, lions, cheetahs, gazelles, etc. We could not get out of the car as it was too dangerous. In fact, once I did close the window because a lion came right toward us. In the evening I watched the elephants at the water hole.

We were up at six to go animal hunting again. When it got light the clouds had cleared and we could see Mount Kilimanjaro. It is 19,000 feet and we were at the foot. It is always snow-capped even though it is only about 200 miles from the equator. We saw zebras and had a wonderful close-up of elephants. As we passed them, a huge male at the back of the herd looked at us, stamped his feet, growled (swearing?) and danced around, as if to say "get out of here." I noticed Joseph put on the gas and left quickly, but he did not say anything.

After breakfast we left for an 80-mile drive to Tsavo National Park (West), the largest in East Africa. We drove across the Kuku Plains and a huge lava flow, and to Kilaguni Lodge, another deluxe place. Each room had a porch where one could sit and watch the animals come to the water hole. It was very relaxing.

We went to Mzima Springs. This is very clear water that is carried underground through molten rock. It is piped and sent on to Mombasa on the coast. There is a little recess underwater where one can see the water and the many fish. We also saw many elephants, and two lions trying to sleep.

The manager gave a lecture before dinner. 18,000 elephants had been in this part of the Park. The previous year a drought killed half of them. They preferred good farm land but were gradually being pushed into the park. They have broken down the trees, making it a plains area, and thus zebras and other plains animals had come in.

The next morning I was the only passenger in the car. Joseph took me to a look out where we could see for miles, then drove around looking for animals. It seemed to be too late in the morning for we did not see any. He took me to another lookout which was not on the itinerary. We had a good discussion about Kenyan politics.

The other passengers joined us on the way back to Nairobi. This was a much better road, and Joseph drove about 65 miles an hour, until the younger passenger asked him to go slower. I laughed to myself, the younger one wanted it slower, and the older one (me) enjoying the speed.

On Sunday I decided to go to the United Church at Levington, a district of Nairobi. It cost about $5 taxi fare. After church I met a missionary, Margaret Finch, who runs a Methodist Guest House which is new. She was disappointed that I had not gone there to stay, but it is far out and I was glad I did not have to pay $5 for each trip. She invited me there for dinner. A Free Methodist Tour group from Seattle Pacific College was there and they took me along with them to the Nairobi Game Park. As this was part of their tour I paid just the entrance fee. We looked for game and saw quite a few zebras and gazelles, but not many others. It was a bit dull after Amboseli and Tsavo. When we returned we went to a wood-carving shop where I bought gifts for Ruth Feuer and Marvel Fagan and had them shipped to the Philippines. I appreciated the way the group from Seattle included me in their afternoon tour.

The tour to see Masai dancing sounded interesting. We went to the Rift Valley, a very wide plateau, about 50 miles across. It is 2000 feet below Nairobi. The road was very steep with no switch-backs. In a garden owned by a British couple the Masai gave a native dance. As they were dressed as warriors I expected them to chase each other around, but they did not. They jumped up and down, back and forth, and up and down, sometimes quite high. It was very odd. Then we had tea, British style.

At the Guest House in Nairobi there were some missionaries from Ethiopia. I learned a good deal about their situation for they knew their time was limited. They have been training leaders so that the church could continue even under the stringent Communist government which seemed to be coming.

At the airport, in order to go to Zambia, I had to exchange the local money into dollars. The man ahead of me had to take off his socks to show how much money he had for they suspected that he was not honest. This was the first time I had ever seen that done.

ZAMBIA

When I arrived in Lusaka, Miss Muriel Bissel, who had been my contact, was waiting for me at the Ridgeway Hotel. She was a retired missionary from Canada and had lived there a number of years. Mr. Claude Susuki, the travel agent, could not reconfirm my plane reservation for Livingston, the town nearest Victoria Falls, because he could not cash my traveler's check. The money had just been devalued and there there was no foreign exchange allowed. Miss Bissel paid all, over $100! Lusaka was full as people came in from all over the country for a celebration. The railroad from Tanzania had just been turned over to the Zambian government by the Chinese, who had built it. Business people were excited.

Miss Bissel had become a Zambian citizen and had a small farm because she was sure God wanted her to stay there. I wondered, will the racial problems in Rhodesia make this difficult in the future? Many years later I was told that she had been murdered by one of her workers. So sad.

In Livingston I stayed at the Musi Tanya, the Intercontinental Hotel. Of course I did not usually stay in these hotels, but there were only two, and this was closest to the Falls and the one Miss Bissel had reserved.

I walked the short distance to see the Falls many times. The spray came up so high that one could see only a part of it. One time I put on shoes that could get wet, wore rain gear, and went out on the wet bridge. The view was magnificent. When I have been asked to compare Victoria Falls with Niagara Falls I answer that it is unimportant. Each has its own wonderful beauty.

Miss Bissel had arranged for a package tour which included a boat trip on the Zambese River. The news outside of Zambia was that guerrillas were going across the river to fight in the civil war in Rhodesia. The Zambian government denied it, but we had police escort nevertheless. At one point we saw three elephants and every one was excited. The sunset was beautiful on the river.

The next day we went into the town of Livingston to the museum. It was excellent, but I thought that I would find information about the life of David Livingston, an early missionary in that area. Obviously the town had been named for him, but, strangely, I could not find a word about him.

We had time to walk around town. I saw a long line of people on a sidewalk so I went over to see what was happening. They were buying meat, something like a hot dog. I wanted to ask many questions: When was the last time meat had been available? How much did it cost? Could they buy as much as they wanted if they had the money? Or was it rationed? I didn't find out. As I was in the luxurious restaurant eating a delicious broiled steak dinner, I asked another guest how it was that the people in town had so little meat available and we were eating like this? He pointed out that the border to Rhodesia was closed and that a train was parked in the middle of the train bridge. Trade between the countries was carried on there for those who could afford it. I wondered, couldn't we have shared a little?

When I went to Kitwe to visit Mendola I expected some one to meet me, but as no one did I wandered about the town and found the market. There was very little meat, some chicken, and the only fresh things were lettuce, cabbage, a few carrots, onions and oranges. This is a copper-mining community, and I expected it to be a little more prosperous.

I took a taxi to Mendola, an ecumenical mission center for all of Africa. The Assistant Administrator housed me in a guest apartment, then took me around the campus. I was impressed by the Dag Hammersvold Library, a memorial to the former United Nations Executive who was killed in a plane crash about ten miles away from there. There were innovative programs designed to help the African people to live fully, and to lead their churches. There was a program for mothers who came for a month, learning child care, first aid, crafts, and gardening. A Journalism department trained students to create their own literature, and the art center taught them to illustrate it. There a man was making dolls to support his family but he would take orders only. An American missionary headed that center. The training class for ministers had 15 students, college not required.

At the YWCA I found that the Canadian woman in charge had lived in Escanaba, Michigan, one of the towns in my district when I traveled in northern Michigan. She and another woman taught women how to make things and sell them in a gift shop. I bought a cloth doll. When I mentioned that the one I really wanted was the one in the art center, the Y.W. friend told me I could have one being made for her. It had two women pounding rice, their arms moving up and down. Although I was retired I wrote to the Board offering to spend a year there in the Library, while they trained the young man in charge in library work, but nothing came of it.

Miss Marjorie Murray and a Disciple missionary, Miss Jane Hooton, took me to the plane. The mother of the latter lived in Indianapolis, across the street from my friend Mabel Metze. Later, when I visited Mabel, Miss Hooton's mother was delighted to have this first-hand report about her daughter.

Back in Lusaka on Sunday morning I went to the United Church. The pastor was an Irish missionary who had his Master of Theology from San Francisco Theological Seminary. One of his professors was Dr. Oxtoby who had taught with us in the Philippines after retirement. I was invited to the Manse for dinner, and Mr. Green, whom I had met at the Falls, was there. We had a delicious dinner and a delightful fellowship. Later I walked to the big Anglican Cathedral. I spent the rest of my time there shopping.

I took the plane to Dar es Salaam, Tanzania, to stay overnight and get the plane for Athens, Greece.

GREEK ISLANDS

After one day in Athens I boarded the ship Orion for a seven-day tour of the Greek Islands. I had a single room, small but nice, with private bath. We discovered that because Greece and Turkey were arguing with each other over oil explorations in the sea it was too dangerous to go to Istanbul. All of us were disappointed because this was the destination we had counted on with this particular tour.

We followed the coast all night and in the morning were at Volos. We took two busses and rode to Meteorie, huge needle-like rocks with monasteries on top. The Monastery of Saint Varlaam was built in the fourteenth century to get away from the Turks. In older days they lifted everything they needed in baskets from the bottom of the hill. Now there is a road to the Monastery. Although this was not a real substitute for Istanbul, it was very interesting, and gave us a glimpse into the history of the Greek-Turkish relationships.

Stacey and I got acquainted early. She was Greek Orthodox, the principal of a Greek Orthodox school near Washington, D.C. Often during the tour we would leave the others and go to churches. She explained the icons to me; we discussed theology and learned a good deal from each other. Her parents were from Greece, but this was her first time to visit the country.

There were three islands on the tour that interested me most, Santorini, Crete and Rhodes. In early days Santorini was known as Saint Irene. It was a volcano which erupted about 1200 B.C., making one side steep, the other sloping like the side of any mountain going into the sea. The tourist ships docked on the steep side. We rode 547 steps by donkey. This was my first time ever to ride any animal. My donkey kept wanting to pass the ones ahead and I had to hold him back as best I could. It was difficult as he understood Greek, not English. If he got too near the wall I pushed him over by pushing my foot against the wall. It was fun and a new experience. All buildings on top were white-washed. There were many,

many tourist shops with a great deal of produce spread outside. I checked around and found a lamb's-wool sweater for $12.50, just like ones I had seen before for $20. Consequently I bought one there. We visited the beautiful modern Orthodox Church. We were surprised to see a road going down the back of the hill and realized that the way we had come was for tourists only. The island was delightful to visit but both Stacey and I thought it quite isolated for living. However, we talked with a British lady in one of the stores. We asked her how she gets on and off the island, and she said, "Why do I want to leave the island? This is home. Oh, once I had a tooth-ache—"

Stacey and I decided to ride the donkeys down again to have the whole experience, although many people were afraid and walked. Going down was much rougher and we had to lean way back to keep from feeling that we were falling. My donkey slipped a couple of times, but I decided that if he slipped I might too, if I had walked. Anyway the steps were dirty with donkey dirt. My donkey did a good job of avoiding the many people who did walk down.

When we arrived in Heraklion, Crete, we visited the archeological museum and the Palace of Knossos. Crete had the earliest European civilization, about 1600 B.C. In mythology Zeus made himself into a bull, and a goddess fell in love with him. The son was a bull and to hide the shame a labyrinth was built in the palace so he could not find his way out. Some sections of this have been restored. The articles in the museum were interesting, many of them artistic. When other people overran and conquered the Cretans, some of them remained as slaves, others sailed to the Asian mainland and became the Philistines.

Landing at Rhodes, we took busses for Lindos, a town at the far end of the island. Stacey and I and some of the others hiked up to the Acropolis to see the sanctuary of Athena. In a cave below we saw a church which had been dedicated to St. Paul. The city of Rhodes was founded after Lindos and became the Capital. In ancient times there had been a huge statue of a man with his feet outstretched across the harbor. This had been one of the Seven Wonders of the World. In Medieval times the Crusaders came and stopped on their way to and from the Holy Land. The Order of St. John stopped on its way back and stayed. There were about 600 monks from several countries, most of them from Spain. The Palace had huge wide steps, many rooms for meetings and a courtyard where concerts were given. We shopped a little and I bought a folding umbrella, having left mine in a Katmandu taxi. There was Greek dancing in the lounge about 11:00 P.M. so Stacey and I watched.

EPHESUS

At Kusadasi, Turkey, soldiers in small boats watched us as we left the ship. It was a little scary but there was no problem. It took about 20 minutes to arrive at the old site of Ephesus. First we visited the ruins of the Cathedral of the Church of St. John. Only some of it has been reconstructed. Then we went to the Ephesus of the New Testament where Paul lived for three years. Here there was a continuity of history that I had known before only on the night I went with the Canon to the Mount of Olives. The mile-long paved avenue, with pedestals where statues had been, the laws engraved in stone for all to read, the crosses when Christianity came in, the library, the market place, the stadium, and the Temple of Diana—it was tremendous. After spending about an hour and a half walking around Stacey and I went back to Kusadasi. I knew I would have to buy a new coat for the U.S. as my old one had become worn out on furloughs. Quickly I decided to buy a leather one in Turkey. I just had time to find one before going back to the ship.

When we returned to Athens I left immediately for Rome, then a two-day tour to southern Italy. We stopped for a panoramic view of Naples, but we did not go into the city. The ruins left by Mt. Vesuvius, which erupted in 79 A.D., were certainly interesting. Much excavation has been done through the years. We walked down the main street and looked at the side streets. We went into the brothel which had pictures of the various postures for sexual contact. (I heard later that this had been closed to women but restrictions had been recently removed.) The temples were not very well preserved or had not yet been reconstructed. One private home was beautiful. The garden was found with statues still intact. It is thought that the eruption happened in the day time because the lamps were all in one place being cleaned. So many things were not broken that the people may have died from poisonous gasses. Many bodies were found and have been preserved by some modern technique. It was all fascinating. We went on to Sorrento, staying overnight at the Hotel Tramontano. This is a very old mansion, beautifully re-done through the years. A famous poet was born in "West Wing" in 1514. A list of notables, Byron, queens and kings, others have stayed here, and, said the notice, we were just as welcome. It sits high on the edge of a cliff on the Bay of Naples. My room was down a hall which went around and around until I almost got lost several times. We ate breakfast out on a balcony overlooking the Bay.

The trip to Capri was in a very small boat that bounced around on the waves although it went fast. We arrived at one end of the island to go into the "Blue Grotto". We got into row boats, three in a boat. I was with two men, one from our tour who was from Brazil and spoke no English but sang beautifully. We went into a little cave, and to quote the tour propaganda it was "suffused with a jeweled luminescence caused by the reflection of the sun rays through the Mediterranean waters". It really was beautiful and when I put my hand in it looked blue, too. The man rowing and the man from Brazil sang together as if they had practiced. Then we went back to the boat and to Marina Grande, the bay town of Capri. We took a very small bus up a very steep zig-zag road where we shopped awhile, then down to the center of town. After some free time we went back in the little boats to Sorrento, and I returned to Rome for overnight and on to the airport for Tunis.

The departure was interesting. The crew closed the door on the Al Italia plane and began the demonstration of life belts. Suddenly they stopped, the door opened, and forty-six Japanese tourists came in, most of them sitting in back. Two sat next to me in the middle group of seats. Just as we seemed ready to leave, the captain was talking to the crew, then an immigration officer came in, and the Japanese leader made an announcement. Suddenly the whole group trooped off again. They had to take their hand baggage with them. Those of us still on the plane guessed that they were so late getting to the plane that the immigration people had gone and their baggage had not gone through the machines. They were back in about ten minutes. We were about an hour late leaving.

Along the way when the two men stewards began to serve drinks I asked for a coke. Before the one nearest me could serve me the other one came down the aisle with his cart, yelling at the other man, and pushed his cart into the other one. They shouted at each other for some time. Finally the one who had been pushed back gave my coke to the man behind me to pass along to me. All in all, it was a very unpleasant trip. I thought I would complain to the airline, but I never did. Somehow we arrived in Tunis on time. My cousin Marion Adoum was at the airport to meet me. Her house was small, and like many others, white with blue trim.

Because I love Oriental Bazaars, Marion took me there the first day. I bought a doll for about $3 and a leather hassock cover, cost about $20. The one I had previously had faded and the cat had ruined it, so I left it in the Philippines. I had found that it fitted into any decor and was comfortable for resting ones feet when relaxing. The cover only was easy to take in the suitcase. A specialty there were bird cages. Marion wanted me to buy one but how would I get it home and what would I do with it then? I have never had a bird and was not sure I would in the future. In spite of her pressure I did not buy one. We rested and after a light supper we went for "tea" at the home of an American family. They had fancy sandwiches, cakes, etc. The father was a geologist and with their six children they were there for six weeks. They seemed anxious for American company. The Bolshoi Ballet would be coming and they had bought Marion a ticket to go with them. I thought it indicated how much they thought of her. They would be going to Cairo for a year's sabbatical from the University of South Carolina.

At one point over lunch Marion and I did a lot of family talking, and I learned more about her father who was my mother's brother. She showed me music which he had published. We talked about her husband whom I had known when they were in the States. He was an Arab, from an important, rich family. She had met him at a World's Fair in Philadelphia. She felt strange to be treated as superior to others. When she went to the doctor he would always take her in right away, no matter how many others were waiting. Some of the vendors in the Bazaar knew her, and I realized that is why she wanted me to buy a bird cage. She was living on her Social Security and pension, not on money from his family. She told me that in the States he taught French, but whenever I had visited them he seemed not to be doing anything. He died in 1972. In my mind she was the primary bread-winner as she sold specialty, high-priced linens in upgrade department stores.

Marion did not have a car, so sight-seeing was by taxi. She took me to a town called Slidi Bon Said, on a high cliff beside the sea. All homes were white-washed and trimmed with blue. Blue was the only color they could use because the town wanted everything white and blue near the sea. There were very beautiful homes and beautiful views. Then we went to the town of Carthage also by the sea. There were very few ruins there. The best ruins are about 100 miles away. I was disappointed, but without a car a trip there was impossible. We had gone quite far from Tunis so we returned by train. As I left she and I were glad to have had the opportunity to visit for all her immediate family had died.

Instead of going directly to Madrid, Spain, from Tunis, I made a twenty-four hour stop in Marseilles, France, where I changed planes. I had read about the Santora doll which is made only in that part of France. Each doll represents the work of a peasant in that area. I was fascinated by the dolls in the gift shop of the hotel but they were quite large and very expensive. I went to a department store to buy some buttons as I had lost one off my suit coat. A salesgirl turned her back on me when she discovered that I did not speak French, and a floor walker pointed upstairs, but with a frown. I found what I wanted, paid the clerk, and walked out a bit angry with the lack of friendliness. I walked on down to the water front to work off the mood, wandering a bit among the many boats which were there because of the regatta the night before. I spotted a gift shop. I thought the clerks could not be worse than the others so I went in. Right there on the shelf were the Santora, a little smaller than those in the hotel and half the price. I picked up one and a young man came over to me. It took only a moment to realize that he did not know one word of English and I did not know French. He began to act out the work of the one I had in my hand. I responded by trying out other dolls, asking him questions by using facial expressions. He was a real ham. I could read the prices. Who cared about language? We were both having far more fun with the non-verbal communication. He was the funniest with a gray haired old woman carrying garlic so I chose that one. It cost about $6. The delightful encounter was worth it.

SPAIN

The flight to Madrid on a small plane was a smooth ride for just one hour. The Emperador Hotel had my reservation, an old but beautiful hotel. It had a marble staircase, with bronze banister and beautiful wood floors. The room had an old-style chandelier, nice furniture, and bath and shower.

The trip to the south had already been arranged. When I checked in I found I had a front seat assigned next to Mrs. Margaret Wilson, who was also traveling alone. We enjoyed each other in spite of the fact that she smoked a great deal and drank a lot. As she has a son who does not drink, she respected my disinterest in it. The leader, Marisal, gave us the itinerary and a map which I lost along the way.

As this was a commercial tour there was not a great deal to distinguish it as we went from town to town. However, Granada cannot be ignored, first because of the Alhambra. It is plain on the outside, but gorgeous inside. It was the palace of the Moors before the Christian Conquest. The rooms have lost their color, but the columns were lacy and beautiful. There were several courtyards with lovely gardens. The "Generalife," a smaller palace, and garden were also outstanding. It is difficult to describe it, as it was distinctly Arabic.

We went to one of the Gypsy "caves." They used to actually live in caves, but they were flooded out and the city made them move. The huts are built to look like caves, with all sorts of copper trinkets hanging from the ceiling. There was no ventilation except the door. With our whole tour group inside and the popular type Flamenco dancing, it really got stuffy. The gypsies insisted that each individual stand for a picture with one of them. I hated all the pictures taken all the time, for every thing we did, and I refused. The second time around I had to stand up just to play the game. But the flash of the camera did not go off. The photographer tried several times, but by this time the battery was dead. Our group started kidding me that I had broken the camera but I said I had a "hex" on it, having no idea the man would understand that word. He became very angry, scowling at me. I tried to explain that he needed a new battery, but he did not understand that, just the "hex!" Mrs. Wilson, knowing how I hated the pictures, tried to keep her laughter hidden. As we left and people were buying their pictures, he hated me. I was confused on how to mend a relationship like that. I thought the leader should have helped, but I did not ask her.

Back in Madrid I went to the Royal Palace. Mrs. Wilson was there and we had an English-speaking guide to take us through. Except for Leningrad, this was the most ornate palace I had been in. The chandeliers were different in every room. Many rooms had silk walls with drapes to match. The ceilings were painted beautifully, and many famous paintings hung on the walls. There were many clocks, more than 100, each of them different. We also visited the collection of armor. I was glad Mrs. Wilson and I had an opportunity to visit again, as this ended our time together.

WORLD METHODIST CONFERENCE, 1976

Dublin, Ireland, was next for the World Methodist Conference. I had not realized that the World Methodist Women were meeting, too. I went to two of their meetings as they are always on the cutting edge of things and inspiring. The President was Mrs. Patrocinia Ocompo, my forerunner at the Seminary.

I took a tour to Lake Kilarney, one of the popular short tours. I sat in the front seat next to a friendly American woman. As we began to share who we were, she said "Oh, you are one of our missionaries." She was Phyllis Foster of Ann Arbor, Michigan, the President of the Ann Arbor District United Methodist Women in the Detroit Conference. In subsequent years I have spoken to her District Meeting, and other groups, and visited her in Ann Arbor. We were interested in the farms as we went along. When we reached the lake area we were put into carriages drawn by horses and rode around the lake. It was an interesting ride and we had lots of time to talk.

The Inauguration Ceremony for the World Methodist Council was fascinating. All the speakers and Bishops and leaders of the various countries were dressed in their clerical garbs, some of which are very colorful, especially those of Africa and Asia. They paraded in the street before coming into the hall. There were about 3,000 delegates, making it an exciting beginning.

During the Conference there were many speakers and discussions. I was especially impressed by Rev. Donald English of Britain who did the Bible Study each morning, and Dr. Alan Walker of Australia. Evening sessions were dramatic, one from Africa and one a Wesley play called "Ride, Ride."

One afternoon Phyllis Foster and I went to see the Book of Kells, which is housed in the Library of Trinity College. These are the four Gospels, copied and decorated in the 8th or 9th Century. One page is shown each day, under glass to preserve it. We stood in line, then had a chance to glance at it. Then we stood in another line to see the page open on the other side of the glass container. As it is in Latin we could not read it, and printing of that day was very different from anything one can see anywhere today. Just being able to see one of the old Bibles so beautifully done many Centuries ago was a thrill.

On Sunday we had a Communion Service in St. Patrick's Cathedral of the Church of England, the only church in Dublin large enough to house the Conference.

In the afternoon I joined the Peace March in solidarity with the Women's Peace March in Belfast, Ireland. An estimated 50,000 people marched through the streets in Dublin to the park where the service was held. I walked with a Catholic priest as we shared our desire for peace not only in Northern Ireland, but through-out the world. The actual service was short but impressive. After reading the "Declaration of the Peace People," we sang "The Lord is my Shepherd." There was a prayer followed by the singing of "The Lord's Prayer." The Dublin City Ramblers sang an anthem written especially for this occasion. I was thrilled to be a part of such a peace demonstration.

The Conference ended with the theme "A Day Yet to Dawn," with ideas and inspiration for the future.

◆   ◆   ◆

Leaving Dublin for New York I had to change planes in Paris, and also airports. I arrived while the plane for New York was loading to find that Air Lingus had not reconfirmed my ticket as I had asked them to do. After some discussion and concern I was sent first class. This was my first time to travel first class and I loved it. There was plenty of room for a nap and we ate delicious food all the way.

At Headquarters of the Board of Global Ministries I spent a couple of days being "de-briefed" which I discovered means briefing them on what had been happening in the work. I went on to Wisconsin to speak in many of the churches I had known. One was in the Neenah church where I had worked before becoming a pastor, and those who were still around were delighted to see me and hear about the work. The pastor was one of the youth leaders I had known as the District Director of Youth Work nearly twenty years before. The Eau Claire Church was another that welcomed me back. While I was there Margaret Gratz took me to Arkansaw to visit with the people I had known. In between speaking engagements I some-times stayed with Cooks in Milwaukee. When I was making arrangements for these visits the woman I had contacted talked with Elaine Cook and asked if we were sisters. Elaine had answered "yes," "well, no." The woman was confused. "Couldn't she make up her mind?" the woman asked me. I was much amused and agreed that perhaps she could not, for in spite of my being about 15 years older we have been close ever since those days in Kendall.

For some reason the Detroit Conference contact was not much interested but I did get to a number of churches in the Upper Peninsula, preaching and visiting many friends. In the Detroit Area itself I had only three places, all with former

Upper Peninsula pastors. I was disappointed, as that was the Conference that I had joined twenty years before.

When I had shipped things from overseas I had them sent to Cooks' address. I realized I really would be over-weight this time. I bought a travel trunk and took the train to Seattle. Walter met me and took me to Olympia.

OLYMPIA, WASHINGTON

THE FIRST TWO YEARS

Walter's mobile home was in a mobile-home park on Black Lake, about seven miles south of Olympia. Soon we went to the home of our nephew Dick Clifton, his wife, Ann Marie, and three children, Terry, Julie and Lisa. Dick was the second son of my brother, Francis, who had changed his name to George Clifton many years before. He had died when he was only 50 years old. His wife, Cecelia, was with us that day. In a few days Walter gave me his car keys and took his Jeep and went deer hunting with Paul Anderson, an uncle of Ann Marie's.

On Sunday I found the First Methodist Church. I liked the Pastor, Rev. Paul Beeman. There was an adult class on world hunger, so I decided that is the place for me.

In Milwaukee I had gone to a doctor because of a minor health problem, and the doctor told me that when I got to Olympia I must see a doctor immediately as it would be the right time to check it. When I saw Dr. Dave Fairbrook the check-up proved to be O.K., and I discovered he was also a Methodist. Thus in the years that followed we often talked about church as well as health.

I was surprised at how much difficulty I had getting a driver's license. I read all the materials and could pass that part without a problem, but the driving itself was a different matter. The policeman said I should turn my head around each time I was to change lanes or make a turn. I told him there would be six cars in front of me by the time I turned around. "Where have you been driving?" "Manila!" But he took two points off of every item for that one thing. Thus I had to take it again. It was embarrassing.

Walter did not have a T.V. and I missed it, so before he got back from hunting I bought a small one and a cart to put it on. Walter had told me to ask a neighbor to help me with things but evidently I asked the wrong one because he did not seem very happy about fixing anything for me.

Thanksgiving was the next week after I arrived. Walter came back with no deer meat as he left it with Ann Marie's parents in Ilwaco. We went to Cecelia's for dinner. Besides Dick's family there was Frances (George's daughter) and her son Earl Eckland III, Cecilia's second husband, and Mr. and Mrs. Savage. Mr. Savage was a former U.S. Representative. He told how he had relied on George for the working man's point of view, as George had been the executive of the local labor union. Mr. Savage spoke highly of him which I was glad to hear.

I bought a furnished mobile home in Shelton which Walter thought was worth the $5,000. The people who owned it wanted to stay until April. Walter thought we would not be ready to move it to his property across the lake before that time. They said I could use the extra room. My things from the Philippines came and were dumped in their yard, and they carried them to the room. I really appreciated that.

There was to be a pot-luck at the church and I said I would bring a cake. Suddenly it occurred to me that if I was going to take a cake I was going to have to make it myself as I no longer had a maid. I bought a cake mix, then discovered that Walter did not have a bowl large enough to mix it in, no large spoon to mix it with and no electric beater. I decided to let somebody else take the cake.

Christmas came quickly. We had Christmas Eve dinner at Dick's home. Ann Marie made a delicious wild-blackberry pie. She and I were happy with "Cool Whip" but Walter would not eat a substitute. I drove over to a little store to buy real whipping cream. This became a perennial habit as long as he lived. We exchanged Christmas gifts in the morning and I was delighted to receive an electric beater. The custom of this family was to eat in a restaurant on Christmas Day so that no one had to cook a big meal that day.

Just after New Year's I headed for Chevy Chase, a suburb of Washington, D.C., for a meeting of the Board of Global Ministries for a formal retirement. We were challenged by Mr. Jim Wallis who led a community in Washington, D.C., which had opened their homes to the poor. His vision of Christian action was new and impelling. There I met Howard Heiner, who was not retired but a former missionary who lived in Tacoma. He and his wife, Peggy, moved to Olympia soon after, and we became good friends. After the meeting I spent a couple of days with Bill and Arlene McTurnal. Bill is a half-brother of cousin Barbara Kline. We had a great visit and they told me they were moving to Tacoma soon.

The next week Jimmy Carter was to be inaugurated President. This was the first time I had been in Washington at the right time for such an event. It was cold that day, about 25°. We stood for an hour and a half on ice during the ceremony. Nevertheless I was thankful to be there. After watching Nixon go in his plane to leave the Capital grounds permanently, the crowd went on to Pennsylvania Ave. for the parade. The next two days it rained and I spent the time in the Smithsonian. I had stayed with a friend who lived just four blocks from the Capitol.

Walter had told me I did not need a car, as he had three; one the Jeep, one that did not run, and a Plymouth. I thought that would be convenient. One time he loaned his Jeep to Dick and went off in his Plymouth. That Sunday we were having a 70th birthday party for Phyllis at Judy's home. I needed a car to get there. Rev. Beeman helped me buy a formerly-leased yellow Plymouth for $3,000.

In due time Walter began to work on the property across the lake. He had it terraced in the fall and it needed time to settle. The couple from whom I bought the mobile home had gone for some time before we moved it over. I left all the building things to Walter as I had no experience at all for that. It was quite a job to get the large window facing the lake, but they did. Over the next few months I painted the ceilings, woodwork, and bedroom furniture. When I was thinking about the carpets it happened that Walter and I were with the older Ecklands, Frances' in-laws. Later Earl Eckland gave me a crash course on choosing carpets. I bought new furniture for the living room, and made a prominent spot for the desk I brought from the Philippines. I made curtains for all the windows. The most challenging were the kitchen curtains made from hand-woven material from the Philippines. I think I had every store in town helping with those curtains. While I was doing all this I took a course in Interior Decorating at the local furniture store. Although I could not afford the furniture displayed, the course was stimulating, and some of the things done were the result of discussions there. When it was all finished I could look out that large front-room window and see the Black Lake, and, in good weather, Mount Rainier.

There were still two operas left in the season. Walter took me as he had two seats in the Loges. Perhaps he had taken Frances before because she seemed to become jealous. I bought seats in the upper balcony for the next season. Walter took Frances then, and usually we would go to the room open only to the expensive patrons and buy desserts. Walter would pay. Frances seemed to expect this.

Richard Deats, a former professor at the Seminary, wrote asking if I had contacted the Fellowship of Reconciliation in Olympia. The group had just been formed the year before and had only two or three meetings and a Christmas Vigil. Glen Anderson was the organizer and he persuaded me to go to the FOR Conference during the Fourth of July weekend at Seabeck on Hood Canal. I found it stimulating, and have continued to go, sometimes joining the group protesting the submarines at Bangor, sometimes leading worship, sometimes just being there getting inspired.

Walter had become a good friend of Ann's cousin Ruby and her husband Forrest Kelly and their four children, Karen, Cheryl, Marilyn, and Mark, in Vancouver, Washington. Sometimes "Uncle Walt" would tell of his experiences at sea. They immediately took me into their family as "Aunt Marion." They are consecrated church people and they seemed excited to have a missionary in the family. Walter and I went to their church when we were there on Sunday. Walter mixed very well with the people. I watched this with curiosity, knowing that Walter was really an agnostic.

Margie Laflin, Walter's goddaughter, came from the Middle West to visit him. He was anxious to show her a good time. As I had the best car I drove to Vancouver and Victoria, B.C. We stayed in a nice hotel which Walter had arranged. The next day we were sight-seeing, but as it was Friday and Walter had a habit of not eating that day, it was 9:00 P.M. before Margie and I had supper. However, the next day after more sight-seeing he took us to a Native American restaurant where the salmon was delicious. In Victoria we went to the Museum, had tea at the Empress Hotel, and the next day went to the Buchart Gardens. After some walking around Walter sat for awhile and Margie and I walked some more. When I mentioned how beautiful one flower was she said, "Oh, well, one flower is just like another to me." I was glad Walter had not heard that as he was trying to be the best host ever. On the way back we stopped in Bremerton to see the battleship Missouri, on which the World War II treaty was signed. I appreciated getting to know Margie; and also it was my first time to visit these cities to the north.

Whenever it had been possible I have had a dog and a cat but I never before had them play together. As soon as I moved into the mobile home I was able to get the best-trained dog I have ever had, and a kitten who loved dogs. Daffy, the dog, and Mitze, the cat, would play tag on a stretch of lawn near the road. When Daffy was chasing Mitze, no one paid any attention, but when it was Mitze's turn to chase Daffy, the cars would slow down to watch. There was a large dog next door, and Mitze would jump up and slap him in the face to get him to play but he could not be bothered. I had an idea that Daffy had told him to leave our cat alone. Mitze evidentaly got poisoned, and the next cat would not play. Daffy trained her not to follow me when I went after the mail, but beyond that there seemed to be little communication.

That first summer, 1977, I went to the United Methodist School of Missions, held at the University of Puget Sound. One of the leaders was a young man from Oregon, Edsel Goldson, serving two Congregational Churches, and a little U. Methodist church. He was from Jamaica, and the Methodists overlooked the fact that he was Congregational, and brought him on for leadership for the class on the Caribbean countries. I asked him to come to our church for the planned mission project in January and he did. I warned him that the Methodists would get him, and two years later he reminded me of that when he transferred to our Conference.

Also at the School of Missions I met the Conference officers of the United Methodist Women. They asked me if I would teach the course on China the following year, as I had at least been in Asia. I agreed, but felt I needed to know more. Mabel Metze and I had been planning to go to China the following year, but she readily agreed to move it up a year.

In preparation for learning about China I joined the U.S.-China Peoples Association, and met regularly with them. Some people had been to China during the previous year, and argued strongly for the Cultural Revolution; others questioned it. There was much discussion of Mao and the Gang of Four. I borrowed ten books from the Hibbards. Gene Hibbard's parents had been missionaries in China and when they returned to this country they had followed me at the Kendall Church. Thus a special relationship grew quickly. I remembered the trouble I had had using chopsticks when I was in Hong Kong. Mary Emma invited me to lunch at Summet, where Gene was pastor. Very patiently he taught me to eat with chopsticks. I was happy for that instruction later.

Before Christmas I gave a talk to a church on "The Christmas Message and Peace," using as the basis The Magnificat, Mary's Song. I wondered to myself if the Communists would consider us imperialists if they had ever read that passage. If they had read it, would they be like most Christians and not let the revolutionary aspect of it reach them?

CHINA, 1978

Mabel Metze, who lived in Indianapolis, Indiana, and I met in Los Angeles where we joined the rest of the group of 96 members of the U.S.-China Friendship Association. We had lectures for two days; the history of China, especially the Revolution; the Gang of Four (Mao's wife and three others who ruled China for several years after Mao's death); and the current situation with Hua as leader. We were warned that China was not yet ready for tourists, as few hotels and few interpreters were ready. We were reminded that normalization of relations between the U.S. and China had begun just five years before. The Association was allowed to bring tourists because they had knowledge about the situation.

We flew via Tokyo to Hong Kong. We took two trains, one from Hong Kong to the China border, then crossed the bridge on foot carrying our baggage, then another train from the border to Canton (Kwangchou). Mabel and I got homesick for the Philippines—rice fields, pineapples, mango trees, bananas, caribao, etc. At the train station we saw a large sign which translated meant "This great country will last 10,000 years." Without stopping long, we flew to Peking (Bejing). Here we were divided into four groups, riding in four busses, with a leader in each one. Sometimes we all went together, sometimes we went to smaller places at different times. We stayed at the Peking Hotel, the only good hotel at that time. It had been freezing the week before we came, but it warmed up to 50° while we were there.

First we went to the Great Wall. This was really a thrill, to actually walk up the steps of that Wall. It was built about 200 B.C. and mended about 1200 A.D., and two sections had been rebuilt in more recent times. This was the only man-made thing that could be seen from the moon.

We visited the Ming Tombs. Large stone sculptures lined the roadway. Only one Tomb had been opened and it was filled with absolutely gorgeous ceramics. One of the interesting things to me was the revolutionary propaganda (education, they called it) which was worked in. In Russia this was done verbally by the guide. But in the Tomb revolutionary pictures were mixed in. Notes, in both Chinese and English, reminded us that the peasants did the work and how much they suffered while the rulers lived in luxury.

Early one morning Mabel and I walked the few blocks to Tien An Men Square and watched the hundreds gathered there doing Tai Chi. We saw no obvious leaders, yet they all seemed to know what to do. We were fascinated. Later the whole group visited the Square. It was huge, so also was the Hall of the People where the Communist Party leaders met.

The Forbidden Palace was also large with many buildings and beautiful carvings. The Imperial Palace was especially interesting, with stairways along both sides of a stone center which was carved with clouds. No one walked on this center as this was where the ruler was carried to the throne. Another part of the grounds had the colorful Wall of Nine Dragons.

The Summer Palace buildings were red, outstanding on a hillside. The very colorful long Corridor is almost half a mile long with the ceiling painted with human figures or animals or plants, and no two alike. It was hard to grasp all that beauty as we walked along. The Marble Boat, a boat of Purity and Ease, was built by the Empress Dowager with funds taken from the Chinese Naval budget. Sun Yat Sen used this as an example of her excesses.

The Temple of Heaven, or Hall of Prayer for Good Harvests, was another beautiful building. Two bronze lions faced us as we entered. The ceiling with its rich colors was one of the most photographed of Chinese interiors.

The guide, who stayed with us for the whole trip, was very proud of the schools and factories, especially those that produced materials for the government. Always there was a "briefing session." First, tea was served, poured from a metal tea kettle. As the leaves were poured out with the tea, we had a difficult time drinking the tea and leaving the leaves in the cup. The speech was always the same: the history of the school or factory; how much they suffered under the Gang of Four; how hard they worked to smash the Gang of Four; and how they could make better things because the Gang of Four had been defeated.

We had an interesting visit to the Tsaihue University Campus. Again, we heard its history. But the buildings were too old to look as though they had been built since the Revolution. In fact, one building looked very much like a Chapel, and we thought this could have been the mission college we had known as Peking University. After the "briefing session," one of the faculty members took us around. We noticed that he sometimes corrected the interpreter on her English. When I had an opportunity I asked him quietly if he had studied in the United States. In excellent English he admitted that he was a Harvard graduate. He had taught sociology in this University for a number of years. During the Cultural Revolution those who had studied in the U.S. or who seemed sympathetic were constantly being criticized as unpatriotic. It was so uncomfortable that he became the Librarian with an office inside. In that way he did not have to deal with the critical students or employees. Thus he could stay in China, be measurably happy, and wait for the political climate to change again.

As we rode around the city Dick Bolen, a young Methodist minister from Southern California, and Mabel and I looked for former church buildings. Most of the ones we saw were being used as housing with clothes hanging out the windows. All churches were closed during the Cultural Revolution. Only two had been re-opened—one Catholic and one Protestant, for one hour only, for visitors and diplomats. We had heard rumors that in some places Bible studies were being held, but that was kept from those in power.

On a free afternoon Mabel and I took a taxi to the American Embassy to visit a young diplomat who had attended the Methodist Church in Shelton, Washington. He had married a Filipina so we had a good personal chat. For about an hour, then, we asked him questions about the relations between the U.S. and China, about the church, the Gang of Four and Hua. We felt it was a good afternoon.

We flew on to Shanghai and stayed in the Peace Hotel in the former French section. This is where President Nixon and his company stayed, the visit that changed the relationship between the U.S. and China. The hotel lacked luxury, but it was comfortable. We had no keys to our room, but there was a guard who watched every time the elevator stopped.

A tributary of the Yangtze River flows through the city. There were boats of all kinds and sizes going up and down, more traffic than I had expected to see.

We woke up each morning about 6:00 A.M. as there was too much noise to sleep. We were amazed at the hundreds of bicyclists and the few cars trying to get through, honking constantly. How any of them got to their destinations we could not imagine.

In one of the suburbs we visited housing for a nearby factory. In one home we found a small two-room apartment where the family shared the kitchen and bath with another family. I thought it looked like luxury compared with what one might find in a corresponding Filipino home but the other Americans were aghast at its primitivism. But they did have running water, a gas stove, and a flush toilet (I wondered if it worked!) All of this was real luxury for any low-income working people in Asia. When we talked to them about finances we discovered that both husband and wife work—as all women did work—and their food and rent and clothes use up almost the entire income. If they save up for several months they might be able to buy a bicycle. We visited their school and the Kindergarten class sang for us. Instead of a children's song that we expected, they sang about how mean the Gang of Four had been and how glad they were that it had been smashed. We realized that the families chosen for us to visit were positive toward the present government, but we all want to look our best for guests.

One of the most delightful places during the whole visit was the Children's Palace. Each one of us was assigned a child guide who took us to all the activities. Several hundred children came from all over the district twice a week after school, and all day on Sunday. All of the extra-curricular activities were done in this one center. There were singing lessons, dancing, orchestra, embroidery, art, magic, manual training and perhaps other classes we did not see. The children had prepared a special program for us, and the dances and music were very well done. In every Children's Palace they did some type of production. In this Palace the third and fourth graders were making electrical outlets. The idea was to teach the children to work with their hands, and to be proud of such work. Much emphasis was placed on production and on criticism of the European nations and the U.S. which were considered consumer nations.

In a large department store Mabel cashed a traveler's check. I looked behind and there was a stairway full of young men watching every move. Having Americans around was still a new thing. A young man said he had been in a mission school but before he could say anything else someone grabbed him and led him away. We wanted to talk with him!

We took a train to Hangchow, not very far away. We were led as a group through an area of the station and the Chinese travelers were a distance away watching us. It was a strange feeling. This was the city which Marco Polo thought was the most beautiful city he had seen. Here we visited a very large commune on the outskirts of the city. Our host was Comrade Shen-chan, Chairman of the Revolutionary Committee of the Peoples' Communes. He started his remarks with "We are tickled pink to have you here." This commune had 23,000 people and was subdivided into 105 production teams. We did not go out to where the people were working, but they were so close together I wondered how they could all keep busy. They were producing tomatoes, cucumbers, and green peppers. The state sets the price of the produce. We went to the Commune-hospital and were told proudly about the "barefoot doctors."

We broke up into small groups of about ten each and visited homes. The host told us that 20-30% still live in straw houses. The ones we saw were made of mud bricks. The occupants of the home we visited were very cordial, and seemed honored to have us visit them. They had dirt floors, a kitchen outside the main rooms, with a stove using grasses for fuel, two rooms, with one electric light hanging from the ceiling of the main room, a picture of Mao, a rough-hewn table and a couple of chairs. There was no running water or toilet facilities. The man told us his father had been a peasant and carried night soil. When we asked him what he did he proudly said he was a member of the Commune and he carried night soil. There was a small garden outside the home which could be used for their own use, or they could sell the produce at the open market.

In the city we visited a ceramic factory, but the products seemed gaudy, not the beautiful art work we expected. There was only one revolutionary figure, and Dick picked it up before I did. We visited a Buddhist Temple which was very old and had many gold-leaf figures. I was surprised at how all of the gods were warriors, as the Buddhists today stress their peaceful teachings.

The last day we were in Hangchou we went to West Lake. This was the most beautiful place we saw in our entire visit. We walked out on a small bridge to the center shelter. Families were enjoying the beautiful surroundings and weather. We would gladly have stayed longer than we did.

Canton (Kwangchow) had more trade with other countries than any other in China. We went to a Trade Fair, a huge room with many objects on display which they wanted to export. As we looked only from a balcony our understanding was limited.

We visited an ivory factory. When I was in Hong Kong twenty years before all the carving had been done by hand, using a small instrument. Now they used an electric drill. Balls, about three or four inches in diameter, had smaller balls inside, working from the outside in. The host talked to us of the Gang of Four and how much better they could work now. I could not figure out why they could put more balls inside now than they could before but I did not ask. The prices of pieces in the visitors' room ranged from several hundred dollars to several thousand. These were sold to museums or to rich tourists.

At the silk factory we followed through the various processes, beginning with the silk worms. In one corner we found a group of young women just sitting. When we asked about it we discovered that they had too many employees but they could not let any of them go. They would work awhile then trade with some one else. On a large black-board were various charts, one an exhortation to work hard.

The Peasant Movement Building was where Sun Yat Sen spearheaded the revolution in 1911, toppling the monarchy. During the 1920's, Mao Zedong, Chiang Kai-shek and Zhou Enlai all began their careers under Sun's leadership. The building was used as a place to educate children about the Revolution. A large number of them came in while we were there. They listened to lectures and copied what was written on the board. As I took their picture, only one child dared look at us. I wondered what he was thinking. Not about the Revolution at that moment, I would guess.

A tragic thing happened to us here, as a man in our small group died. It seemed that he had overworked his heart and he died in his sleep. When his wife was informed she told us that he had said before he left that if he died before he returned to spread his ashes over China. The Chinese leaders liked that. Dick Bolen and I decided we should have a memorial service which I taped for his wife. I read from Psalm 139, not using the New Testament because there were a large number of Jews in the group. Dick gave a short message. The service was short and simple, and many of the Jews as well as the Christians felt it was appropriate.

It was interesting to me, as I read books about China and read some of Mao's works, that although the old order was broken down by violence, Mao soon learned that violence does not build a new order. Mao himself said that they had killed many of the people who knew how to do the things that needed to be done, and they killed the stock and destroyed the machinery. It took a nonviolent approach to build the new order. However, violence was so much a part of his philosophy that he started the Cultural Revolution.

As we left China Mabel and I agreed that one idea stood out, the idea of "serving the people" instead of "getting ahead" or "taking care of Number One." It seemed that although orders came from the top, small groups were used which became support groups, and could be controlling or from them changes could be made.

Mabel and I had realized that we could not go all that way across the ocean without stopping in Manila to see our friends. We stayed in the guest house which was built when I was there. One day when I went to Manila to see Ruth Feuer and other friends I happened to see a former student, Vilma Fuentes. She had received a Masters in Journalism and was working for the ecumenical publishing house. She was writing some children's books, a result of the Christian Education classes at the Seminary. We continued to stay in touch.

One day Mabel and I went to Manila to talk with our former President, Emmy Nacpil, now a Bishop. We had the best theological conversation with him that we had ever had, better than when we were all on the faculty together.

Although we had not planned it to be so, we were there during Graduation. We couldn't have planned it better! The class I had as first-year students greeted me warmly, shaking my hand. But the second-year class, which had been such a creative group, greeted me with both hands. One of them spoke, he said for the group, that when they were in school they had had so much fun in my class they thought they hadn't learned anything. On internship, they said, they had learned more from my class than from any other on how to carry on the work! That was good news for any teacher to hear. Graduation was exciting.

All of this was a highly charged emotional two weeks for both of us. We flew back to Seattle via Tokyo, and Mabel went directly on to Indianapolis. We both looked forward to teaching what we had learned.

◆   ◆   ◆

In order to teach in the School of Christian Mission I read the ten books on China borrowed from Hibbards, then we had to read about ten more required ones, some on how to teach, etc. It was required that all who teach go to the Regional School, that year at Billings, Montana. Four of us would be teaching classes on China. We discovered we had very different backgrounds. When the School started in July we decided to work as a unit, rotating so that each of us taught each class. In that way classes had the opportunity to hear Gene Hibbard's experiences in growing up there in China and get his wife's recipes; to learn a little of the language from Mary Gates who had been studying it; to hear from a college student who had gone on a trip the previous summer with a college group and professor; and to see my slides. The students appreciated the way we did it.

Later I went to the Ecumenical School of Missions held in a college near Portland. The leader was the one who represented China in the National Council of Churches. I found it interesting and was glad I could add a little, too. Also, Harold, whom I had dated in Berkeley, and his wife were there. He was the pastor of a small Baptist church in Eastern Washington. It was strange to meet such a person more than forty years later. What would life have been like with him? I was glad we had let it drop.

Somewhere along the line, I was not just sure when, Rev. Paul Beeman asked me to join the staff of the First United Methodist Church of Olympia as an Associate Minister. He said I was doing a professional job at the hospital and he wanted me to continue that. He also offered me the choice of Christian Education or Visitation. I chose Visitation, as in retirement a change of work was welcome. Paul wanted me to start in September, but the finance committee said October.

At the School in July the Conference Officers of the United Methodist Women discovered that I had not been "Itinerated" as most missionaries were when they return from the mission field. The women made up a schedule for me for September so that I would visit each of their churches, especially those on the east side of the mountains.

In Coeur d' Alene, Idaho, I talked to every class in the Sunday School about the Philippines, changing the presentation from the Kindergarten to the High

School. Then I preached to the adults in the worship service. This was really quite a challenge. I stayed with an older couple who had been missionaries in Indonesia. In the Spokane Valley Church I was scheduled to preach in the morning, then show slides in the afternoon. It happened that the pastor got caught in an ice storm in Portland the night before, so I went ahead with the entire service. He came in just as I was finishing showing the slides of the Philippines. When I went to Sand Point, Idaho, I discovered that I had known the pastor, Harold Huff, years ago, dating back to the Arkansaw days. He had been in Graduate School in Madison and had been serving a small charge on the same sub-district.

I went on down the road to Colfax and stayed on a large wheat farm. I learned about wheat farming which was a completely new subject for me. I also heard that they could not provide housing for their migrants because the government had set such high standards that they could not afford it. The workers had to rent whatever they could find. I showed slides of China in an evening meeting. I stayed in a mobile home in the yard which was for guests. On to Richland where I had lunch with Ruth Steach who could not arrange anything in her church because of the schedule. However, I felt the time was worth it to get acquainted with her. At Tieton I stayed on a fruit ranch with Katherine Havnaer and her husband. A few people gathered for an informal discussion. An evening meeting at Toppenish completed the trip. I came home with a car full of peaches, pears and tomatoes. I spent the last two weeks of September canning, freezing and making jellies. Walter enjoyed the results as much as I did during the ensuing meals.

FUMCO—FIRST UNITED METHODIST CHURCH OF OLYMPIA

Rev. Paul Beeman and Rev. Corliss Hanson were co-pastors of the First United Methodist Church of Olympia. It was difficult for them to find time for calling on people at the hospitals. For about two years I had helped them, visiting Methodists at the hospitals twice a week. Paul told me I was doing professional job and he wanted me to join the staff. I said I would do it for a year or two. In October, 1978, both Eleanor Swoboda and I were hired for part time; she as Christian Education Director and Youth Worker, and I as Minister of Visitation. Also I was to keep track of new people. We each received half the minimum salary of a retired member of Conference. Each year we took two months in the summer off without pay.

When I was introduced to the Congregation, Rev. Corliss Hanson said: "She came to us a stranger and we took her in. That's the way I would like to think it happened, but perhaps it was the other way around…Marion really is one of those rare phenomena who felt a call into the ministry of the Methodist Church long before officialdom was ready for her. Perhaps the church never did get ready for her or for the steady stream of called, committed, Christian feminine candidates for the clergy who were to follow in her wake…She is a part of the ministerial team and spends hours each week visiting in local hospitals. If you have not yet met her, you will have the opportunity to do so this Sunday when she will preach at both services. Somehow it doesn't seem at all strange that her topic will be 'Giving and Receiving, A Reciprocal Relationship.' After all, that's what her life has been all about." It was into this type of supportive relationship that I began to work.

The pastoral calling at the hospitals was a favorite part of the work, continuing what I had been doing as a volunteer. I called on all who were listed as Methodist, whether members of our church or not. Several situations come to mind. I visited a young man who had been injured in a fight. He was looking in the Bible for the 23rd Psalm. I helped him find it, then read it with him. He was realizing he had made a wrong choice by fighting.

One time I walked into a room as the family was gathered about the room. The woman was talking on the phone and I heard her say, "I feel at home now, the Methodist Minister just walked in the room." They were from New Jersey and she had become ill while they were traveling. The connectionalism of the Methodist Church was apparent.

One evening I was about to finish doing my regular telephoning of new people about 9:00 P.M. I did not reach the woman I expected, but her niece, instead. She said her mother and aunt were at the hospital because her uncle was not expected to live. I asked if there was a minister with them, and she said "No." By the time I got to the hospital it was 10:00 P.M. I spent about half an hour with them. He died a few days later. Although I was asked to perform the memorial service I asked one of the pastors to do it as Walter and I were having company from New York. Later the wife joined the choir and her sister was active in another group. I didn't usually make calls at 10:00 P.M. but this one was unusual.

After calling one day I wrote this:

> Have you ever waited?
> Really waited, I mean?

Today I waited with a young couple,
>> Waiting in agony and expectancy for a New Life.
Then I waited with another couple,
>> Waiting for her mother to die.
>> Waiting in agony and expectancy for New Life.
All my life I have waited for peace in the world.
>> Waiting in agony.
>> Where has the expectancy gone?

Also I called on the home-bound, but as we had about 50 of these, and some needed more attention than others, it took me some time to call on all of them. I solicited help now and then but found that visiting those in nursing homes was threatening for many people.

As Olympia is the State Capital there is much movement going in and out of jobs, and thus more movement within the church. I began having a coffee-hour before the first service once a month for new people. Some lay people came and visited with them. By telephoning people the day after they came the first time; trying to visit them during the first week; and then making them feel welcome at the coffee-hour, people said they were "hooked." In time they teased me calling me the "hooker." All this led into the class for new members.

At first Paul was teaching the class for new members but after some time he asked me to take it. I was free to develop my own lesson plan. I used the "Methodist Quadrilateral," that is, Scripture, Tradition, Experience, and Reason. We found a Fellowship Friend for each one who would help them get acquainted. After five sessions the class with their Fellowship Friends had an evening pot-luck in one of the pastors' homes, so they could become acquainted with these new people. After four months we had a reunion, partly for fun, and partly to see how well they had become assimilated into the life of the church.

A committee had divided the church into cluster groups before I arrived. They named the leaders the Lay Ministers of Pastoral Care. I discovered the name frightened many, so I called them Care Clusters. To get someone in each cluster to accept responsibility for the care of others in the group was quite a task. At one point I taught a four-weeks class on counseling which helped some, but I was never satisfied.

Work with older adults was one of my tasks. There was a group of adults meeting one evening a month. They had started as young adults, and had been meeting together for years. New people found it hard to feel at home. We developed a new group to meet at noon once a month. This developed into a lively fellowship and both groups had good leadership.

On Sundays Walter usually went to Dick and Ann's for dinner, but I found it was difficult to include me. I looked for some people to eat with, and started a regular group to eat dinner together after church. One person agreed to make arrangements with a restaurant for the next Sunday; some-times we changed places, sometimes not. Most were women and widows. As soon as a new widow seemed ready to be out on her own, I invited her to come. Several told me later how much that meant to them.

As a volunteer I had been chairman of the Missions Work Area, with a program every Sunday evening in January. Another former missionary took it over and we worked closely together. I became chairman of the Social Action Committee.

In 1980 Corliss was appointed to another church. That left only Paul and me. At the end of December that year Paul wrote me this note: "You are an esteemed colleague; I value your ministry among us more than I can say. Your hospital and new member calling, your work with shut-ins and other members, your leadership in groups, and your consistent social concern make for a rare blend. You are primarily responsible for much of the growth, strength and balance in our church. Your skill is matched only by your devotion and my gratitude. Affectionately, Paul. P.S. Your leadership on Christmas Eve was superb. Thank you." Of course, none of this would have been possible without Paul's excellent leadership.

Rev.Paul and Betty Beeman and Rev.Richard and Peggy Smith

Some friends.

Led down the aisle for retiremen byl Bo Newsom !

Christmas Peace Demonstration in Olympia

THE OBERAMMERGAU PASSION PLAY TRIP, 1980

With the summer free, Miriam Peterson and I went to Europe the summer of 1980 to see the Oberammergau Passion Play. This Passion Play was begun 400 years ago as a celebration to thank God that their town had survived the plague, which had devastated most of Europe. It has been given every ten years ever since, except in time of war. I had read about it in a German class in college, and ever since had wanted to get there.

Miriam and I met at the airport in Chicago and flew to Frankfurt, West Germany. Here we parted for three days, as she had planned a Romantic Road Tour, mainly to Rothenburg, an old walled town which is being preserved as a medieval town for tourists. I had visited it on a previous trip.

Meanwhile I visited friends. Linda and Chris Sekiguichi, whom I had known in the Philippines, were living in Frankfurt, where Linda was teaching children of the military, and Chris was working in communications. Linda met me and after we picked up Chris, we drove onto our U.S. Army base, and went up an elevator to the top of a high tower. I was impressed by the extent of our military presence, and they told me the French and British are the same. I wondered, World War II was over 35 years ago. Does Germany need this much protection? Or are they, and we, afraid of Communism? Or do we just think we must have a strong base in Europe? Why doesn't Germany kick us all out?

Next I took the train to Neuendettelsau, to visit Dr. and Mrs. Anderson. He had taught on our campus in the Philippines during a sabbatical and was President of the Protestant Theological Seminary for Bavaria. At one point he told me about his military experience during World War II. He had to go into the army or be killed. He was sent to Norway. He felt sorry for the Norwegians as they had been taken over by Hitler. He went to church the first Sunday, expecting to find a friend in the minister. But the minister would have nothing to do with him as he was the enemy. He was disappointed. He didn't feel like the enemy, yet he realized how he might feel if he was in that minister's place. He did not think there was any such thing as a "just war."

The Andersons took me around to see some of the villages, one of which was still walled, then took me to the train for Munich. I was sad to hear that he died about ten days after my visit.

Not many times have I stayed in a hotel like the Hilton in Munich. It was beautifully furnished. On the wall was a large picture, off white, with one dark blue line running straight across it. It must have been art, but even I could do that with a ruler. When Miriam joined me I was sorry to hear that she had not enjoyed her trip to Rothenburg because the hotel, like the rest of the town, was primitive. That was the idea, we supposed, to let tourists know what it was like in the past. This was quite an overnight change, from Rothenburg to the Hilton.

After we met with our tour guide, Igor, in the morning, I asked for directions for Dachau, one of the Nazi death camps. It was so close, I did not want to miss it. Miriam did not want to go, but when I decided to go alone, she changed her mind and went along.

The suburban train was crowded. I wondered if they were tourists who had lost friends or relatives here or in one of the other camps. Or, just like we had, they had heard of such a place and wanted to see it. We saw a long list of names, and I chose Gertrude. I sat on one of the beds in the dormitory, wondering what it would have been like to be Gertrude. Had her husband, a healthy, strong man, been taken out for work as a slave? Where were her children? Perhaps she had been taken away without even being able to say good-bye. Her teen-age daughter? A beautiful girl of 17? As they were pushed on to the train, had she seen her daughter being put aside for the soldiers' enjoyment? And now she is alone. Others have gone and not come back. What is ahead? Fear could have overcome her.

I went to the museum and saw horrible pictures, people starved to death, skeletons piled up. Then I went over to the huge all-black oven. I stood at the top of that incline leading to the heavy iron door. What would Gertrude be feeling? How many people would have been pushed down that space at once? 10? 25? 50? I could only imagine the fear, knowing that when that door opened and she was pushed in, she would be cremated alive. And surely she was praying—or had she given up?

I went back to find Miriam, who had gone to the museum to see the pictures. That is all she could stand. We left for the train, not able to talk. As we walked along that long section between the two very high barbed-wire fences, we felt keenly the desire for escape and yet the impossibility of it.

In the evening our tour group gathered for dinner. There were 4l, a congenial group, with a few young ones. One couple was on their honeymoon. Miriam and I were not the oldest. Later, when we were alone, Miriam said she was glad she had gone with me. We had had a little glimpse of the suffering of over 300,000 people, mostly Jewish, but also a few Christian ministers, who had died in that one camp, only because Hitler imagined himself to be superior.

THE PASSION PLAY

Our tour group travelled to Ettal, a town about three miles from Oberammergau, and were housed in the Hotel Ludwig Der Buyer. After checking in, Miriam and I took the optional tour to Linderhof Castle, the only castle of King Ludwig which was completed. He was building seven castles, but was drowned before they were finished. This castle has a beautiful pool in front, and it is very ornate. The rooms were very small. One had a small table which went up and down on a trick floor so that he would not have to see his servants. He was very much a loner.

When we set out for the play, we discovered it had been cold the week before we came. The concierge insisted that we rent blankets to keep warm. We used them as cushions which made the bare seats much more comfortable. I had taken my opera glasses, as recommended by a friend, and Miriam had some small field glasses. We were glad, as we were in row 30.

The whole experience was tremendous. The action was sometimes slowed down by the choruses, the tableaus, the reaching back to the Old Testament to bring in the beginning of the ideas, or the relationship to other happenings. All this added to the art and beauty of it. We had borrowed an English translation which we had read before we came, so it was quite easy to follow the story. All the parts were played beautifully. Jesus was superb.

It was Peter that moved me most in the morning. I am a person that likes to get things done, to see that something is accomplished. It was easy, then, for me to identify with Peter, with his anxiety to get this Kingdom going.

When Judas came to the Garden to see Jesus I became as excited as though I had never read the story. The interpretation of his actions was different from anything else I had ever heard and made me feel almost sorry for him. Jesus had been talking of a Kingdom, and like the other disciples, Judas thought of it as an earthly Kingdom, that Jesus would win their freedom from Roman rule and would "redeem Israel." Judas saw only poverty and hopelessness. Here in Jerusalem Jesus was doing nothing to arouse people against Roman rule, but was confronting the Jewish leaders. Judas did not want to go on this way. Friends of the High Priest won him over, to turn Jesus in, and sell him for the price of a slave. At the Garden, Judas expected Jesus to show his power. He had seen so many wonderful things done, surely Jesus would overcome the crowd he had assembled. When Jesus did not do this, he was confused. When Judas returned the money, he asked for Jesus back. They told him it was no longer any of his business what they would do with Jesus. Judas was then repentant, and his soliloquy was excellent. Then he hanged himself. Here was a play 400 years old, reinterpreting the Gospel story in its own way, long before modern biblical criticism. Ever since, I have wondered, how did Judas expect Jesus to respond? Obviously, not what he got.

Peter, also, seemed to expect Jesus to show his power. He, too, had seen so many wonderful things happen that he thought it would still go on. "We were witnesses to his transfiguration on the mountain. Now what shall we see?" he asked. He was the one who began to fight with the sword, and was surprised by Jesus' response. He intended to be loyal, and stayed close enough to see Jesus, but he is confused and frightened. And, it was hinted, perhaps the disciples' lives were in danger.

On the way to the Cross, Jesus carried the whole cross, while the other two carried the crossbars only. Actually, historically, only the crossbar was carried, as the post was already there for the many crucifixions carried out by the Romans.

In the afternoon, at the Cross, at first I worried about the actual men hanging there, until I discovered that they were standing on a platform and their arms were resting on the crossbars. I identified with Mary. I think for the first time I really sympathized with her, watching her first-born son being treated as a criminal. She must have thought about his boyhood, how she really hadn't understood him when he left home, but then she realized how many people he had helped. I watched with her; she cried, and I cried, too. After Jesus died, his body was put in her lap. "My son…your suffering and bitter death went through my soul like a sword." And mine, too. The speech ended with her knowing it was atonement. The Tomb scene was beautiful, with only the voice of the angel. The Ascension scene seemed a bit more like Hollywood.

Both Miriam and I have worked in Christian Education, and thus with many children through the years. We thought about the children growing up in this town, where their parents were the players. Surely as they played together, they would play these scenes, and early on would know all the lines.

I had seen two shorter passion plays in the United States, one with Miriam in South Dakota, and the other in Florida. But this one, all day, gave one an opportunity to feel with all one's emotions, and to identify with the characters. It was worth the 50-year wait.

TO GENEVA

After the Passion Play we went to Salzburg. We took a sight-seeing tour, mostly walking. We visited the Cathedral, saw the old monastery, then went on to Mozart's birthplace. We saw his violin and harpsichord. I couldn't find Miriam, and I began to get worried about her. Finally she came in. She had stopped to take a picture and followed the guide with the wrong umbrella. After the tour Miriam and I went to the Hohensalzburg Fortress. As we sat down to drink some apple cider the yellow jackets swarmed around. One was trying so hard to drink my juice that he fell in. The waiter dug him out and I drank it.

The clerk at the hotel was able to get tickets for The Nutcracker, at the Marionette Theatre, for eleven of us, and no one wanted to be responsible for them. I thought: "Let's give them to the men." Then I decided that with Women's Lib, we could do it ourselves. So I took care of the tickets. The Nutcracker Suite was superb. The costumes were excellent and they danced around as though they were real people. They curtsied at the end. This was a different version, with much more humor than the regular ballet one.

We drove on the Autobahn to Vienna. On a sight-seeing trip we went to several of the parks, and to the Schoenbruhn Palace. There was an exhibition of some kind going on, and we could see only a part of it. I was disappointed for the group, for when I was there before I had seen much more. It was beautiful.

Igor worked out a special trip for dinner that night to a Hungarian Restaurant where we had music and some of the group dances. There was much local color. We discovered that there were large ethnic groups in Vienna. We went to ride on the world's largest Ferris Wheel. There were large enclosed cabins, which went up and around very slowly. This was for tourists only, as the local people took the faster, more exciting games below. About 9:00 P.M. we went to the Stadt Park to have coffee and cake, and listen to Strauss being played by an orchestra. It was delightful.

On a free day Miriam and I took a taxi to the Hofburg Palace to see the Crown Jewels. Previously I had been in an apartment section, but it was not open this time. We wandered around the center of the city, window-shopping, people watching, etc. The clothes looked expensive to us—dresses for $450 or more, and shoes for $100. Igor assured us that there are cheaper places, but we had to admit these were desirable.

We went to the Grinsinger Restaurant in a suburb for dinner. There were a number of different groups, with a couple of musicians that went from group to group. A French group was near us. They sang French songs, sometimes we joined in, in English. When we sang English songs, they joined in as they knew them in French. Before this Miriam and I thought we were the only ones that did not drink, but that evening there were five of us at our table who did not. We gave the wine away. It was a noisy, fun evening.

Three stops along the way from Vienna to Geneva, Switzerland, stand out. We were going over passes out of Austria, and arrived in Cortina in northern Italy. Suddenly it looked like the tropics. First I saw a flame tree, with its beautiful red flowers, then palm trees scattered around, and orchids, bougainvillies, Bird of Paradise, and other flowers. I could have been back in Manila. How does this happen, I asked Igor. He explained that we had come over mountains, and we would be going over more tomorrow. In between was this section where the winds from the Mediterranean Sea blow into this area, with no mountains in between. I thought it seemed impossible, but here we were in a southern climate.

It was in the morning that I dropped my room key. We were on the elevator with another couple from our group. We all had our hands full, holding wraps for the mountain, dark glasses, and the room key to turn in while we were gone. The elevators in Europe were often small, holding only four or five people. In order to get out of the elevator, we had to manipulate three doors. For some reason, I was the one opening them. I got the first one slid open, then the second. The third one had to be pulled on the handle, then pushed. In trying all this I dropped the room key and it went down the elevator shaft. It was not retrieved until we returned from the mountain.

We went on the cog lift, that is, in small cars. This was in three sections and we went up to a peak of 10,000 feet. The last section was almost straight up the rock cliff. It was a bit scary, and I got a little bit dizzy, which I did not admit to anyone. We stayed at the top about half an hour or more, then took the car down. Several others of our group came down with us. It was scary coming down, too. This is the same cog lift that a U.S. Army pilot flew into in 2001, and got world-wide attention. It was scary reading about it.

On the way to St. Moritz, Switzerland, we went over four passes, three with hairpin turns. The roads were very narrow and there was a good deal of traffic. Our bus driver would swing around the curves on the wrong side of the road, and cars would have to back up and wait for us. Those of us who have driven in mountains looked at each other in horror. I thought St. Moritz was one of the most beautiful cities I had seen. It is at the foot of mountain cliffs and on a beautiful lake. Miriam and I walked down to the lake immediately on arrival, and several other times as well. Some of our group walked all around the lake, about five or six miles. The steep hill from the lake was all we could manage. As it was Sunday morning we thought about going to church, but discovered there would be a concert following. We did not know German well enough to understand a sermon, so substituted the music.

We crossed over other passes to reach Brig, then took a train to Zermatt, elevation 6,500 feet. There were little electric trucks that ran through the pedestrian streets like mad. Our room in the hotel was the only one at our end that had a kitchenette, so we heated water for coffee and tea for those in neighboring rooms.

The day was clear and sunny when we took the cog-wheel train to Gernergrat, elevation 10,000 ft. From there we could see the whole range of mountains, the Matterhorn being the highest, elevation 14,685 ft. It is very distinctive, rather narrow. Two very sharp sections join together at a pointed top. Fortunately, although it had taken some time, I had already learned that every mountain did not have to look like Mount Rainier for me to appreciate it. We stayed at Gornergrat about an hour, then returned by the cog-wheel train to Zermatt. The next day the sky was cloudy, and although we went to France, we could not see Mount Blanc. We were all disappointed.

We went on to Geneva. We were taken on a city tour, but Igor did not know the city and we did not stop anywhere for pictures. Miriam and I went alone to take pictures of the Monument to the Reformation, the World Council of Churches, and the beautiful park at the lake. Also we loved the flower market, and were able to do quite a bit of shopping for Christmas presents in the many gift shops.

My old suitcase was getting broken, and I had been using an old strap to hold it together. I left Miriam sitting on a busy street corner while I went to a large department store looking for a new strap. After considerable wandering I found the English Service section. A clerk took me to the luggage department where I found just what I wanted. It took me three-fourths of an hour to buy the little item. Miriam was getting worried, thinking something had happened to me.

At the final dinner there were lots of pictures taken. It had been a good tour group, and we had lots of goodbys. The tipping for our driver had been done the day before, and we thought rather brazenly. The tipping for Igor was much simpler. Miriam and I stayed an extra day and had a nice trip by boat on the lake. We flew back to Frankfurt to pick up our round-trip fare and on to Chicago and home.

◆   ◆   ◆

In July, 1981, Rev. Richard Smith came as the other Associate Pastor, from Nashville, headquarters for many national church programs. His experience there led to his work with programming. The three of us made a good team.

I preached only occasionally. I left the personal faith growth aspect to the other ministers and I stressed reaching out in faith to the world. However, one special experience stands out. In appreciation for the excellent work that the United Methodist Women (UMW) did, I had been attending their District meetings as well as the local ones. When the Annual Conference UMW met at Olympia one year, I was asked to preach the morning sermon. Having both the Bishop and the District Superintendent in the congregation amused me, for I was the one preaching to them. I quote the thank you letter from the Conference President: "Thank you so much for the beautiful service on Sunday. I can't ever remember being a part of a more beautiful service. The litany, your message, the beautiful setting, the beautiful music and the lovely dancers! I think I will remember it always and want to thank you for all you did to make it the success it was. I felt the violin solo was perfect for the postlude. May God continue to bless you! Shalom and Joy, Ann Hammons." One never does all this by oneself, but many others helped plan it and participated. The Conference UMW had already given me a pin (as had the Detroit Conference UMW) and now the local church gave me a special recognition. With all of these money is given to the national UMW in the name of the recipient.

Being ecumenical in experience and in spirit, it did not take me long to discover the ASSOCIATED MINISTRIES, which included the mainline churches in Olympia, as well as the Roman Catholic Church. Each year we had a Day of Awareness which high-lighted some social issue, and hopefully led to action. There were many subgroups in Olympia working on various issues as a result. For two years I was responsible for peace issues. Both Days of Awareness were successful in subject and in attendance. The FOR (Fellowship of Reconciliation) was the continuing action group.

The newspaper, THE OLYMPIAN, published a section once a week called the "Pastor's Perspective." Most of the pastors in the city were invited to participate. I found these challenging, and tried to make my columns challenging to the reader. One had to do with my own college experience of being in both a "liberal" and "conservative" group of Christians at the same time. I had become convinced that both created walls that kept them from understanding the other, and that both were talking about the same things, but using different language. Another had to do with peace issues. I quoted from Tertullian in the Third Century that war was not the way of Jesus, then referred to the Quakers, then the modern peace movement. One reader wrote a blasting letter. I realized, even more than before, that Jesus is still far ahead of all of us in our understanding of God's ways.

Another ecumenical group was the WIDOWS AND WIDOWERS organization that met once a month on Saturdays at FUMCO. The wife of the mortician was the sponsor. Since some-one from our church needed to be there I volunteered. As time went on I invited new widows and widowers to come to my office to talk. This became a safe place for tears. It was good to see some, who were very upset at first, later comforting others.

The CHURCH WOMEN UNITED, an international organization, was another interesting group. Women from the mainline churches met several times a year. One meeting was in the Episcopal Church, which was completely full of men as well as women. I was asked to give a prayer at the beginning of the service. I quote: "Before we pray, let me share with you something about the written service. This was written in Kenya. One of the editors says: 'I must reveal that I personally removed from the material such local references as 'God is a Great Hen' (symbolizing, I suppose, that God is the source of all blessings); 'May we always be in communion with the Living Dead (I assume they mean the Communion of the Saints); and 'May our women be as fat gourds' (the Womens Liberation Movement would kill us).' When they finished laughing, I went on, "God, we give you thanks for laughter and humor. As we laugh at the figures of speech of another culture, help us to accept their laughter as they laugh at us because of our strange words and ways. God, do you laugh at us, too, when we go our own narrow ways, each one thinking that we know the truth about what Your Son taught when he was with us? Do you laugh as you see how little all together we know about you and your way? O God, bring us closer together, with humor and laughter if you will, that we might see ourselves and each other more clearly, and having found our home in You, we will search together for a deeper understanding of your way for us. Amen." Response: The magazine of the United Methodist Women, published this.

I found several opportunities for continued training in order to keep up with current trends. For several years I went to the classes held in Des Moines. The professors were flown from Claremont Theological Seminary, Claremont, California, teaching Old Testament, New Testament, Teachings of Jesus, and various theologies. It was stimulating, and I got to know many of the pastors.

In order for pastors to be secure in hospital calling, a week at Swedish Hospital in Seattle was offered at no cost. We stayed in a hotel not far from the hospital. Each morning we had a lecture by the Chaplain and a discussion of the situations the pastors were facing. In the afternoon we toured the hospital, spending time especially in the cancer section. We were free to examine equipment and ask questions. Some of the afternoons we interviewed cancer patients. We shared problems afterward.

Another was the Good Samaritan Hospital in Puyallup with an emphasis on rehabilitation after a stroke or accident. Five men and I were there for a week. I stayed in the home of the U. Methodist pastor and his wife. We had lectures and discussions. Some of the assignments gave us an experience of what it would be like to be in the place of the patient. At lunch the cooks had all kinds of things to assign to different people. The most disturbing to me was a bib. Did they expect me to slobber? I felt a loss of self-control. In the discussion afterward we shared our feelings. At the end of the time each of us met with the Chaplain. He told me he hesitated to have a woman join the group, but he was glad I had come. These hospital training experiences built on the old "Clinical Training of Garrett" days, and helped to bring me-up-to-date and provided new challenges.

Paul Beeman had been pastor of the Olympia Church for 11 years and he recognized that it was time to leave. When he left in July, 1984, he wrote me this note: "A Mind insatiably alive, Energy endlessly expendable, Friendship forever welcoming, Committed always to a justice realizable in God's world—the most balanced Christian life I have known. With Deepest Affection, Paul Beeman."

Rev. Larry Speicher came as Senior Pastor. Formerly I had been calling on new people during their first week, but Larry began to do this. That relieved me, but there were times when I was not sure of my "space." We would go out for lunch and work it out. He depended on me a great deal for knowing about the families in the church, not just the new members, but older ones, too.

An exciting program developed suddenly. As the staff discussed the new Performing Arts Center which had just opened, we suddenly decided to have an Easter Service there. The whole congregation became involved as we prepared. We had three services, one at 8:00 A.M. at the church, and duplicate services at 9:00 A.M. and 11:00 A.M. at the Performing Arts Center. We were overwhelmed as we saw the entire place fill up, even including the fourth balcony. Many people came to one of our services as well as their own. When we passed around a paper for people to sign if they wanted to have a contact with the church, 80 people signed it. We telephoned them that week and had open-house for them. Many came and later joined the church. This was a less-threatening introduction than a traditional service would have been. One of the values for the community, we thought, was that they could see that main line churches were not dead.

As I was to be 75 years old by July of 1986, I decided it was time to quit working. I bought a new car, a red Plymouth. Larry told people he would have to buy a computer when I left. They did, but only for finances at first.

When I was preparing my last sermon as a member of the staff, I had a startling experience. I quote from notes I took soon after. "I took the last page out of the typewriter. I had, of course, asked for guidance before I started, all the while I was thinking about it. As I took the paper in my hands I said, 'Oh, God, is it good enough?' The answer came clearly and quickly: 'It is I who put your fingers on those keys.' I preached in confidence, but still amazed at the number of people who said specific parts were helpful. Thank you, God."

A note from Richard Smith after participating in some of the community activities indicates more of the wonderful relationships we had working together. "I do appreciate, Marion, all that you do to support these kinds of efforts in our church and community. I don't write you very often to tell you this in such a formal way. but I thought I surely needed to do that and this was a good opportunity. It's been a marvelous experience getting to know and work with you. I am grateful. Sincerely yours, Richard."

I did resign in 1986 and the farewell was unbelievable. There were three sections: the morning worship service at 10:00 A.M.; a dinner in Fellowship Hall at 11:45; and an honoring program in the Sanctuary at 1:00 P.M. Several people participated in the worship service which I had helped plan. Carrie Richardson sang during the delightful luncheon. In the afternoon letters were read from friends far and near which the committee had secured from my mailing list. Gifts included a painting of me by Mary Ann Bigelow, a painting by John Cash, and a money gift of $1215. It was wonderful to have the family there, Dick and Ann, Fran and Earl III, Ruby and Forrest, Earl Ecklund and Ruby, and even Walter came to the church for part of the time. Super!

Ruth Gray, recently widowed, succeeded me. She worked on her Master of Divinity Degree part-time and was later ordained.

All through these years other things were happening that were not related to the work. After Walter moved his mobile home onto the property he came over for dinner more easily. As he never bought a TV he would often stay after dinner to watch baseball or football games, or artistic programs such as ballet. Sometimes we watched programs about other countries and I was often surprised that we agreed about the political situations. As he had been a chief engineer in the

Merchant Marine, I expected that a sailor and a missionary would have different opinions, but that was not so.

THE POOL. Following the advice of the doctor for my arthritis I began swimming in the pool. The Athletic Club allowed one to pay for the pool without joining the Club. I went early in the morning, then dressed for work arriving about 9:00 A.M. I decided I was too old to try to learn any new strokes and to enjoy the ones I already knew: the side stroke and the back stroke. Sometimes I floated on my back and relaxing, thought about something at the church. Often ideas would come that I shared with the staff. Later, after I stopped working, I joined the water aerobics class, as I thought I got better all around exercise.

OPERA, Seattle Rep Theatre and Act Theatre, all in Seattle, with Walter and Frances, were regular enjoyments. Walter and Frances also went to Intiman Theatre, but I could not manage them all. Saturday evening performances at the Opera were the most difficult because we did not get home until very late, and I needed to be at work early the next morning. I got extra sleep later.

THE SEABECK CONFERENCE of the Fellowship of Reconciliation was a regular function each year. One of the most exciting times was training in nonviolence. After some training at the camp we went to the gate at Bangor where the nuclear submarines are based. We gathered in small groups and sang and prayed. The guards who had run to get clubs in case we came in, were stymied. In the meantime some of the group had climbed the fence in back and were planting a peace garden. They were arrested, but kept only overnight. The next year we were not allowed in front of the gate but had to be across the street. We made one big sign that all could read with about 50 of us holding it up. One year there were fewer of us and we were at the back gate. I gave a short message about Jesus weeping over the city of Jerusalem because they did not know the things that make for peace. These experiences have added to the depth of feeling I have for that annual gathering.

CROP WALK got started. In the years after World War II, I had been a County Chairman for the Christian Rural Overseas Program, where seeds for producing farm produce were sent overseas. In ensuing years Walks had been developed by Church World Service to ease the burden of poverty in Third World Countries. The first year of the Walk in Olympia I helped as a registrar and advertised it in the church. The Walk grew as more and more churches participated.

THE SHAKESPEARE FESTIVAL at Ashland, Oregon, has been one of the recreational delights through the years. I have gone with a number of different people; when Elderhostel began we signed up for that. Always one class was taught by an actor which gave us insights into what went on behind the scenes. A favorite lecturer was a Jewish Rabbi.

On May 18, 1980, Mt. St. Helens erupted. It had been beautiful, with a pointed top. Although warnings were sent out, and roads closed, about fifty people ignored them and were killed. It happened that the next afternoon I called on a woman whose son and family were on the mountain and she had not heard from them. I had planned to make other calls but stayed with her all afternoon In the evening it was known that all her family were all killed. She thanked me often for "holding her hand that afternoon" as she expressed it. The devastation was immense, and now and then in later years it was good to see it coming to life again.

THE INTERNATIONAL ASSOCIATION OF WOMEN MINISTERS (IAWM) met in 1982 in a small church college in Canada. A trip through the Rockies was included. All of my friends had taken such a trip. I decided this would be a good group to go with. Although I had belonged to the organization since Garrett days, I had been to only one meeting at that time. This would be a good renewal. I was the only retired one of about 40 women ministers. More were from the U.S. than from Canada.

We discussed a number of issues relating to women in the ministry, with many telling of their problems and successes. A few of us had headaches and stood near the coffee pot drinking coffee and enjoying each other. At the end of the week we discovered we had been drinking decaf coffee, and the lack of caffeine was giving us the headaches. These stopped when we had the opportunity to drink regular coffee. We had to agree that we were coffee addicts.

Just before we left one of the officers told me that they were asking me to be in charge of the meeting the next year, in connection with the World Council of Churches, to be held in Vancouver, B.C. They thought I lived close enough to make arrangements.

We proceeded to Jasper and walked through a park, then on to the hotel on Lake Louise for lunch. We arrived at Banff in the evening. I roomed with the Canadian woman who had taken care of the money. She needed help in figuring it out. I discovered she had made a mistake in the exchange rate. She had charged the Americans considerably more than the Canadians. Some of the women had been very critical of everything and I thought if they knew this they would have rebelled.

I said nothing until one woman needed some scholarship help and was feeling guilty. I told her she had paid too much in the first place.

On Sunday morning we went to the Church of Canada. The organist was a former Catholic nun who had been excommunicated because she had been vocal for women to become priests. She was thrilled with our group.

I had planned to stay a day in Vancouver before going home, intending to take a city tour. Instead I spent the day making contacts for the next year. I discovered there would be a women's center. I was able to talk with the woman in charge, telling her about our needs and desires. I contacted the housing group, asking for the YWCA. I spent some time just relaxing at the beautiful St. Elizabeth Park. All in all, I was satisfied with the whole trip.

Three trips to Vancouver, B.C., were needed to make arrangements for the IAWM meeting. On one I took Judy Kreger with me. We found we were not being given the YWCA for housing as I had asked, but rather a small family-run hotel, Bosman's Motor Hotel, which proved to be excellent. We went by ferry to Victoria, checking on prices for cars and walkers, and ferry schedules. We drove all around the city of Victoria, as well as to the Buchart Gardens.

The IAWM gathered in the Hotel the weekend before the World Council of Churches began. Our theme was three-fold: Looking Inward, to find unique things that women can offer the ministry; Looking Outward as we join in some of the World Council of Churches meetings; and Looking Upward as we women joined together in Worship.

The Center for Women, called the Well, was in the Lutheran Church across from the University Campus where the Council meetings were held. The woman in charge of the Well had arranged for women clergy of other countries to speak the first two afternoons at the Well. I had not really expected such a rich blessing. Our most outstanding speaker was Dr. Constance Parvey, who gave us a fascinating history of the ordination of women through the centuries. All who met with our group were very appreciative of our work. At times we listened to the Plenary Sessions on the TV arranged for us in the meeting room of the Hotel, and at other times we attended the session in the Auditorium. Worship was with others at the Well, or in the Tent, or by ourselves with Dr. Charlotte Caron of Saskatoon.

THE WORLD COUNCIL OF CHURCHES itself was inspiring. The entrance of the various church leaders from around the world in their various costumes was magnificent. Although there had been some opposition to having Russians from the Eastern Orthodox Church included (they must be Communist), these objectors discovered it was the Easterners who brought the Westerners to worship when emotions ran high. To watch the leaders of churches around the world dialogue and work on issues was a wonderful experience. People everywhere were heard from and listened to and the pain and sorrow and joys of people were shared by all. Worship was held every morning in the Tent and always the Lord's Prayer was said in one's own language. They had been working for some years on papers on Baptism, Eucharist, and Ministry, and they came to some agreement. We did not stay for the whole session which extended for three weeks. I returned for two days at the end. This whole experience was outstanding.

One day in a summer, I do not know just when, I was just sitting out in my yard, relaxing and meditating. I had a pen and paper with me, and I wrote this prayer: "This closeness, this feeling of security, this serenity You have given me—how thankful I am for it now. The day is peaceful, too, and this seat under a tree facing the lake and mountains beyond seem to accentuate the peacefulness of it. A shot from Fort Lewis! As if You were reminding me that though You have given me calmness You did not mean that I should become complacent. We Christians have sinned against You, for we have become conformed to this world. Oh God, search our guilty hearts, make us face the conflicts honestly, and use our little, worthless love as one with Thy Redeeming Love."

SEARCHING FOR A RETIREMENT COMMUNITY took some time, I discovered. Walter was not well and it seemed I should make plans for a time when I might be alone. As we were three miles from the closest bus I wondered what would happen if I could not drive, as was true of several friends. I wanted to be closer to Seattle, so that it would not be so far to drive to the Opera and plays and other attractions. I wrote to the Seattle Senior Assistance Office and asked for a list of Retirement Homes. Denominations were ignored as I wrote and received literature. I visited several Communities which helped me to decide that I really wanted a cottage where I could do my own cooking. The one that appealed to me was Wesley Homes, in Des Moines, fifteen miles from Seattle. I paid my down payment, then told Walter. He was relieved, knowing that if he died I would be cared for.

WALTER'S 80th birthday was March 1st, 1986. Early in the year Ann and I decided we should make this a big affair. This was a good opportunity for people to express how much he had meant to them. We sent out invitations to all the people on his mailing list, asking for cards if they could not come. He received many cards but also some very special guests. Margie Laflin flew in the day before from California. She said she wanted to have some time with him before all the others arrived. He had paid her tuition for college and they were very fond of each other. He was delighted to see her, and whether that made him suspect that something was in the air we did not know. On Sunday two couples arrived from New York, Bonnie Albertson and her husband-to-be, and Alice (Albertson) Waller. Their father had been in the Merchant Marine with Walter before they were born. They were sure this would be the last time they would see Walter and they wanted him to know they appreciated how much he had done for them through the years. Walter told me once that the ones he would have liked to have had as daughters were Bonnie and Margie. He truly loved them both and became, I think, a surrogate father for both. These girls who meant so much to him had come to see him—he could hardly believe it!

We all left for the dinner at Alice's Restaurant. As we were driving along on the country road south of Tenino, Bonnie wondered if there could be any food this far away from everything. After all, she lived in a suburb and worked in New York City. Here she was going to dinner out in the woods. There were thirty of us, filling the small room. Bonnie could not believe how much food there was, and how inexpensive it was compared to New York. As always, it was delicious and everybody had a great time. We gave Walter the many cards from people who could not come. He shook his head in wonder, as he could not believe it.

Bonnie and her Bob liked to ski in the Vermont mountains. Mt. Rainier was an amazement to them. They said that every time they turned around, there was that mountain. Although it was early March we learned that the road was open. We drove up to Paradise in two cars. The snow banks were deep, and everything was closed. One of the workmen told us of a place inside where we could eat our lunch. It was clear enough for us to see the top of the mountain, which thrilled us all. We had never been there when snow was everywhere, and we were glad we had the opportunity to show off our mountain to the New York skiers.

After the birthday party Walter became increasingly confused. In late July he went every week to Vancouver to see the Kellys. They were surprised but enjoyed it. Then he went to California to see Margie. On the way he stopped in San Jose to see Wayne, Anne's brother, and told him he was not going to live long. He visited a former shipmate who did not remember him. Margie had been looking forward so much to the visit, but when he arrived he was concerned only with the fact that he had been forgotten. The next morning Margie and Larry heard him fall, and took him to the closest hospital. She called me and told me Walter had a stroke. I had church responsibilities on Sunday, so on Monday I flew to Margie's home. When we went to the hospital Walter seemed to accept the fact that I was there, as usual. As I knew that a month was not a long time for recovery from such a stroke, I went, as planned, to Great Britain for an Elderhostel.

Margie was not yet strong from her surgery, yet she went to see him twice a day. She said he had never let her do anything for him and she was glad to do this. He did appreciate having her there. I felt comfortable leaving him in her care. Bonnie would have been the only other person in the country I would have left him with. Margie and I were in communication over the phone a number of times. On that morning of August 14 I had a very deep sense of peace. I was hoping it meant that he would last until I got back, but when I got the word he had died, I thought perhaps it meant that he was at peace. I had thought how despondent he would have been if he had to stay in the house without getting out in the yard. Perhaps it was better that he did not linger. He left an envelope "in the event of death" on his desk. Also a letter to his friend Bush in Oklahoma, not finished, saying that the old jeep had given out, and he had wondered whether it or he would go first, and he guessed it was a draw. Margie took care of the cremation and sent the ashes to me.

THE GREAT BRITAIN ELDERHOSTEL

It was late July, 1986, when I left Walter in the hospital. With Margie seeing him twice a day, I felt fairly secure about leaving him. Kay Proctor, a friend from Olympia, had stayed overnight with me, and we took a British Airways flight to London. After we were settled a card with a quiz was given to each of us. This was a contest, but Kay and I and the young man sitting in the third seat decided to play with it just to pass the time. As he was from the east coast and we from the west, and I had lived in the middle, we made a pretty good team. The first part consisted of meanings of words, relationships between things, trivia, and was not too difficult. We shared only a little. The last section was the "tie breaker." We decided to do this together. With my calculator we did all the math for that section, guessing at all our answers. We ended with 2352. Kay put that number down. Our young man and I did not, but thought awhile. Finally I decided that four numbers could be a date and therefore, 1986 might be the answer. After awhile he said it might be that, and when he realized that I had come to the same conclusion, he put it down also. But Kay said he had trouble with meanings of words in the first section. It had all been in fun, but we handed in the cards the next day anyway.

After we arrived in London we waited for some more Elderhostelers to arrive, then took a chartered bus to Brighton, Sussex. Our accommodations were modern, in Palmer Hall of the Brighton Polytechnic. We were at breakfast the next morning when the local leader said, as he passed my table, "You won." He went on to take a message to someone, and on his way back I asked him "Won what?" "I don't know. Didn't you have a contest on the plane?" "You are kidding!" "How else would I know?" Then I discovered that the travel agent, whose address we had given as our own, had sent word that I had won the contest! 350 people on the flight and I won! The prize was $700 to be spent at Herrod's Department Store, where, it is said, the Queen shops. Kay and I had signed up for a week's extension in London, and I would have time to shop. Even when I got the official papers I had difficulty believing it.

Our first field trip was to the center of the town of Brighton, a resort town by the sea. In the 18th Century George IV had the Royal Pavilion built in the style of the Mogul palaces of India and furnished in the Chinese style. I was especially interested in the beautiful colorful lighting fixtures.

The nearby Arundel Castle was huge, built in the llth Century by the Earl of Arundel. For over 700 years it has been the home of the Dukes of Norfolk. We enjoyed the beautiful portraits of the family. The gift shop had everything. I bought a doll representing Elizabeth I. The doll for Henry VIII was irresistible.

Our main study was about English Gardens. We learned about their history, then we visited Wakehurst and Sheffield castles with their beautiful gardens. It was costing too much to keep them up so the families turned them over to the Kew Foundation. The castles themselves were closed but there were acres of gardens. We spent three days walking among the trees and flowers, many from other parts of the world. These gardens were more beautiful, I thought, than the French formal gardens I had seen previously.

Another field trip was to Hastings. This is where William the Conqueror defeated Harold in battle, and came to rule in England. We visited Battle Abbey. The massive gate house still dominates the town, and the monks' dormitory stands roofless but well preserved. All Abbeys were destroyed by King Henry VIII when he broke from the Roman Catholic Church. As we looked over the cliff we found all along the coast were white cliffs horizontally striped with black flint. This was a unique sight.

At the end of the week we left for Galashiels, Scotland. We were housed in the modern dormitory of the Scottish College of Textiles. The week we were there they were teaching people to machine-knit sweaters. I would have loved to have taken part, but our study was the Scottish Borders.

A number of us went to church on Sunday morning, the Catholics to the Cathedral, and we Protestants to the Church of Scotland. This was not a very large church, but had a balcony running around three-quarters of it. About a dozen of us sat toward the front of the center section. The Scots must have thought we were poison for all of them (about 25) sat around under the balconies, far away from us. Afterwards no one spoke to us, not even the minister. We felt that foreigners certainly did not belong in that church.

One of the first field trips was a mile walk to Abbotsford, the home of Sir Walter Scott, which he built in 1822. The library and study were most interesting. In the armory Kay found a sword with the name of her husband's family.

Early in the week we went to Edinburgh to see the city and to shop. The Castle dominates the landscape. We rode up to it, and walked around. We went in St. Margaret's Chapel, the oldest building on the grounds. The inside was simple and beautiful.

The Scott monument is outstanding. The Queen's State Apartments were open to the public, and have paintings, tapestries, and old furniture. The beautiful crown jewels had not been used since England conquered Scotland years ago.

We took two trips with a guide who knew the history of every tree and waterfall and hillside in the whole area. It had been a battlefield between warring Scots and English forces. It was very desolate country, we thought. Both Kay and I became extremely bored until we passed a mansion with the name of her husband's family. That gave us a little life. On one trip we went to the English Border and Hadrian's Wall. The materials described the area as dramatic, but except for that bit of history, we disagreed.

We went to Edinburgh again to take a nice boat ride to visit Incholm Island and the Abbey. It had been a beautiful Abbey and the people who took care of it were glad to have visitors. It was a delightful place to relax. In the evening we went to the Tatoo. This was advertised as a military festival, but only one band was in military costume the night we were there. Bands from all over the world came to play, but there were none from the U.S., as there was fear of terrorism. We felt this was an exceptional opportunity to witness Scotland's exciting festival.

For the third week we traveled by car, train and bus all day to Camarthan, Wales. It was built over an old Roman town on a river which runs into the sea. Our accommodations were terrible. Fortunately we had single rooms as there was no place to put anything. We kept our clothes in our suitcases, but a wet towel had no place. There were two other groups there, and class distinctions were seen at meals. The group from France was seated for dinner, and had better housing. The music teachers had better housing but ate cafeteria style with us. We evidently were the cheap ones, with the cheapest housing.

All along the way I had called Margie to find out about Walter. At one point he had been back in Intensive Care again, but was better. I asked both Margie and the doctor if I should come home, but they both said "No." It was here at

Camarthan that I had word of his death. When I asked Margie should I return, she said, "Are you crazy?" So I stayed on.

We went to church Sunday morning. We Protestants went to the Methodist Church. The Catholics waited for us impatiently in the bus, but the people were so friendly and wanted to talk with each one of us that we found it hard to leave. It was such a contrast to the Scottish Church.

Dylan Thomas, a well known 20th Century poet, lived in Camarthan. We visited his house and work shed and read some poetry. I bought a book because one poem, "Death Has No Dominion," fitted my mood at that time. We went to a Welsh Choir of 40 voices and although we had heard such choirs before, hearing them sing right in their own home situation was a thrill. I went to another room as I heard some women singing. I was delighted. They, too, had beautiful voices. I thought they should be advertised, as well.

One trip was to the gardens of King Hywel Dda, who codified Welsh law in the 10th Century. We were especially interested in the freedom women had, and the compassion of the King. Another trip was to St. David's, a town on the far west peninsula. The first church was built there about 550 A.D. The present one was built in 1181. King Henry VIII did not destroy it because a member of his family was buried there. The cross in the village was a Celtic cross. We were told that St. Patrick was sent to Ireland from there, but that could be legend. We had a chartered bus back to London. We had no final dinner, which is traditional for Elderhostels, because when we got to London we were all in different hotels. Thus we said our good-byes on the bus. Kay and I were the only ones who had arranged for an extra week in London. Our hotel was the St. Ermins Hotel, considerably upgraded from the others. We arrived in time for dinner, which was included in the Elderhostel cost. The cheapest dinner was $17, so we ate with much thanksgiving, and decided to eat at other places at other times.

We were glad to have the time in London for neither of us had spent much time there previously. In Herods, where I had to spend the money I had won on the plane, we walked floor to floor and we agreed with other tourists that there was nothing anywhere like the floor displaying foods. The first thing I bought was a blue wool suit. While I was trying it on Kay thought it did not fit well in back. I suggested I might be able to adjust it, but the young clerk said, "No, I can not sell it if it is not perfect." On her lunch hour she shopped for me at another store. No wonder the Queen shopped there! Also I bought a dress with a long full skirt. This was also an opportunity to buy a Seiko watch. I had a serving dish which matched her China shipped to Margie. And I did all my Christmas shopping which delighted the receivers.

We could not use the money for travel, but we could for plays. We went to several, especially "Guys and Dolls" and "Hello Dolly." We walked the center of London. At the Changing of the Guard at Buckingham Palace I was disappointed as there was a high fence between the actual ceremony and the rest of us. It had not been there before the fear of terrorism. We took a number of short trips, to Westminster Abbey, and a trip on the river where we could get an excellent view. We went to Windsor Castle. The Queen was in residence that day so her apartment was not open. However we did go to the section for her dolls and doll houses. Kay got bored and wandered off, but I was entranced. For me to view the Queen's doll collection was a rare gift. We also took in Stratford, Blenheim Palace, and Oxford.

Canterbury Cathedral was a place I had wanted to go for a long time. One of the women clergy I had met at our women's clergy meetings in the U.S. lived at Kent, just outside London. She told me she would show us the Cathedral. We agreed to take the same train, but when it stopped at Kent she got on but did not look for us. When I found her I led her through three cars ahead. All the while she was ahead of me talking in a loud shrill voice telling me why she thought we were not there. Inasmuch as the British were apt to complain about how noisy Americans were, I was glad that all the people watching could hear her British English!

The Cathedral is as beautiful as I had expected it to be. The leaflet says St. Augustine arrived in Kent and soon established the first Cathedral in 597. This was destroyed by fire, and in 1070-78 the present building was built. There have been many additions and changes through the years. The latest remodeling was repairing the library from war damage. Some windows are old, designed to tell illiterate people about Jesus. Some are new, such as the Peace window, replacing glass destroyed in World War II. It represents the gathering together of all people of all races and their indivisibility in Christ.

We had lunch at the Mayflower Restaurant, which is supposed to be the place where the Mayflower contract was signed. Then our friend took the train back to

Kent, and we went to see an old church nearby. St. Martin's Church was built by St. Augustine about 562. It is built of stone, and very plain inside. Evidently it was not important enough to destroy, added to, or rebuild. We walked back to the train station in a pouring rain. Even raincoats and hoods did not keep us dry.

Back at the St. Ermins Hotel we continued to enjoy the ambiance of the old hotel, and also the many Japanese and other racial groups staying there. I was especially intrigued by the sign that said that in 1903 the World Methodist Conference was held in that hotel. This Conference included the black Methodist denominations as well as white. Thus some of the speakers were black. Other patrons complained to the manager, saying that blacks should not be there. The manager and the owners decided that the blacks were welcome and could speak. Ever since that time the hotel has welcomed those of other races. Would that all our Methodists through the years could have that legacy!

◆   ◆   ◆

It was hard to come home and realize that Walter would not be coming home. When I cleaned up his kitchen things, I realized how he had prepared for the time I was gone. Yet on his desk he left a half-written letter to his friend Bush, saying he would not live long. Yet I was glad he did not suffer longer than he did.

We had a Memorial Service in the Chapel for the family and a few friends. Our Pastor Larry conducted the service, using a short biography which I had written. Although Walter had been active in the local Opera Guild, those who came were surprised at how much going to the opera in other countries had meant to him. People from the Power Squadron were also appreciative of his volunteering with them. He had indicated he wanted his ashes buried in the Vaughn Cemetery, where other members of our family were buried. We could not arrange a time for this when the family members could be there. I asked Rev. Richard Smith to go with me. At the graveside I gave a very short service for the few friends he knew there. Our cousin Barbara could not find the place.

I wrote to friends: One hates to see them go, yet I am glad that he did not linger long as an invalid. Eating dinners alone, and not having any one to yell and scream with when there are football games on T.V., have been moments of real loss. Also the trips to Seattle for Repertory Theatre and Opera without him are not the same. I have been grateful for the ten years of companionship we have had.

Sometime during the winter that followed I received a check refunding me for the excess taxes that were charged as Americans in England. Kay and I used it go to see Eugene O'Neill's "Moon for the Misbegotten" in Seattle.

It was in this year, 1986, that the former missionaries to the Philippines held their first reunion. We met in Nashville, and have met every two years since, usually there or somewhere in the East. Always we have had some worship services but have spent a good deal of time sharing experiences. Each time I have been reminded of how few of the people I worked with were Methodist, and only once or twice have these been there. However it has been a time of bonding with those who have shared Filipino culture.

THE WORLD EXPOSITION 86 was in Vancouver, B.C. With that so close, Phyllis Hoogan, Judy Kreger and I went together. We stayed at Bosman's Hotel where our women's clergy group had stayed previously. The first day we just walked from one section to another, visiting especially the Chinese, Canadian and African Pavilions. The second day Phyllis did not want to walk or stand in lines. She took a cable-car over the Pavilions, while Judy and I enjoyed the Hall of Ramses II. The rest of the day we did nothing. Neither Judy nor I were satisfied as we had missed some of the very new things being demonstrated. Judy returned with family members, and I went for two days by myself.

Later in the summer I went to a meeting of the International Association of Women Ministers in California. The emphasis was on homosexuality. Like most of the others, I had been confronted with it, but had little understanding. I learned that the name Metropolitan Church usually meant it was a church for gays and lesbians. I began to wonder about the children and youth I had known in years past. The girls at Westminster College, for instance, who would have a "crush" on me or on the gym teacher. We would try not to let them get too close, but without hurting their feelings. I wondered if they had been lesbian. Of course neither they nor I understood it at that time. And I remembered when Rosalie (with whom I lived in Neenah) was concerned about her fourth grader who was showing feminine characteristics. She tried to help his father to be a bit tolerant. Almost all the speakers had trouble with their mothers, and I wondered aloud to a psychologist if that was part of the problem, but she thought it was a result, not the cause of that style of life. I have been thankful for this beginning for it has led to much more thinking and understanding of the whole issue.

When I retired Amory Peck asked me what I was going to do, and I answered that I wanted to read the mystics. She thought that would be interesting, and we formed a group of five which met every two weeks. The Methodist Publishing House had published excerpts from many, and we bought those and chose which ones we wanted to read and discuss. Two of the women Chaplains from St. Peter's Hospital joined us, for they said they had heard these names all their lives, but as nurses they had not had an opportunity to read them. They added a lot to our group. The excerpts did not include anyone after Dietrich Bonhoeffer. We also studied Matthew Fox, Doug Hammerskjold, Simon Weil, Thomas Merton, Teilhard de Charden, and Henri Nowen. Each of us selected which ones we wanted, and excerpted a book. This took a good deal of time, but was exceedingly inspiring. After two years Richard Smith decided that there should be a program for people who would like to study something deep, and he started a Sunday evening study of Liberation Theology. This appealed to a larger number and our group joined it and enjoyed it.

Another fall project was taking over the Church Library. I found all the children's books mixed up with the adults' books. The new Church School Superintendent and I worked together, ordering new children's books. We put them in the hall-way, where the children could find them. We were delighted the first day to find them a mess—the children had really gone over them and taken about half of them. The cards were all duly signed and in the right place. It was money well spent. The following year I found a helper who remained the librarian for many years.

THE TRIP TO NICARAGUA in the spring of 1987 cost just the amount which was given me when I retired. Therefore I used that money for the trip. President Reagan was hiring soldiers (called contras) from Honduras and northern Nicaragua to fight against President Ortega. Our government had supported Samoza, the dictator. The Revolution, then, was against our interests. Our country had a policy of "containment." Any country in this hemisphere which was being helped by Russia or Cuba was to be destroyed. If a war seemed not advisable for us, we hired others to fight it. The whole thing was done in secrecy, intrigue, and denial.

Seven of us from our church and seven others decided to go to Nicaragua to see what we could find out. Peggy and Howard Heiner, missionaries there, had encouraged us to go. Our tour organizer was GATE (Global Awareness Through Experience). We had a day-and-a-half stopover in Mexico City with Sister Stephanie who had organized GATE. We had a look at Nicaragua's history of relations with the U.S., including fourteen years of occupation, and also the present contra situation. She packed up materials and food for us to take, so that when we got on the plane for Managua we had 54 pieces of baggage for the 14 of us, with no extra charge.

In Managua we women discovered our housing was less than sparse, then learned that the men's housing was worse. But we decided we were not there to vacation in luxury. As we walked to the center of town, we found that where we expected the center to be there was all brush and low trees. There was one build- ing being built. Many countries had sent money to help rebuild the city after the earthquake of 1973, but Samoza had simply kept the money and not rebuilt any- thing.

Peggy Heiner had arranged interviews for us. Chief among these was our sponsor, Guillerma Auguiell, Director of CEPAD (The Nicaraguan Council of Churches Development Agency). This was formed after the earth-quake to get the churches working together to help to ease the suffering of the people, and it had continued to be active.

Our first visitation was with two nuns who introduced us to the split in the Catholic Church between the hierarchy and the priests and nuns who were work- ing with the poor people. Under Samoza the hierarchy of the church had been very powerful. Now after the Revolution they were treated without respect. The priests and nuns felt that this government was much better than Samoza's in tak- ing care of the poor.

Peggy had tried to arrange a meeting with the Cardinal, but instead he sent a young assistant who read a paper. This began, "It is a waste of time to talk with you..." The Church hierarchy was opposed to the government and approved of the contras who were fighting it. In response the government had closed down the Church's newspaper, radio, and television station and had expelled one out- spoken Bishop. After the paper we questioned the representative who was ada- mant in his stand. He made no mention, and did not answer our questions, about starvation and oppression under Samoza nor the work for the poor being done by the Sandinistas. He pleaded: "What can a church do without its television station?" We could think of a few things!

As we were there two Sundays we went first to the church of the hierarchy (the Cathedral had been destroyed in the Revolution) and talked with people who greeted us, telling them what our purpose was. I was struck by the fact that all people were welcome to take Mass. The second Sunday we went to a church where an outspoken priest works with the compesinos (the very poor) and openly supports the present government. This was in Spanish, but we could watch both the priest and the responses and realize that he understood them and was speaking to their situation. The art work around the wall was delightful.

One of the people we interviewed was Maria de Socorro who worked for the government in the Ministry of Housing. She told us of her personal experience of working for the U.S. company Tropigas. She began to study the abuses by Samoza and became part of the Sandinistas who would overthrow him. She told us how Samoza's army would take suspected subversives up in helicopters and just throw them out. This made her angry and led her to open her house where the revolutionaries could hide. They formed an "underground railroad," part of it coming through her back yard and home. This helped the Revolution to succeed. She told us about the government housing which she was supervising. She was a delightful personality, and a well-educated, capable person.

One nun, Luz Beatrice Aurella, headed a center where she was training Bible leaders. She stressed the importance of the Christian Base Communities. She explained that small groups in a church started reading the Bible together. As the Catholic Church had not stressed Bible reading, this was a first for many. As they read the New Testament they took it very seriously. "Blessed are the poor" meant the poor were not to be ignored. They asked: When did we see you hungry? The answer: Today. Centuries of interpretation were wiped away and the Gospel came alive. These small groups then reached out to include the poor and those ignored by society. Some of them became economically secure. It was these communities that the Bible leaders were helping. The movement became known by theologians as Liberation Theology.

We had some time to wander in the city, alone or in groups. I was especially excited to find a children's library, encouraging young people to learn how to

read. For a former librarian this was an important find. I took several of the group
to see it.

One of our trips was to a refugee family living in tents a short distance from
Managua. The government had given them a small amount of land for farming.
They belonged to the Church of the Brethren (one of the historic peace churches)
from the northern part of the country. They had refused to fight for either side.
They told us there were many others in the town nearby. It was interesting to us
that conscientious objectors were not only allowed, but that the government
actually aided them.

We were in for some surprises politically. We had heard only of President
Ortega and the U.S. unspoken assumption that there was only one party. When
we talked with a man who had been elected to the National Assembly we found
that there were 12 political parties. Four of these were to the left of the Sandinistas. The others were more conservative. Every party gets at least one vote. There
was a joke going around the National Assembly circles that the only representative of the Marxist-Leninist Party stood up one day in frustration and declared
that Ronald Reagan was the only person who recognized him! His own colleagues
ignored him! With 67% of the members of the National Assembly, Ortega really
had little opposition. From our point of view there was no freedom of the press.
La Prensa, a right-wing newspaper had been closed. It was discovered that the
U.S. CIA had been subsidizing La Prensa to stay in business and support the contras. The Marxist-Leninist paper had also been closed.

When we visited the American Embassy (which looked like a fortress), we discovered that the current Ambassador was strongly in favor of the contras, and
believed that Ortega had a completely Communist government. He was hostile
as he answered our questions. We had heard that the previous Ambassador had
been called back to the U.S. because he had tried to persuade President Reagan
that Ortega had done some good things. We thought this one wanted to keep his
job, and would refuse to look at anything good. One morning every week a vigil
was held outside the American Embassy to oppose the contras. Several hundred
were there when we joined it, mostly Americans who work there, and some other
tourists. Among others I met a retired pastor of a Seattle Church and also an
active Presbyterian missionary, Chess Campbell, who later took over much of
Peggy's work of arranging contacts for tourists.

We went to Matagalpa for a few days. Peggy thought we should pick coffee, but the leader of the pickers said they had all the Americans they could handle. I was very relieved, for I did not look forward to living out in the open with no facilities of any kind, which this seemed to involve. Instead the men found a boy with a bat, and played baseball with the boys in the street. Others of us sat in the park, people-watching and visiting with people when we could. We did visit a children's day care-center for pickers, and were much impressed by the care given them.

It was here that we learned how the contras worked. The CEPAD worker told us that the night before contras had burned a government clinic which held all the polio vaccinations for that entire area. We had thought that the contras were fighting the Nicaraguan Army; we found instead that they avoided the army. They went in small bands to villages, burning schools and clinics, killing community leaders, such as school teachers, health workers, priests and pastors. In order to prevent farmers from getting their produce to the villages they placed mines in the roads, maiming and killing any who passed. We met with the family of a minister and his two daughters who were injured in such an accident on a Sunday morning as they went from one church to another. They were in the U.S. for medical treatment, taken there by one of the mission societies. But hundreds were not so fortunate. We discovered that the contras were not really as much an army, as they were terrorists paid by the U.S.

We went on north to Jinotega where much damage had been done. We visited a women's sewing cooperative. The government gave them materials which had been sent from Europe. They made dresses and men's shirts. We spent some time at the market, but the others were not as fascinated as I was, for though it was small it told much about their culture. There were half a dozen government soldiers to protect the town from further inroads by the contras. The men spent quite a bit of time with them as one of them was good with Spanish and they could communicate quite well. Also we were intrigued with the local photographer with his very old-fashioned camera taking pictures of people.

Some of our most interesting short trips were to cooperative farms. The government had confiscated the large holdings of the Samoza and other rich farmers who had moved to Miami. The people we met knew Peggy as she had brought groups to them before, and they were anxious to tell us how good the government had been to them. At one farm we found a large pile of lumber. They had cut down some trees, and with the aid of a cross cut saw had prepared lumber. They admitted to being disappointed in us. They were waiting for some Methodists from Oregon to help them build their houses, and they thought we would be the ones. I was delighted later to meet the leader of that group which did arrive the following week. At one of the farms we found a road-side stall selling vegetables and discovered that the farmers had already built houses to live in and had comparatively good farming soil. They were proud of their achievements.

Another cooperative was a shoe factory. Again, Peggy had taken many groups there, and the workers were happy to see her. When necessary in all these situations Peggy translated, but in some places, as in this one, a large part was in English. One man, as we were leaving, said very emphatically: "You bring all these Americans here to talk with us. Why don't you people go home and tell your government what is happening here?" "We will," we promised. We asked ourselves, will Reagan listen?

The place where Peggy had arranged for us to spend the night was unavailable, so she asked the women in the sewing cooperative if we could stay in their homes. When she was deciding where each of us should go I agreed to take the home where they could take only one person. Others went in twos. My family consisted of a mother, (father had been killed by the contras) a son about 20, two daughters, one 18, and one 12. After giggling for awhile, we decided to sing. They sang some of their songs, then I sang some of mine. We had a great time. When it was time to go to bed, I found I had a single bed in the living room, with everybody else in the other room. I was shown the toilet and the shower. In the morning I took a shower the Filipino way, pouring a can of water over me. It felt wonderful. I dressed quickly expecting to go to the restaurant for breakfast. My hosts insisted I have a roll (which the girl had run to the bakery to buy) and a cup of coffee with them. By this time we were able to communicate a little better and they indicated that the older girl had killed a contra. They were very proud of this. I noticed the Ten Commandments hanging on the wall. I started to try to read them in Spanish. The young man helped me to get the right pronunciation. I acted them out to make sure I had the meaning, and he joined in. Then we went to the Beatitudes and we did the same thing. They really loved it that I was trying their Spanish. At breakfast with the group we shared experiences, and I thought I had the best experience of all. When I mentioned having a shower, I was met with amazement. I laughed at them—they just did not know how. Although they had been in pairs, some of them found the experience difficult. We left our friends and went back to Managua.

The Heiner son and daughter-in-law opened their home to us, and we ate and relaxed there for a couple of days, thinking about what we had learned. The government controls the banks, the exports, and land distribution and other functions. There are still some large farms, especially those growing coffee. There were other capitalist ventures. I especially took note of the Esso gas station on one of the street corners. There was a mixture of socialism, capitalism and cooperatives all together. The Soviet help came in military hardware. There were quite a number of Cuban doctors, but the one we met said they were all so busy they did not have time for politics. We visited the market, and I bought Christmas presents and two dolls depicting farmers.

On our way home we changed planes in Mexico City. I shopped in the airport and found a lovely, very Mexican, nativity scene. When I asked how much it was the man looked at me closely and then said, almost to himself, no more Christmas. He offered it for $15 and I quickly took it.

Back in Olympia we gave our report about a month later, after our slides were in order and integrated. We were surprised that the entire Great Hall was full that evening, as people were really anxious to hear what we had learned. About a month later we gave the report to the Renton United Methodist Church, as one of their laymen had been with us.

◆   ◆   ◆

Getting used to February weather in Olympia was a little bit difficult after Central America. However, almost immediately I heard that there would be a demonstration in Washington, D.C., protesting the Government's policy in Nicaragua. I began to make plans to go. The husband of Marilyn Jackson, one of the Vancouver girls, was in the Air Force and assigned to the Pentagon. She had been asking me to come to see her. Also my cousin Marion was living in the same town, as she had been brought to this country by a woman who had married into the same Arab family. Putting all this together, in April I was on my way.

THE ANTI-CONTRA DEMONSTRATION IN WASHINGTON, D.C., was the perfect timing for a visit with Marilyn. We had a good time visiting

Mount Vernon and other places. I was glad for this opportunity to see my cousin Marion Aduum, as her health was deteriorating and she died the next year.

The FOR group gathered for the demonstration at a specified place, and Richard Deats was there with a large sign. Besides a few others I knew, I was happy to find two friends from the Philippines, Melinda Quiambao, a child when I left, who became a doctor, and Romy Del Rosario, who became a missionary. We had a great time renewing friendships, then began walking with about 150,000 others down Pennsylvania Avenue past the White House to a park. They walked fast and I had to stop and sit down awhile, and thus lost our group. When I got to the park I found Richard and his sign, but he had lost the others. I went with him in the evening to an FOR gathering where an Israeli young man told us of efforts for peace with the Palestinians. A woman who lived beyond Marilyn's house took me home rather late in the evening. President Reagan paid no attention; in fact, he consistently insisted he knew nothing about the contras, even though he had been consulted twice a week, according to Oliver North, who became the scapegoat.

◆   ◆   ◆

In October SOUTH AMERICA beckoned when I learned that Gene Muench, a retired District Superintendent, was leading a trip, and that Katherine Havnaer needed a roommate. I had visited her farm when I was speaking in churches, and now that her husband had died she wanted to travel. A few things stand out in Columbia, especially the amount of gold in the museum, exquisitely carved. We visited the Salt Cathedral, which some explorers had made from a salt mine. Gold was so plentiful that it was traded for salt. The church was impressive, with little chapels. One of these, the Holy Family, dimly lit, inspired our group to sing "Silent Night." We were surprised at the harmony.

In Peru we had two outstanding trips. The first was to Machu Picchu. From Cuzco we took a train through the canyons and took a small bus up the hill on very steep switch-backs. We went through various restored buildings, then began to climb the steps. The view of the old community was amazing.

The other trip was on the Amazon River. We took a plane to Tabatinga, Brazil, paying $10 as we left, for the privilege of landing there, we guessed. Then we and our baggage got into decrepit taxis and after a ride on a very rough unpaved road, dodging children, bicycles, and animals, we reached the Amazon at Leticia, Columbia. We climbed down a very slippery bank and into little motor boats. We had a fast ride in strong wind and 90° heat and got into the M/C Buccaneer, a small boat for 35 passengers, which made the trip on the river once a week. The cabins were first class with air-conditioning. The round about way of arriving was to save the ship from paying enormous fees to the other countries if they docked in any of them.

The trip down the river was fascinating. We stopped at the little village of San Pablo which had about 2,500 people. Missionaries had been working there for a number of years. We noticed a priest and a good-looking Catholic Church. There was a leprosy hospital and also a general hospital, which we visited. This had a delivery room, an operating room and several wards. It was very clean. We walked around the town and when we were ready to leave a number of children gathered on the shore with things for us to buy, mostly small wood articles their parents had made. I bought a small bird. The air-conditioned cabin felt good after this.

The next day we went up a tributary for about a mile and a half and disembarked at the little Indian village of Bora. Kathryn's notes are better than mine, so I quote. "At the center we watched a dance to a native drink, a dance to snakes, and a dance to an anaconda. The people were in native dress, or undress, skirts for the women with the rest of their bodies painted, and shorts for the men, whose bodies were painted…The clothing was made of the bark of the fig tree (my note—maybe palm tree?) much like tapa cloth and decorated. Then we walked past the school which was half-way between two villages where we saw more dances and were able to buy trinkets. From there we straggled back to the river bank and back to the ship."

After a hard storm during the night, with sheet lightning, we landed in Iquitos. We were surprised at the modern-looking buildings. Kathryn made an interesting observation. "One of the intersting spots was an appliance store with all sorts of appliances that would be used in an outport sort of town, or in the jungle. There were fancy Kerosene stoves, some with three burners, some that operate much like Coleman camp stoves; sewing machines, operated with a foot pedal and belt; and kerosene refrigerators…There were models of battery-operated portable radios and tape recorders." I was not so impressed because these things had often been used in the Philippines. I did not think of them as "jungle," as Kathryn and most Americans would.

We went back to the airport for a 6:30 flight to Lima, but discovered it would be 1½ hours late, then another 2½ hours. We tried to have supper at the restaurant in the airport, but we could not communicate with the waiter. We had a dry sandwich and a drink. When Gene asked for our bill, the waiter brought 6 beers. After we got through laughing, Gladys, who had had a bit of Spanish, asked for the ticket in Spanish. He brought chicken sandwiches. Gene went in and talked with the cashier. Finally we got our bills paid but none of us were sure we got the right change. A storm over the Andes was responsible for the delay.

Outstanding on this trip was Iguaco Falls. We were in Argentina, facing the Brazilian side of the falls. We walked down to the platform and saw the falls spread out and thought that was magnificent. The noise was deafening. We found this was only a small part of the falls, as there were 255 in all. Rios, our guide, took Kathryn and me and a few others down a winding trail that went to the upper end of the falls. It was a leisurely walk, stopping often to take pictures. The further we walked, the more falls we saw. Finally we came to the main falls, "The Throat of the Devil" where it is 240 feet high. It was gorgeous. We walked out on a boardwalk walk, getting sprayed a bit, but thoroughly enjoying it. An elevator took us back to the trail at the top, and a bus back to the hotel. What a special hour it had been!

As we came in on the plane to RIO DE JANEIRO, BRAZIL, it looked like a huge jewel. The pilot turned off the lights so we could really see it. We were met by a young blue-eyed blond youth named Ibo. When later we asked him about his parentage we found that his family was German and that the southern section of Brazil had been a rescue spot for many Europeans fleeing wars. We toured the city, taking a funicular (cable-car) to Urca, then to Sugar Loaf, which is 1300 feet to the top. From there I took a picture of the Goddess of the Sea. Walter had sent me a picture of it years before and he told me how much it meant to the men on the ships when they could see it as they were coming into Rio.

Nancy Tims and Marion Way took us to the Racinha Community Center on the edge of the Racinha slums. Jim Tims had broken his leg when he fell while he was painting the outside of the new building. This was built with Call to Prayer and Self-Denial Funds, annual funds raised by the United Methodist Women.

The pre-school children sang to us and were excited to have visitors. The older children were eating supper, a gruel made of corn, potatoes and carrots. The children were of working mothers and had all three meals there. The charge was 10% of wages, about $2 per month.

The slums had about 200,000 people. The average salary was about $200 per month. They build shacks of cardboard until they can afford some bricks. Some have electricity and some have water, as we could see plastic hoses running all over. It seemed a little better than Tondo in Manila.

There were 11 million people in the great Rio area, and 50 Methodist churches, some of them in the slums. There are various programs for all ages, including a camp in the mountains. 130 street children were to go to the camp the following week. Many of the churches help the children with their homework, as they are in school only four hours a day in large classrooms. The Methodists are working with the Catholics in a prevention program for abandoned children. The Catholic Church is active in working with the poor. They feel the Pope has too much emphasis on Mary and a lack of ecumenical outlook.

Frances (a fellow shopper) and I went to a vendor just outside the hotel and bought sweatshirts. The doorman did not want us to go, and watched us the whole time. We discovered he had reason to be worried, as five of our group had gone together to the beach. A gang of four young fellows grabbed Helen's bag she bought at the Center with her shoes inside. She had intended to walk in the water. They knocked LeRoy down, slit his pants pocket and took a bill-fold with $8, but did not find the one with other money. They also took his watch and Chuck's camera. When I saw pictures of those beaches with people on them, I was cynical. When were they taken?

We went to Corcavado by bus and up the mountain by train to the Statue of Christ the Redeemer. The statue is 94 feet high, and the mountain is 2,500 feet high, so the statue overlooks all of Rio. About halfway up the 292 steps to the statue I was out of breath and feeling a little weak. There was a small restaurant there and a waiter was standing watching us climb. He told me to wait a minute and he brought me a leaf like a mint and told me to hold it under my tongue. In a few minutes I felt better and continued the climb. Several times we discovered that there is a positive use for coca, for it does help in high altitudes. It is the improper use and export that causes problems. On the way down we got off the train at a waterfall. It was a lovely spot, and had a gift shop. Kathryn stayed outside, uninterested, but not I. I bought a cute doll, entirely made of palm bark, which looked as if it had been woven.

We visited Brasilia, the modern Capital of Brazil. It was formed like a plane. It had one long avenue with all the government buildings, and two side wings where the workers lived. We visited one of these, and each had its own stores, schools and other services. The Catholic Church was outstanding. The supporting beams were on the outside, at the top reaching out to represent the crown of Christ. We were much impressed by the beauty of the whole city.

◆　　　◆　　　◆

In early 1988 I went to an Elderhostel in Hawaii at the Brigham Young University. It was the Cultural Center that I most enjoyed. We had free tickets, and I went whenever there was free time. The different tribal groups were in costume either on the shore or in boats on the man-made river, playing on their own musical instruments. I went in boats, either with other tourists or by myself, going from tribe to tribe. When I returned, as I did several times, some of the people would welcome me. Even though I did think it was almost overdone, I loved it anyway.

The second Elderhostel on that same trip was in Hilo. Here the Kilauea volcano proved especially interesting. At that time the volcano was not erupting in the cone and we saw just a large open space. What captured our attention were the cut flowers put there very recently, perhaps that morning. We were told that there were many people who worshiped Pele, the goddess of fire, and that the next week-end there would be many people there. We had been hearing about how modern the culture had become, and yet we had a taste of pre-modern worship. We had wondered why we could not get flights to Honolulu on Saturday and we found it would be completely full of these worshipers. At the Black Sands Beach we saw this volcano flowing underground to meet the ocean, a fascinating sight.

◆　　　◆　　　◆

A while later I went to another Elderhostel near Portland, Oregon. There were two emphases, one to learn to speak Spanish, the other on Nicaragua. Bob, the leader, had told us in a letter to bring slides if we wished. I brought mine of Nicaragua. It was fun to find that Bob had been the leader of a group of Methodists from Oregon that the people on the farm had been waiting for. I showed my slides, including those of the lumber we found on the farm, and their disappointed faces. Then Bob showed his of the men and the farmers building their houses. Then I continued with mine. The group was fascinated on how it worked together.

It was the middle of November that I had a telephone call from Wesley Homes that a small cottage was available. The next week I went to see it and yes, I liked it at the price of $31,000. It was the smaller part of a duplex. A large storage room was shared with the woman on the other side. One drawback was that there was no place for a washer and dryer, but I was assured that when the woman (who was 90) moved out the room would be remodeled.

WESLEY HOMES

THE COTTAGE

On December 31, 1988, I moved to the cottage at Wesley Homes. It was Saturday, and four men from the Olympia Church moved me, using a rented truck. One man said he rented them for his work, and when I tried to pay I found it was already done. They were through about noon so I took them to lunch at the nearby restaurant. I got off easy—the whole move from Olympia to Des Moines for the price of a few lunches!

Considerable work had been done to the cottage, with new fixtures, countertops, carpeting, walls and ceilings painted. As the living room was large I had a room divider made, giving me a place for the dolls, and a separate section for the typewriter and the mail that collects. I bought new furniture for both the living room and the bedroom. As Earl Eckland had helped me with carpeting before, he helped me with furniture construction this time.

This retirement community, Wesley Homes, is related to the United Methodist Church, but the Executive is Lutheran, and many staff members and residents are of many churches. There are about 550 residents, with two apartment buildings, one called The Gardens, the other The Terrace. There are 52 cottages, and The View with 15 upscale apartments. It is a "Continuing Care Community," with all the health care one needs until the end of life.

I quickly discovered there were lots of interesting things going on all the time. I joined a group going to a pool about a mile away for water aerobics. A program committee brought in two programs a week, musical numbers, slide shows, lectures on timely topics, etc. Busses went to Seattle for Symphony, and several theaters. There were one-day trips here and there, and also mystery trips where you did not know where you were going until you got there. We had good public bus service, a few times a day right to our front door, at other times a short walk down (and up) the hill.

While I was getting settled I prepared to teach a course on the Philippines at the School of Christian Mission. By this time books about the Marcos administration had been published which gave me a view of the inside happenings. Afterward I had several opportunities to speak, and also taught a course on the campus assisted by a woman who had lived in Manila.

One of the new experiences was a camp on the Washington Coast, which became a summer activity for several years. The first year we had a study of the political disruptions of nations around the world, led by Herman Will. It was amazing how many civil wars continued. Another outstanding leader was retired Bishop Jack Tuell who gave us a history of the Methodist Social Principles. Always the hikes along the beach were wonderful, and also the walks at night to see the stars. One of those nights the sunset was blended between the sky and the ocean so that you could not tell where one ended and the other began, and all in beautiful colors. I have seen many gorgeous sunsets, but none other like that.

World Communion Sunday, when all churches around the world celebrate Communion, meant a great deal to us overseas, as it helped to keep us from feeling isolated. When that Sunday passed at the Des Moines church without being mentioned I talked with the minister about it. The next year he managed to be away and turned the whole service over to me. We decorated the church, some wore costumes, and I preached a mission sermon. Every year since that it has been celebrated, each succeeding pastor asking for my help, if only for dolls for decorations.

Soon at the Church, I became chairman of the Social Action Work Area. With a Peace Advocates group, we kept the church alive with letters to the Legislatures for people to sign, which we put on the wall in the room for coffee hour. As the first war in Iraq threatened and we continued to send messages against it, many did continue to sign, but some became very wary and did not want us to use the church stationery for the letters, and found other objections. As far as we could we made the changes, but continued fighting against the ensuing war. As the time became close, we were able to get permission to use a small park with a large American flag for a demonstration, the Unitarian Church joining us. As people passed by in their cars some were belligerent, swearing at us, and giving us obscene gestures. Only a very few indicated they were with us. Some of our group was hurt by it, but for some of us it was just the continuation of the control of thought by the government. The war was fought, (1991), and Iraq was kept out of Kuwait. Many soldiers came home ill and it was some years before the Pentagon admitted this and took care of them. However, for some in the government the war was not finished, as Saddam was still in power. Gerie Brown, my good friend, and I seemed to be the only ones here at Wesley who were concerned.

THE IRELAND ELDERHOSTEL 1990

Millie Gillmor, my friend in Olympia, had long wanted to go to Ireland. When she found there would be an Elderhostel for three weeks in the summer of 1990, she asked me to go with her. We added several days to spend in Dublin. We flew to the Shannon Airport, beginning the trip at Limerick. We learned that we would be studying the history of Ireland, from Neolithic times to the present. The first week we stayed in Limerick and took trips to the surrounding areas. Most interesting in town were the lace makers. It was fascinating to watch them work with the tiny threads and fashion such beautiful designs.

We were introduced to the Neolithic remains in the Lough Gur area. These are thought to be from about 3000 B.C., the late Stone Age. After seeing some small circles of rock, we went to the Great Stone Circle with a diameter of 135 feet. A posthole in the center was thought to have held a stake to make the circle. Many of the stones were very large. The whole mound was higher than the area around. It was a wonder how they were able to get the stones there and put them in such a methodical way. It must have been used as a place for community gatherings and probably for worship.

Several Dolmans were in this area, as well. These were rocks piled in a certain way. Some of them used were as burial grounds. Others were rocks piled upright with a large flat one on top. At sunset at a certain time of the year the sun shone through. 1200 of these survived, and later we were able to see the sun shining through one of them at sunset. These, too, showed a high degree of knowledge. People through the years did not realize the significance of these and sometimes used the rocks to build their houses.

In the town of Galway we visited a glass factory. I bought a tiny vase for $18, and discovered it would hold one stem of a rose if the thorns and leaves were cut off. So much for the idea of buying vases for Christmas presents!

We said goodby to our housing in Limerick, and headed for Mayo County. In an area where earlier there had been many thatched roofs, we saw only one. All the others had metal roofs. In that area, however, we saw children collecting turf. This was used for heating the cottages during the winter. The donkey carried the peat on his back, as a cart would sink into the bog.

The stop at Kylemore Abbey was delightful. It had been the home of Benedictine Nuns for 300 years. It was a beautiful building, and the Abbey High School for Girls was known throughout the area. We found an excellent gift shop. The women in our group bought all the Molly Malone dolls they had, as their collection and prices were the best we had seen. I would have loved the Molly and her cart, but it would take up too much room, so I bought the "Immigrant." This Abbey had been built after King Henry VIII, and had not been destroyed.

We went on to Castlebar in Mayo County for our second week. This is known as the poorest county in Ireland. We spent more time in classes than we had previously, with a history professor giving us the history from the middle of the 12th Century. At that time the King of England was asked to come and help the King of Ireland keep his power. The succeeding troubles were outlined for us, which helped us understand a little of the continued fighting.

We had other activities when not in class. Some children entertained us with Irish dancing. One day I walked down the street and found little houses almost alike, all joined together and all had lovely lace curtains. A trip took us to a wide valley. We were told that during World War II many American planes were lost in that place because they would come to this area for a rest and try to land as it was flat. They would crash in the bog.

It was this week that we learned about Saint Patrick. Because I found his life fascinating, and it is not well known in the U.S., I am including a brief summary of it. He did not drive the snakes out, because Ireland had separated from the rest of Europe before the snakes arrived. There are many stories and it is difficult to tell fact from fiction.

As we heard it, Patrick grew up in Southern Wales. His grandfather had been a priest and his grandmother was a Frank, thus his family were strong Christians. In the year 401 A.D. pirates sent by the High King Niall of Ireland raided the southern coast of Wales in search of slaves and other things of value. The household of Calpurnius, who was of Roman descent, was raided and the seventeen year old heir, Succoth, and the servants were carried off. Succoth was sold to Milcho, and for seven years he took care of the pigs. These years he got up earlier than required and prayed. His father's Christian faith became real to him. As he worked and lived with the slaves he learned the ancient Gaelic language and learned their worship and stories. He learned to love the people and to love Ireland.

After receiving a sign in his sleep he walked 200 miles to the coast and secured passage on a ship which wandered for 25 days before reaching Wales. It was wonderful to see his family and friends again, but he was not satisfied. Finally he went to Tours in France and became a monk. It was there that he became Patricius, or as we know him, Patrick.

He was about 40 years old when he was sent to Ireland. When the ship stopped the people were ready to kill any stranger who got off because of fear of pirates. Patrick called out to them in their own language which surprised them. Knowing the language, loving the people, he became immediately popular. He went to see Milcho, who was astounded, and offered to pay his expenses. He traveled all over the country. He beheaded the devils, healed many people, performed many miracles according to the legends. He put a sun on the cross so that when they worshipped the sun they were also worshipping the Son. He christianized the holy places. As the word about him spread his Christianity had more magic than the Celtic worship.

On a hill that is now known as Crough he spent the forty days of Lent praying and fasting. The week after we visited, the last Sunday of July, 80,000 pilgrims would come from all over the country to climb the hill on gravel road, the last part on their hands and knees, in a great national pilgrimage. There is a crude statue of St. Patrick at Tara.

One trip was to the Ballintuber Abbey, founded in 441 A.D. by St. Patrick. Although it was burned and destroyed numerous times it refused to die. Sometimes monks were there, sometimes only priests in the village. However it continued to hold services, in the wreckage, out of doors, or wherever it could. In 1889 it was restored and in 1966 it celebrated its 750th anniversary of its founding. While entering a little chapel in back yard of the church I found this carving in the rock: "Were Christ to be born in a thousand stables it would be of no avail were he not born in our hearts."

Our third week was spent in Sligo, the childhood home of William Butler Yeats. With the help of an English Professor we read and discussed Yeat's work, mainly the plays. Most of the group had never heard of him before, but those of us who had majored in literature in college were glad to renew not only the works, but also to see the area he wrote about.

We went to Drumcliffe where Yeats is buried. His grandfather had been the rector there, and many summers were spent with him. Drumcliffe has been important because of the monastic establishment founded there by St. Columba in 574. The Round Tower is close by. During the 8th and 9th Centuries the Vikings fought with the Celts. In order to survive the people climbed into the tower. The only entrance was very high, and they entered only by ladder. Then they would bring up the ladder so the Vikings could not enter. There were a few windows high up. There were many over the country, but this was the only one remaining. On the other side of the road was the Cross, beautifully carved, of Adam and Eve and the snake. We were told that Yeats was granted his wish when he was re-interred in Drumcliffe Churchyard in 1948.

At the end of the Elderhostel Millie and I went on to Dublin for a few days. We walked around the town. As we read its history we found that although it had been occupied by settlers from the earliest days, it had become developed as a town when the Vikings established it as a base for their pirating adventures in 840 A.D. Trade grew between Dublin and Europe, making this a desirable place for kings to establish themselves. From early days the Catholics were increasingly persecuted until they had the least land and were extremely poor. In the ensuing struggles Dublin became the center for independence from England and for Catholic civil rights.

We walked to the National Museum and we were able to see the display of the early Irish metalwork of the 7th and 8th Centuries. This was a special display, bringing in items which had been in museums in other countries. Many of these things were discovered in 1980, and carefully restored by the British Museum. How can one describe the carvings and gorgeous designs of the Ardagh Chalice, and the Tara Brooch and others worn by kings of those early days? No wonder one archaeologist had called it the "Work of Angels"—and how fortunate we were to be able to see this special exhibit.

We took a trip to Newgrange about which we had heard when we were studying the Neolithic Age. This dates from about 2,000 B.C., with far more technology than the ones on the western shore. It is a round mound, the sides covered with small white rocks, with a smattering of dark ones. The top is of green grass. We saw the mound first, then the huge rocks surrounding it, perhaps a hundred feet from it. Originally they hid the mound but only twelve are left. They are smaller than the mound. About 1700 A.D. a local king told his workers to get those huge rocks and bring them for his castle. As they did so, cutting them to be able to move them, they discovered the hidden mound in the middle. They became curious and found a carved stone at what seemed to be an entrance. They told the king, who opened it to the public as it has been since that time.

The carved rock proved to be an entrance to the center. It had three recesses, with huge blocks of stone covered with much intricate carving. As it was plundered by the Viking raiders about 860 A.D., it was impossible to know what might have been inside. It had been kept dry by the roofing constructed in such a way that the water from rain ran off to the ground, and rocks on the ceiling kept it from coming in. Above the entrance was a hole. Exactly at sunrise on midwinter's day the sun shone through that hole, and lightened the passage way and the center. Archaeologists from all over the world gather to witness this technology of an ancient time. Every midwinter's day I think about that sunrise.

In Dublin we walked past the American Embassy, the most beautiful one I had seen. We became interested in the doors on the houses. We wondered if the owners compete with each other to have the most beautiful doors. Many of them had pillars, with arches above, and were painted red, or white or green. The houses themselves were not ornate, so the doors gave them an individuality not otherwise apparent.

We also found the statue of Molly Malone and her cart. A well-known Irish song is about her:

> In Dublin's fair city,
> Where the girls are so pretty,
> I first set my eyes on sweet Molly Malone.

> She wheeled her wheelbarrow,
> Through streets broad and narrow,
> Crying cockles and mussels, alive, alive, oh!

I was doubly glad to have the Molly Malone doll.

It was a hot day, the hottest Dublin had ever seen, people said, about 90°. We found some shade to walk in and noticed that everyone had ice cream cones. We decided it was a good idea, but found that there was no more ice cream left in town. No store had predicted such a drain on their resources.

In the evening we went to the Abbey Theatre which had been founded by Yeats in the early days of the 20th Century. We saw the play: "Dancing at Lughnasa," depicting the clash between old-time festivals and newer ideas of what young people should do. We wanted to go to that theatre because of its reputation of being "bothersome, passionate, argumentative, adventurous and at times right-down contrary," even as Yeats himself was said to be. The next morning we flew to the Shannon Airport and on to Seattle and home.

◆   ◆   ◆

VOLUNTEERING

A number of the residents had found places to volunteer outside the campus, and I looked for such an opportunity. I found one at the GERO-PSYCH UNIT of a hospital a few miles away. We were peer counselors, working with older people who preferred to talk with people their age, rather than with younger ones. We had three months of training in non-directive counseling by a psychiatric social worker. I was surprised at how closely it related to the training I had 40 years before at Garrett. This was an excellent opportunity to bring that knowledge up to date.

At first I had three clients. We had a tendency to call them patients, but as we were not doctors or nurses we could not use that term. We visited them while in the hospital, then kept in touch with them when they went home. Depression was a major factor. We watched for any other signs, such as suicidal tendencies, and for signs of improvement. We met each week with the social worker and discussed our situations in the group. The new psychological medications were just coming in, and we learned some of the positive and negative reactions of those taking them. We stayed with these same people for about three months, or until they seemed better.

The clients were challenging, including a man who was always blaming someone else for his lack of success, and suing or threatening to sue any-one who got in his way. I was relieved when he went to another hospital; they did not let me visit him, as they were now responsible for him. One woman told me to go away but I ignored that. Later she asked me if I was the one she told that to, and when I answered yes, she grinned but did not repeat it.

One client became a special person. It was discovered that her problem was not psychological, but rather an inoperable brain tumor. She went to an assisted-living home close to us, and I went each week to see her. One time I went to have coffee with her at lunch and found her in her room with the breakfast tray still there. She wanted to go to bed, but as she was trying to lift herself from the walker to the bed she fell. I held on to her so she would not hit her head but I did not know how to lift her. I rang for help and immediately two nurses came running. They got her in bed but she was sent to the hospital later that day. She was moved to a nursing home nearby and I went to see her every day, knowing that she was terminal. I "wore two hats," the hospital one, where you do not talk religion, and the clergy one where you do, sometimes using one, sometimes the other. One day I saw her daughter who was grateful for the "clergy hat" so I increased that until she died.

One time I was asked to see a man in a nursing home in Federal Way who was having flash-backs to his days in the Philippines at the time of the "Death March." He talked freely to me as I understood the horror of that experience. In a few weeks he did not seem to need this service any more. I stayed with this program for two years.

As Chairman of the Social Action Committee at the church, and with the help of Brian Linn, who headed the Peace Group, we decided to go to Yakima for the HABITAT FOR HUMANITY project. This was within driving distance, and already organized so that our work built on the work of others. About twenty of us went, including three of us older ones, mainly to give it a push. We had the use of the Baptist church for sleeping (on the floors) and cooking. We were building sheds to keep the building materials, and some of us painted them. It was discouraging to see the sand during a sand-storm cover the paint. We were assured this was just a first coat.

For devotions, I had searched the Old and New Testaments for passages about housing. Because of my past experience with Quaker projects I felt that we should know something about the problems of the people we were working with. For one evening session I invited the man, who was the manager of the Spanish radio station, to speak to us. Most of the group went in, expecting to go to sleep, but he kept them wide awake. I especially remember his explaining that the asparagus workers were paid by the amount they picked. When it rained the asparagus had not grown to a thickness that the market would buy, but the workers had to cut it anyway and work all day without any pay. In succeeding years an hourly wage had been set by the Legislature, and the small, weak asparagus was sold as a very special delicacy at a higher price. The church has continued through the years to help in building homes there, but I have not heard about anyone continuing to study the social situation, except to see the decrepit housing they are replacing. In fact, this lack of studying the local social and economic situation has been my major criticism of the Habitat for Humanity projects over the country. We feel good building the houses, but we might not feel so good if we realized we were taking part in an unjust situation.

We began a CROP WALK in the Burien and Des Moines area. Church World Service, the ecumenical relief agency which all of our main-line churches cooperated with, had developed this Walk to raise money for emergency relief programs, long-term self-help projects, and refugee relief. When I was the pastor in Arkansaw at the end of World War II, I was County Chairman for this Christian Rural Overseas Program which sent seeds overseas to rebuild farms destroyed by the War. In intervening years it has become a very popular money-raising program, as walkers theoretically raise money for the miles they walk, although we find people just give what they can. We had started the year before but the pastor who was chairman could not seem to form a committee, and it meant one or two people were doing all the work, which that year were two of us from our church. For one year I pushed myself in as chairman, formed a good committee, and then turned it over to the pastor again, which worked fine for the next five or six years. That one year we had 265 walkers, and raised $21,767. One-fourth of the money stayed in the community, which we divided between the two food banks. The Walk in that form lasted about ten years.

While I was involved with the peer counseling one of the women ministers challenged me to work with the homeless women in Seattle as she told about the start of a project. Kim, a Korean pastor, had begun the CHURCH OF MARY MAGDALENE. This was on Saturdays in the sub-basement of the First United Methodist Church. She came to our church and spoke for a Christmas Tea, and I told her I was considering helping, and she encouraged me strongly. The day I went happened to be the First Anniversary. In due time I was able to recruit Dorothy Kimbrell and Dorothy Travaille, both from Wesley. Churches were asked to give money but also to bring dinners to be served at noon. As the only food they had was perhaps a sandwich at night, she felt a dinner was essential. The women we served were at least one step ahead, some more, than those I had as peer counselor. Most of them were dependent on medicine to keep them going, but because of side effects they often did not take them. Or they were trying to become sober. Or they were simply unemployable. There were as many different reasons as there were people. About 50 to 60 came each week. There was a light breakfast provided, then an hour of singing hymns. Dorothy Travaille played the piano for many years. An interactive sermon followed. A Korean metal bowl was on the table, and the women were asked to write on slips of paper one thing they wanted to change during the week. One paper was to be burned in the bowl, the other to be put under the bra. Soon Kim found they did not have bras, nor money to buy them. She asked churches to give money so they could be provided. She called this her "Panty Theology." After a dinner served by various churches, some classes were given. such as crafts or sewing. Dorothy Travaille also taught crocheting or knitting. Much of the time some of them sat around and Dorothy Kimbrell and I talked with them. We left about 3:30 after vacuuming the rug and straightening up. After about three years I found I was getting tired, as Kim would be gone and I would have charge of the entire day. The doctor decided it was time for me to stop. However it was a fulfilling experience, for unlike the hospital, it combined my clergy training with the counseling. The program was strengthened with the addition of Mary's Place, where the room was open all week.

The weddings of two great nieces have been fun. Lisa and Marty Gates were married 1990, in the Clifton's back yard with many friends and relatives present. I had the service, as I had had Terry's a couple of years before in the Lutheran Church. I had not done any pre-marital counseling as this is a bit hard when it is your own family. It was a beautiful wedding. The reception was held there, in the garden. Marty had been a car salesman, and worked in the finance part of that business. Lisa had training as a para-legal, and worked ever since her internship with that company.

Julie and Matt Knox were married in 1991 in the Lutheran Church. I did not have this wedding, as I think the church that Matt and his parents went to did not approve of women ministers. The reception was quite formal, held in an upstairs room of a local restaurant. Both Matt and Julie were runners in college and they started running together. She was a laboratory technician. Matt majored in forestry and worked for the city of Kent as an ecologist.

Frances, who lived on the other side of the cottage, moved to the Health Center as she was falling. The back room we had been sharing was remodeled, making it into a utility room for each side. This was much more convenient as I had been washing clothes in the basement of the main building. Now I had my own washer and dryer, and other equipment. A number of cupboards and storage shelves were included, which enabled me to take things out of the attic. In fact, the stairs to the attic were eliminated. In the process, I found that Frances had been paying the hot water bill for both sides for the twenty years she had lived there.

Christmas Eve, 1992, our family was invited to the home of Vincent and Anne de Bellis who owned Alice's Restaurant. They had built a winery and their lovely home above it. As we walked up the long outdoor stairway I was behind Dick, who was laboring up the steps. I walked up slowly but he was having an extremely difficult time. I saw Vin, our host, watching him, too. As soon as he got to the top he sat down. He said he had car-sickness, but neither Vin nor I believed him. Ann did have some feeling of car-sickness, as we had taken a different road which was more winding than the other, so she did not worry about Dick. We discovered that Dick had been having headaches, but he had an excuse for that, and he had other pains, always with some excuse. Vin and I both told him to be sure to go the doctor soon. He called in a few days and said he had made an appointment for a physical in a month. I was horrified—wait a month? I was ready to call his doctor, who was also mine, when I found that he and Ann had lunch with some good friends and he was so weak that they insisted that he go to the doctor the next day. He did; cancer was discovered, and he began chemotherapy that day. They tried everything, but by March he was gone at age 57. He was too young, as it had been with his father (Francis) and with other members of our family. I had his memorial service which included slides a friend had prepared, giving it a bit of humor which Dick would have appreciated.

ISRAEL, EGYPT ELDERHOSTEL 1993

Andrea Staley, a cottager, and I had become good friends. She wanted to go to Israel; I wanted to spend more time in Egypt, so we decided to do both. We went with an Elderhostel, hosted by Archaeological Seminars. It was Bible history, taught by American Jews. We had classes in the morning, when we traced the history from Abraham and Sarah. It was pointed out that the people of Israel had had conflict throughout their history. The early wars were to gain territory; then the Exile occurred; and as they came back from the Exile, there were tensions between the people who had stayed and those who returned. The influence of the Greek culture created tensions between those rulers who gave in to the Greeks and the rebel Jews who objected. This led to the Macabean Revolt. The Jews were free but fought among themselves. Rome was asked to intervene. For the last class they brought in a young man who was a Christian working on a Doctor's Degree, studying the very early Christian church. I found this course fascinating.

The afternoons were spent on field trips. We saw some of the excavations done in Jerusalem, such as a beautiful mosaic flooring for a home, and other homes which must have been for the rich. One day we went to the Wailing Wall and realized that men only were putting their prayers in the wall. Later the Rabbi would come and take them out and say the prayers. There were a few women in an upper area. We sat on the steps of the south wall, and discussed the sacrifice of animals which would have been carried out there. As we got to one section of the temple wall we were shown some rock formations below which were a part of the First temple, and discovered by one of our instructors. We were taken to a very old cemetery, and to Gehenna, where garbage was burned, the basis for being burned in hell.

The Church of the Holy Sepulcher, for Jewish, Christian and Muslim worshippers, was a highlight. Although I had been there earlier, I was more impressed this time, seeing actual people there worshipping. I really felt on Holy Ground.

Another holy ground was the Israel Museum and the Shrine of the Book. To actually see the fragments of the Book of Isaiah was a thrill. The history of these scrolls has been interesting for they were found in caves, sold to anyone, and the

Bishop of the Church of Syria had control over most of them. Many scholars, both Jewish and American, complained that they were not available for study. After a number of years of arguing the Jewish scholars acquired them. Our leaders said "after all it was their history."

We went to the room which is thought to be the room of the Last Supper. This is a different place than the one I went to before, but at that time we were told there were two possible places, and I presumed that this was the other one. It is still a bare room upstairs. We imagined the Disciples eating there with Jesus.

The model of the Second Temple period was a large outdoor reconstruction of the Temple and the city around it. It helped us to see how large the Temple was in relation to the homes around it. This did more than a picture could do to see what it must have been like to be in Jerusalem in those days.

The day we went to the reconstructed town of Tel Maresha was outstanding for all of us. We went to the area of David and Goliath, southeast of Jerusalem. Tel Maresha had been built during the Hellenistic period. It is thought to have been the birthplace of Herod. It had been an oil-exporting town, on an ancient roadway. It had been destroyed by the Persians, and no other city had been built on the site.

We went to a certain place where a home had been. We went down a hole, perhaps six feet deep, at least enough for some of the men to hold on to me and let me down easy. Andrea made it better than I did. We searched for pottery on the dirt floor. I found a little piece of the handle of a cup. Andrea found a larger, more important piece. During the day we shook the pieces on screen, washed them, saw how they were sorted by the scientists, and saw one large completed pot. Actually we did not do all this in order; we had to put it together chronologically afterward. I found it fascinating—for one day. I could not go to a site each year, as some of my friends did and spend weeks digging for artifacts. However, this day gave me an appreciation for all who discover ancient cultures.

We went to Jericho one day to look at the archaeological work being done there. However, it was boarded off so one could see very little, yet we could appreciate it. We were taken to various places which had been important in the early days of the city.

The Mount of Olives was in Palestinian hands, and therefore too dangerous for us to go there. I was glad I had been there previously, and also to Bethlehem, but Andrea was happy without them.

Before leaving Jerusalem I was able to meet with our United Methodist missionary whose job it was to see that tourists understand the conflict with the Palestinians. Most of the Christians were Palestinians. It was hard for them to realize that people came to look for the ancient sites, and paid no attention to the Christians of the current day. They wondered why.

We went on to Tel Aviv and spent a large part of the day shopping in a large mall, almost like an American one. Then the next day we went to Masada. Herod had built a palace on the top of this hill in case he was deposed, or if he was attacked by Egypt. We took the cable car to the top and looked at all the ruins which were excavated in the early 1960's. We walked through the storehouses and to what had been the old Synagogue. We had only a glimpse of what had been Herod's palace. This became the last fortress of a group of 960 Jews, including women and children, who were survivors after the Romans took Jerusalem in 70 A.D. They thought the Romans could not reach them. It took some time, but in 73 A.D. the walls were breached. Before the Roman soldiers were able to get to the top, the survivors all committed suicide. The leader had said "Let us die unenslaved by our enemies, and leave this world as free men in the company of our wives and children."

We flew to Cairo for the second part of our Elderhostel. We stayed at the Club Med, on the grounds of what had been the Manial Palace. The grounds were beautiful. The Palace Museum was close to the hotel. I wandered alone on the grounds and to the Museum, as we did not go as a group, and Andrea did not wish to go with me. I thoroughly enjoyed it. We had some free time and wandered around the streets somewhat, not far enough from the hotel to get lost. Our lectures were held in one of the buildings of the hotel, and the lecturers were from the American School, an excellent college which invited outstanding professors from the U.S.

It has been hard to summarize the information given, as we had much on the early history, art, etc., of Egypt. Ramses II may have been the Pharoah in power at the time of Moses—but we were told that no records have been found that mention slaves or Moses, or the Hebrews. (Slaves might have been forced labor, and when the Hebrews defeated them they might have taken it out of their history).

When a statue of a ruler in the ancient days was made his physical features were that of a virile young man. Only the facial features identified him as the one who currently sat on the throne. He was naked except for a loin cloth in order to show how perfect he was. One foot was always in front of the other, as though he were walking, and active. When the Great Wife was depicted her feet were always together, to indicate a passive nature.

There were many gods, often the head of an animal on a human body. When a person moved he changed his god to be the god of that area. The god for the area across the river was a cow, and thus it was that the Hebrews who knew, and perhaps worshipped, the Egyptian gods, built a calf as they waited for Moses to return. From 525 B.C. to 1952 Egypt was ruled by Persians, Greeks, Romans, Muslims, Ottoman Empire, British, but not Egyptians.

Our first trip as a group was to the American School where we had lunch, and had time with some of the students. The second trip was to the pyramids. When I was there previously our friend, a Professor at the American School, took us there in a car. This time we had to ride the camels. Andrea got on easily, and for some reason they put me back of her on the same camel. She enjoyed the ride, but I complained that I was hitting against the back hump and wanted to get off. If I had been on a separate camel I think I would have enjoyed it more.

We went to the Mohammed Ali Mosque which was made of alabaster. It was very beautiful outside and inside. Also we went to the Coptic Church, and heard the history of it from the earliest times of Christianity. It is an old building but has some beautiful carvings and lights. The Museum next door was especially interesting to me, as it housed the Gnostic Gospels. I had read a book about these very early Christian writings, and the collection of the sayings of Jesus by St. Thomas shown in the display was fascinating.

After some investigation I discovered that the Presbyterians had several schools in Cairo. We visited the Ramses School for Girls. Like colleges in other countries, it included elementary and high school students to prepare them for college. We met teachers of each group. Some of the college women wore the headgear of the Muslims. This was not required, but one of the girls told us that the boys did not know how to act when they did not wear it. The girls said wearing it was an easy way to tell the boys to behave themselves. I asked about the relationship with the Coptic Christians, and the Principal said they have not been very friendly. They thought as they were the original Christians the Presbyterians were upstarts. We appreciated the time the President gave us. From my experience of colleges overseas, I thought this one was excellent.

For the traditional Elderhostel final dinner for this section, we discovered it was the beginning of Ramadan, the month of fasting. The only place we could have a dinner was the Hilton Hotel. We loved that. Our last day in Cairo was Sunday, and we found an English-speaking church, St. Andrews. We met three missionaries, one of whom was the assistant to the pastor. I was especially interested in meeting three young men from Sudan who had left their country because they would have to go to war if they stayed.

We flew to Luxor. Most commercial tours take a boat, but the Elderhostel said there was too much rebel activity, and they were not sure of our safety. Here we stayed at the Hilton. The dinner table was elegant, with a procession of waiters in gorgeous costumes parading in to serve us. Our room was next to the elevator, and was noisy as we could hear it when it went up or down. Just as we were feeling sorry for ourselves we would go to tea or dinner, and the beauty of it would take away any negative thoughts.

The statues at the Luxor Museum were amazing that they could be so complete although so old. We also went to the temple at Luxor and were shown the Muslim Mosque built right on the old stones. Karnak, the Temple of Ramses II, was outside Luxor. It was entered by a row of rams on pedestals. A statue of Ramses II greeted us, and also the statue of Pinedjam, a goddess. We wandered among those huge beautiful columns, 134 of them, 80 feet high. Some of them were beautifully carved, with the bee and a blade of grass, indicating that the north and south of Egypt had been united under Ramses II. The obelisk, also carved, was made under the time of Hatshepsut. There were beautifully carved walls. A section which had been a dining hall had been used by the Coptic monks at one time.

We took the ferry across the river to the Valley of the Kings. We went into several of the tombs. As I stood there and looked at that ancient writing, I had a new respect for the Rosetta Stone which I had seen in the British Museum. I imagined standing there wondering what all that writing meant, and later being able to read it and translate it. Amazing.

The funerary temple of Ramses II was known as the Ramesseum. It looked almost modern with the center section built up like a tower. The Colossus of Mennon, now with two statues remaining, was one of the Seven Wonders of the ancient world. Then we went on to the Valley of the Queens. To me the most interesting of all was the Tomb of Queen Hatshepsut. Of course a woman could not really rule, so she called herself King. Actually she was the guardian for the young king, but she ruled the country. Her tomb is above ground. A row of carved columns are in front, and inside the walls are carvings that have retained some of the orginal colors. It was all beautiful.

On the way to the dam at Aswan, we stopped at three temples: the Edfu, Esna, and Kom Ombo. All of them had carved columns and walls, dedicated to a certain god. In Aswan we stayed at the New Cataract Hotel, very modern and lovely. They took us to the dam and we walked around, taking pictures. We went to the quarry, and were amazed at the size of the rocks. Here we saw an unfinished obelisk giving us a good idea of its size and carvings. We learned that Egypt, in 1965, had asked the U.S. and Britain for help in building the dam but we refused, and Russia helped them. Thus Egypt and Russia were good friends during the Cold War. Here we had the final dinner for the entire Israel-Egypt Elderhostel.

Andrea and I flew on to Abu Simbal. Ramses II had conquered the Nubians to the south, and built this monument to show his strength. When the dam was built the entire monument was moved by cutting it in pieces, then raising it and putting the pieces together. It was called the Miracle of the Sun. There were four statues of Ramses II, but the head of one was not so well preserved. The others are superior. Inside of the temple was a beautiful monument to his wife Nefertari.

We stayed in Abu Simbul just one night. The next afternoon we left for Cairo and on to New York. When we arrived there late, all other means of transportation were also late because of a snowstorm the previous day. We were directed to a special line where a woman checked our baggage, told us the plane was ready to start, and to run. Even I ran, which surprised Andrea, for I walked slower than she did. When we got on the plane I realized we had been in that airport two and a half hours and still we were the last ones on the plane. We finally relaxed and slept all the way to Seattle.

◆   ◆   ◆

It has been fun to have former parishioners visit me when they are coming west. This time it was the Patnodes whose farm I had visited and baptized their four children. She later became treasurer of the Arkansaw church. They stayed at a Motel 6 nearby to which I had directed them. We visited the night they came. The next day I took them around Seattle to the Pike Place Market, the Space Needle, and Seattle Center. By the end of the day I was exhausted, but tried not to show it, and they were surprised I was still upright! They had figured my age by the ages of their children.

When I first arrived at Wesley I found the programs very interesting. Before long my friend, Gerie Brown, asked me to be on the committee. After a few years the Chairman felt she must give it up, and I took over. It was a good committee and we planned programs for two evenings a week. I continued this volunteering for nine years. For one thing I really enjoyed the contacts with all the people who came. Also I felt that I was helping myself and other residents to keep our minds active. It entailed so many details it was hard to find some one else to continue with it, but I finally did.

THE FLORIDA ELDERHOSTEL, 1994

As my niece, Ann, was too young to go to an Elderhostel on her own, I took her with me to one near Orlando, Florida, taking advantage of a special airline discount. We flew to Orlando and arranged for a tour to Cape Canaveral the next day. We were able to see the rocket that was being prepared to take off in about a week. We went into the Air Force Space Museum, looking at pictures on the wall. In the midst of a crowd of people a man from behind put his arms around me. I thought "The Nerve!" I turned around, glaring, to find one of the retired ministers who attended the Puyallup potluck each month. His wife said she wished she had a picture of my face when I turned around. I wished she did, too. We were happy to have this opportunity to see a rocket and visit the various aspects of the Center.

We went to Epcot, part of the Walt Disney theme park. The "Spaceship Earth" greeted us, and we went inside to find a history of communications from the earliest days. We took the bus around to the various buildings. The "Showcases" that interested me most were those of China, Japan, Morocco and Mexico. In the afternoon we went to Sea World and saw the Whale and Dolphin Show.

Our Elderhostel was at an Easter Seal Camp, "Camp Challenge." The director was one of the young men who had been helped through the years. With one leg shorter than the other, he got around quickly with his golf cart. The outstanding course was on genetics, with the up-to-date finding on the DNA, helping us to understand the elementary facts. All this was very new and difficult to comprehend but it did help me to read an article about it in Time Magazine.

Another course was on the plants of central Florida. I was surprised at how similar they were to the Northwest. The instructor showed me a map which depicted the nine growing areas in the U.S., the one from the northwest, number 9, swinging around toward the south and to the central Florida region. The weather was colder than we had been having in Seattle, so I asked some of the friends from New York State, "Why come south?" They responded emphatically, "This is warm." Some of them had been on the last plane out of their town before a heavy snowstorm had come which had tied up everything. I was glad I had taken one sweatshirt along, just in case. I wore it the whole week, thanks to the washer and dryer in the back of the cabin. We evaluated this as a very good Elderhostel, as we learned much.

◆   ◆   ◆

A big surprise awaited me at Conference that year of 1994. We were meeting at Gonzaga University in Spokane. As I had come in to the afternoon session a little late I was sitting in the very back of the auditorium. Suddenly I found one woman District Superintendent on one side of me, and another on the other side. They lifted me out of my chair and led me to the front and up on the platform where all the women ministers in the Conference had gathered. Then they sang a song about being a "foremother," and presented me with the Ruth Award, given to a lay or clergy woman who has been supportive of Women in Ministry. The whole Conference gave me a standing ovation. The Award is named for the woman to whom it was given first, and I am the third to receive it. It was an overpowering experience.

LAKE POWELL

In September my niece Ann and I went with Julie's parents-in-law, Randy and Jean Knox, on a trip to Utah and to Lake Powell. They were younger, outdoor people. Ann and I went along at our own pace. First we went to the mountains of the Capital Reef. We stayed at the Wonderland Inn, a nice motel. We followed trails, some along the Fremont River, among gorgeous red sandstone formations. Many of the cliffs are named, such as the Castle, Chimney Rock, and Cathedral Valley. Capital Dome was outstanding because it was white against all that red. One day Randy and Jean lead us up a trail; they went on ahead while we dragged behind. They waited for us on the far side of Hickman Natural Bridge, a huge arch with a span of 133 feet.

At Hite we rented a houseboat which Randy had reserved for us. It was supposed to hold eight people but we thought it was a bit crowded with four. We had brought food with us. We spent four days on Lake Powell, mooring the houseboat, then taking the small motorized boat to investigate the nearby canyons, all this in the midst of the red cliffs. When we found petroglyphs high on the canyon wall, the others climbed to them while I stayed below and took pictures. The four of us enjoyed each other and the entire trip.

MARDI GRAS, 1995

Jane Arp, the friend I had visited in Thailand, and I went to an Elderhostel in New Orleans, the week before Fat Tuesday. We went a day early so we could have a cheaper flight by staying overnight on Saturday. A-bed-and-breakfast had been arranged for us. At breakfast the woman of the house gave the visitors a personal history of Mardi Gras. Her husband had been a member of one of the krewes, the name for the organizations that put it on. It cost at least $1,000 to join a krewe. Her two daughters had "come out" as southern belles, a wonderful experience for the family. Now, she said sorrowfully, an organization had been formed that allowed people to join for just $10, and people from many places, not just New Orleans, are joining and the banquet is open to anyone. She felt this was the end of Mardi Gras.

We walked to the French Quarter, along the way seeing some of the old houses, built before the Civil War, with dates to indicate this. We found the outdoor market, and spent time wandering. In the Square we saw the oldest Cathedral in the U.S., and also a statue of Andrew Jackson who is said to have saved the city. We saw the mimes standing for hours without moving. We walked along the river and listened to the jazz being played to all who would listen. The old two-and three-story buildings with their iron balconies, often with flowers, were beautiful.

In the morning we went to the main street to watch a parade. A vendor came along with so many things to sell we could hardly see him. The floats were fascinating with all sorts of decorations, and people on all of them throwing out necklaces and other things to the people on the street. We were interested in the people near us who were so anxious to receive some of the necklaces that they shouted and jumped up and down. This began as a way of the wealthier people throwing out baubles to the peons. It had become a fun experience all around. After the parade we walked down Bourbon Street, known for its drinking. We saw none of that, just couples beautifully dressed. In the evenings when there was drinking, the reporters went there, so that the only thing that was shown on television was the drinking.

In the afternoon we took a taxi to the hotel, specified by the Elderhostel, to register. We stayed overnight in that hotel, and the next morning we were taken around the city, mostly to the French Quarter. We were told bits of history as we went. The cemetery was especially interesting, for the whole city is below sea level, and people are buried above ground. A family has one tomb with the members buried one on top of another. We crossed the lake and went to the Abbey in the town of Saint Benedict, which was our home for the week. We learned the history of Mardi Gras from early French days. It has always been a party just before Lent. The monks were happy about the popularization of it. Three of the old-time krewes stopped "rolling" because they did not want to admit other races, and worse than that, the women. There had been some krewes that consisted of Native Americans only and one for women only, but to have them all with the men was not acceptable to them. Some of the older krewes were worried because they had been raising money with Bingo, but the casinos were taking that source away from them.

One parade we saw made fun of the city government. We were surprised, yet we were told this was usually done. The queen was beautiful, and when I went close to take her picture, she handed me one of her special necklaces.

An unusual event was a boat trip on the swamp. It was an open boat, without a cover. One could see the tops of the trees, as well as the swamp itself. We were surprised to see water lilies growing. We were asked if we wanted to see an old man who lived on the swamp, and of course we said "yes." He took cypress roots and polished them and sold them to all who came. As one of the women said, she was really surprised to find a gift shop on the swamp. We bought about everything he had ready.

Because I was on a mileage ticket, I could not fly out at the end of the Elderhostel as Jane did. The monks knew of a bed-and-breakfast nearby, and I stayed there Friday and Saturday nights. On Saturday all the other guests left and the hostess took me to the parade of the krewe Orphaus, one of the new, popular ones. The town of Mandeville had organized 1,000 of the community leaders for a krewe. This was the best parade I had seen. I took so many pictures that I did not receive many of the baubles. We went to my friend's favorite restaurant to eat dinner; the waitress asked if we were local, and I said I was from Seattle. I was overheard by a family sitting at a table nearby. They brought me some of the best necklaces, including the one which was the most special of that parade. They said they had plenty from this time and from other years. I realized that they knew, and perhaps were themselves, some of the community leaders who put this on. When I told my friend that I would be giving a program, showing my slides and that I had been given a lot of the cheap ones to throw out to my friends, she gave me some of her best ones. All this generosity was a pleasant surprise. I did not find a place to go to church on Sunday morning, but one of the monks took me to the plane in the afternoon.

◆　　　◆　　　◆

WESLEY GARDENS

The first three months of 1996 were spent getting ready to move to the five-story apartment building, The Gardens. There was a ruling that when you reached 85 you had to move from a cottage to the building. There was never any explanation, though the suggestion was that one was not capable of living alone, or the younger person of a couple could no longer take care of both. At any rate, I was caught, for I would have liked to have stayed in the cottage a year or two more.

Two auctions and three rummage sales the year before had enabled me to clean out my storage cupboards and give away things I had not used in the six years I had lived there. Getting rid of equipment was a task, although relatives were glad for much of it. I sorted out the dolls I had in storage and those on the shelves, and sent Cheryl about a hundred of them. It took some time for the truck to come from Vancouver for the things for those families.

Packing all the dolls and books, as well as everything else, looked like such a big task that I hired one of the homeless women I had known at the Church of Mary Magdalene. She was capable, but did not respond to people easily and was unemployable. She came out by bus and I met her at the bus station so that she did not carry all her belongings up the hill. She was wonderful help. The maintenance men moved me over in a short while. In the morning I looked at all those boxes taking up half the living room. I called my helper and asked her to come back. I paid her several dollars more than the minimum wage, and took her to dinners at noon at the restaurant nearby. She loved the pies and in order to get pie for her I had to order one for myself, every day! In all it cost me quite a bit of money but I realized it was worth it, not only for myself, but also for her, as she used the money to go to computer school, and then did all the computer work for the Church of Mary Magdalene.

Because the west side of the building had a beautiful view of Puget Sound, I thought I wanted to be on that side. There was none available and I took the one on first floor, looking out over the lovely rose garden and gazebo. Soon I found I could not have chosen better for it was so very convenient when I was taking care of the programs. And I discovered it was a relief when I did not have to weed a flower garden or eat so many T.V. dinners.

FRIDAY HARBOR ELDERHOSTEL

Ann and I went to an Elderhostel in Friday Harbor while I was still getting organized. We spent an extra day on the way in order to shop in the gift shops in LaConner. Judy, Helen and I spent many hours in LaConner but only to eat at a restaurant that Helen liked. Neither of them would condescend to shop. Ann and I went from one end of the street to the other, going into every store. Neither of us bought anything but we certainly had fun looking.

Friday Harbor was new to both of us, a beautiful little town with a huge marina, the chief port of the San Juan Islands. One of our classes was on the

DNA, giving us a chance to know what had been happening since our last class in Florida several years before. There were four doctors in the group and they added much to the discussion. We also learned the history of the San Juan Islands and discovered that England and the U.S. went to war because they were arguing about which channel would be used for shipping. The immediate cause was the death of a pig, and thus it is called the "Pig War." We went to a reenactment of the place where the war was supposed to be fought, with two men in costumes, one British, the other U.S. The countries argued and argued but did not fight, and the armies would get together and have a good time while they were waiting. They never did get around to fighting each other.

In another class we studied whales. A scientist led us, showing us pictures of the different families of whales, and playing tapes of their calls. One afternoon Ann and I drove around the island to a spot where Dick and his staff had worked, making a sign telling about the whales which can often be seen at that particular spot. He later made a silk screen of the whales, and another of the lighthouse and the waves. I received both of these as presents.

◆   ◆   ◆

It was very sad to lose Helen Larm. Every two or three months for some years I had been picking up Judy in Seattle and driving to Mount Vernon to stay overnight with Helen (a cousin of Judy's). Her husband had died some years before and for years she had taken care of her mother who died and for whom I had the graveside service. Helen was alone and ill. She always said she was fine, but we judged it by breakfast. If she made something like muffins, she was fine. If it came from the store, she was not. When we heard she was to have surgery we went and came back the same day, for we did not stay long. After her surgery which shortened her life, both of us sent cards every day. We loved Helen and it was hard to lose her. I was astonished to learn some time later that she had left money in her will for me, and even more astonished when I got the check for $4,500. By adding $500 to this I was able to replace my old car which was burning oil profusely. With a car salesman in the family, I went to see Marty, Lisa's husband. I bought a Ford Taurus, old and with quite a bit of mileage, but it had been well taken care of. I drove it for seven years and still got money out of it when it was sold.

Faith moved from her cottage to the Terrace, the other Wesley apartment building across the street. She had been Vice Chairman of the Resident Council, and she persuaded the Chairman to appoint me to take her place. She said I would not have anything to do. That was true, as the Chairman was making all the decisions often without even taking a vote. The next person elected as Chairman was a woman who had never been on the Council, and I stayed on as Vice Chairman. She was the Chairman for one of the floors. Two of the people from that floor came to me independently, asking if I would help her as they thought she was not a good leader, and they said she could not read. I found that she did not understand what she was reading. When things were to be done I would go over them with her, and found her very conscientious and she would immediately set to work. We had a new Treasurer that year who was astonished that there had not been a budget. She worked one out, and in spite of some resistance the Chairman saw it through. It proved to be a great advantage. It was an especially hard year because the lower level was being remodeled and it was difficult to make all the adjustments necessary to the new arrangement. The end of the year was made even more difficult as she developed cancer, telling only a very few of us.

In July, 1997, I was elected Chairman for the next year. With the program responsibilities this took a good deal of time. Many of the reconstruction problems had been solved but there were still things that needed to be done. I made out a "wish list" for the things we needed, such as a loudspeaker for the new Stanton Hall downstairs, card tables, new hymnals, a new organ, refinishing of the table used as an altar for vespers. Working with the new budget, finding money for all these and smaller things, kept the Council busy.

The Executive, Ron, was pushing us to have the same Constitution as the Terrace Council. I could see a real advantage in that it would solve a long-standing situation that I thought needed to be changed. But I hated to work on constitutions so I asked the Vice Chairman, Howell Lowe, to do it for me. He was excellent at it and it was not finished until he became Chairman the next year. It solved the problem easily. The two years had been a strain and I was glad to be relieved. From that time on I served on the budget or nominating committees, or none at all.

A new volunteering project was that of a mentor for a third grade girl at Parkside Elementary School, about two miles from Wesley. It had Kindergarten through Third Grade, with a large percentage on free lunch students, indicating the poverty of the families. Studies were showing that if someone took an interest in children who were at risk when they were young, they were less apt to become involved with gangs when they were older. I spent a lunch hour once a week with a girl who was of mixed ethnic background. When she named all the members of her family, she did not mention a father. She did not read well, and sometimes I read to her, sometimes I found something easy for her to read and help her begin to feel successful. I discovered that this was her fourth school as her family was evicted when the rent was not paid. I wondered how she could possibly learn to read with that much shifting around. Her mother wanted her to go to Parkside as it was known for helping such children. One day she was very cold as she had slept with only a thin covering for her younger sister had wet the bed. Just after Thanksgiving she moved to Tacoma. I reasoned that a Christmas present is not considered charity. The women in our church who make quilts to give away gave me three quilts, one for each of the children in the family. The week before Christmas I went to the home. I brought in the quilt for my girl first, and she was thrilled. Her brother, two years younger, looked despondent. Then I brought in the other two, and when he found that he had one he wrapped it around him and his eyes glittered. He had a quilt of his own! The younger sister was shy, but also happy. When school started up again my girl moved to a Tacoma school.

The next girl was a large girl, an ethnic mixture, including Samoan. She liked to read and did it well. When we were not reading I found it quite a challenge to make the time really special. Some of our residents were writing to these third graders as pen palls. The teacher encouraged this as it taught them to write letters. Just before graduation I found out who my girl's pen pal was, and together we took her out to lunch at McDonald's. We each gave her a book; hers was "Heidi", mine was "Winnie the Pooh". She hugged us both to thank us. The next year she would be moving to another school. This teacher, whom I greatly admired, would be retiring and I decided not to try to work with another student.

Having time to read was a problem. But I did read two books about this time which I found different. "Orders to Kill," by William Pepper, was an amazing, disturbing, extremely well documented account of the assassination of Martin Luther King, Jr. blaming the Attorney General. The King family had become convinced that Pepper really was right. The government continued to say he was wrong. The book was convincing, yet one hated to think that anyone in our government would be involved.

The other book was an historical novel "The Queen of Sheba," by Roberta Kells Dorr. She wove into one story the accounts from the Bible, the Koran, and the many rumors about this always interesting woman. Mrs. Dorr had lived in the Middle East for 20 years, collecting as many stories as she could find. This was a very new perspective.

HAWAII ELDERHOSTEL, 1997

In the early part of the year, while I was still Vice-chairman of the Resident Council, I realized the years were passing, and I decided I wanted to go to Hawaii once again. I joined an Elderhostel group, but there were only two things that I felt worthwhile. The general subject was preservation. A Hawaiian woman talked with us. She was trying to find the good things in her native religion and bring them into her Christianity. I thought she was doing a wonderful job of bringing Christ into her own experience. I quoted to her Gene Hibbard's father when he went to China, "God had been there before him." She looked at me with big eyes, and said "I wish a missionary had told me that. You have made my day." From what she had said, it seemed that all missionaries had thought she was leaving Christ behind, which she resented. She thought of herself as a true Christian. As we were trying to present Christ so that people of other cultures could understand Him, it seemed to me that her studies could have been valuable.

The other experience was entirely different. We had gone to the north of the island of Kauai to the Kilauea Wildlife Sanctuary an hour before it opened to the public. We walked around, reading the signs and watching the birds from many parts of the world. Then the manager called us together and told us the albatross were nesting. He did not let the public go there, but he would let us go as he thought we would be responsible. He led us to an area where about 50 female albatross were nesting, some with the male sitting with them. He showed us the large lawn made for the male birds. Just then one came in and landed on that lawn with each wing spreading about six feet, which was true only of this type of albatross in the Pacific Ocean. He quickly folded his wings and his body showed no sign of a wing there. He had a large hooked beak and he was almost white. He walked over to us looking from one to the other. We were motionless. Finally he decided we were no threat, and he walked over to his female and the nest with its very large white egg. The incubation is done by both male and female. We walked quietly away, knowing that we had seen a rare sight.

◆   ◆   ◆

Marcus Borg was a challenging scholar of the Jesus Seminar, which was trying to discover what Jesus was really like as opposed to the traditions that have grown up around him. One day I went to Seattle to hear him, expecting to hear him tear the gospels apart. Instead I found it one of the most positive and inspirational days I had had in many years. One of his books was "Seeing Jesus Again For The First Time," which was thought-provoking.

Another inspirational time was when Helen Oak, one of my cottager friends, and I went to a "Five Day Academy for Spiritual Renewal," because of our admiration for one of the leaders, Rodney Romney. Each day we met in the same small group. As we were sharing personal experiences, one woman said she had not come from a Christian home. She admitted to sometimes feeling that she did not belong when people talked of the great value in being raised as a Christian. I joined her in this. The leader, a pastor, was shocked. One morning Rev. Romney told of his experience of going to a certain cabin by himself and working out his forgiveness of his father for being a failure. During the quiet hour, I sat outside realizing that I had never forgiven my father for his failure. It was hard because my mother through the years had blamed him for the failure of their marriage. Does one forgive even that? I watched a large wave come across the Sound and as it came closer and closer I forgave bit by bit. It was as if an old weight had been lifted, one which had been in the background and rarely brought into my consciousness. I did not share this as it was too personal and too new. Helen did a nice painting to summarize her experience.

MISSISSIPI RIVER, 1998

It was summer when Kay Proctor, a friend from Olympia, and I took the "Mississippi Queen" from New Orleans to Saint Louis. We were told this was the most crooked river in the world, and as we sat outside on our little porch we often did not know east from west. Sometimes it seemed the sun came up in the west, at another time it set in the east. We laughed over it. Some of the sunsets were beautiful. I was amazed at how long the barges were, carrying produce up and down the river. Samuel Clemens had been a pilot in his early days. He had heard the call many times: Mark One, Mark Two, Mark Twain, meaning two fathoms or twelve feet. Every steamboat pilot's desire was to have twelve feet of water. He adopted Mark Twain as his pen name when he started writing.

Natchez, Mississippi, had not wanted to take part in the Civil War and it surrendered without a fight. Thus more than 200 homes have not been destroyed. These homes reflect the wealth of the early cotton planters. One home we visited was Stanton Hall, the most palatial mansion in Natchez. As we entered we were met by a lovely young woman in the costume of the Civil War days. A large long hall went through the center of the home, with parlors and dining room on the sides. I was especially intrigued by the beautiful French metal decoration on the porches.

Memphis, Tennessee, was another interesting stop. We went to the Peabody Hotel to see the ducks. The story was that in the 1930's, the manager of the hotel and a close friend went duck hunting, and had a little too much to drink. As a prank they brought some of their live ducks to the fountain in the center of the hotel lobby. The result was great enthusiasm and this became an event known in hotel circles around the world.

Some people took a tour to Presley's Graceland, but we decided to walk around town. We walked to the Schwab Store which has been there since 1875. It was a general store, with everything. We heard stories about some things being so old they fell apart if someone bought them.

Other stops were not so interesting. We arrived in Saint Louis on the Fourth of July, and saw the wonderful fireworks.

◆   ◆   ◆

At the church we wanted to do something special for Peace and Justice Week, and I decided to write some vignettes. I wrote five on various subjects. I had quite a time getting people to practice. It all went very well except for the two youth who never practiced and talked too fast. I was sorry, for one had come in on crutches to indicate she had been hurt in a land mine, which was one of the subjects we wanted to emphasize. I felt like I was running around like I did when I was 37, not 87. I was completely exhausted afterward. Just then a resident became ill and said I would take over her responsibility. I just said, "Sorry," and spent a couple of days with Judy in Seattle to get some rest. Someone else picked up the project.

Once when I was in the Philippines I took a couple from the U.S. to a town where wood carving was done. The man was fascinated by the canes. I bought one too, reasoning that Walter might need it, and if not, maybe I would. It was beautiful, hand carved and inlaid with mother of pearl. When one day after a bout of flu I could not raise my foot the nurse said 'Go to the doctor" and he said "Go to a specialist." The specialist said a muscle needed to be strengthened. I went to the spa every day, sat on the steps and tried to raise my foot. It took two months to get it flexible and for the pain to leave. I was happy for that cane which I could show off to take away the attention from my foot.

A sad time was when Phyllis Hoogan died. She had been in a nursing home for six months and had just returned to her home in Ballard. She had a stroke and was gone before I could get there to see her. She had said for years that she wanted me to have her service, as I had for her husband. This was hard. I had known her for 70 years. She would never discuss faith with Judy or me, as she said she had her own ideas and would not change them. None of her family were Christian. I used the 23rd Psalm, as I thought that is one part of the Bible that everybody knows about. One granddaughter played the cello and another sang a solo unaccompanied, simple and beautiful.

UNITED METHODIST COMMITTEE ON RELIEF, 1999

A different kind of experience was when I went with fourteen from this Conference as Volunteers in Mission under the Board of Global Ministries. We went to Baldwin, Louisiana, to volunteer for the Methodist Committee on Relief (UMCOR). In order that all money given could be used for relief, we paid our transportation and also our board and room. We rented a van and one of our women drove us 250 miles west of New Orleans. I roomed with two black women for which I was glad, for they have continued to be good friends. We joined other volunteers for meals, totaling about 35 for that week. Only six people were hired, and all the rest of the work was done by volunteers. We found that the types of work needed were: work in the warehouse, which included rolling blankets in plastic; packing boxes of dried food; measuring and folding and boxing yards and yards of mosquito netting; taking apart the kits to make sure they had just the right amount of things in them; sewing bags for school kits; and telephoning. Outside there were gardening, grass-cutting, and making a porch for a house in the community.

Phyllis, one of my roommates, and I volunteered to telephone. The One Great Hour of Sharing was approaching and our task was to call the ministers and make sure they had the information and supplies needed. I called the ministers in North Carolina; she called those in Texas. As she was from Texas she used her Texan drawl. Because there was a one-hour change between North Carolina and Louisiana, the offices closed an hour earlier, and I could quit working at 4:00 P.M. instead of 5:00 P.M. I went around and took pictures.

On Sunday morning we drove about 40 miles to Lafayette to attend church. We arrived in time for the service where a woman was preaching. She was excellent and afterward I found that she was a niece of one of our District superintendents, a woman whom I knew well. We were both glad to make such a connection, as was her aunt when I returned.

◆   ◆   ◆

THE CANADIAN ROCKIES

We had gone to UMCOR early in the year, and it was still spring when Faith Callahan and I went to an Elderhostel in the Canadian Rockies. We flew to Banff and had a day for shopping which I thoroughly enjoyed as there were many gift shops. I went alone as Faith does not care to shop. Two deer walking down the middle of the street, with the traffic waiting for them to get out of the way, was amusing to me.

We went to Sulphur Mountain, riding in the little glass-enclosed gondola, which holds only four people. Although it was somewhat cloudy, the views were outstanding. We had a light lunch there, spending most of the time with the two women who had ridden in the gondola with us and who remained our good friends throughout the trip.

The road to Jasper was beautiful. I was fascinated by the various features of each mountain. We saw many deer and caribou grazing, and one black bear. We had time to walk around the town in Jasper. The trip to the Columbia Ice Fields was a different kind of experience. We rode in a "Snocoach," a special bus with huge tires. We got out and spent some time walking around in the snow.

Spring was late that year, and the lakes were still frozen over. The most disappointing was Maligne Lake, as I remembered how beautiful it was when I was there before. The mountains were beautiful but the lake had no color at all. At a stop near the Maligne Canyon there was a walk that the leader said was quite steep and difficult. Several of us decided not to take it, but Faith did. I walked along the pathway beside the Athabaska River and took some good pictures of the falls which were small but lovely among the rocks. I discovered later that the walking group had not seen the river in such a rocky area. There was a large gift shop there and I bought a few gifts for Christmas.

When we left Jasper in the morning it was raining, and when we went a little higher in altitude the mountains had fresh snow. They were gorgeous! The clouds moved around and at times the sky was a beautiful blue, and combined with the fresh snow, it was extraordinary.

We took the side trip to Lake Louise. Again, the lake was frozen, and we missed seeing it at its best. The mountains were not very clear and only a few of our group wandered outside. The hotel itself had much to keep one occupied, as there were a number of gift shops and lobbies that encouraged one to relax.

We stayed at Canmore overnight and took the Rocky Mountaineer Railroad, a two-day trip to Vancouver. Our group was placed in one car with a guide to tell us where we were and the important scenery. The first day the mountains were beautiful, then we and the train stayed overnight at Kamloops. The second day we followed the Fraser River, discovering the various trees, and enjoying the river. We loved it. We had a day in Vancouver which we spent wandering about the mall and loafing.

On the flight to SeaTac I asked for a wheelchair, and Faith walked along. This was much easier to get from one place to the other, but at first Faith was a bit embarrassed by it. However we went to the front of the line for Customs, without any wait, although the other lines were long. When we got to the airport train the man wheeling me whisked everybody aside, making room for the "invalid." That time I was a bit embarrassed! When we started out for the baggage section my driver put Faith in a wheelchair too, and drove us both. It was so easy that both of us were happy, as was Faith's son-in-law, who met us.

◆   ◆   ◆

There had been much speculation about what would happen when we began a new millennium in 2000, such as what would happen to the technical operations. Would they be shut down? I had been saying for several years that I wanted to live at least until January lst just to see what would happen. There had been so much preparation that actually nothing did happen. A man had been caught with explosives coming across the border a few days earlier so that the people who wanted to have a New Year's Eve Party at the Space Needle could not do so because of security measures. It was a rather calm New Years Eve in Seattle with no fireworks.

The year 2000 was an exciting year for me as I had received my Master of Divinity Degree from Garrett-Evangelical Theological Seminary in Evanston, Illinois, in 1950, the only woman in that class. The 50th reunion could not be missed. Dr. Barbara Troxell, a professor there who had interviewed me on the phone earlier, had asked me to come a day early. She and other women professors rolled out the red carpet for me. They met me at the train in Chicago, took me out to dinner, and arranged for me to stay overnight in the dormitory. The next day they had a special luncheon for me, with most of the women faculty and some of the women students. I just answered questions, and they were happy to know that the pastor of the First United Methodist Church in Seattle was a woman. And also that the pastor of the United Methodist church near the University of Washington was a woman. This gave the students encouragement.

Later in the afternoon about fifty former students and their wives came. It was especially good to see Bob Trobaugh who had been the Conference Director of Youth Work in Wisconsin while I was the District Director. In recent years we had been exchanging Christmas cards. Shan Rice had also been a friend, and there were other friendships to be renewed. At the banquet, which included the President and the Trustees, I gave the Benediction. Because several people said they appreciated it, and a Trustee said she had been waiting to hear something like that, I include it here:

"Let us go forth, giving thanks for the excellent training we have had; thanks for the encouragement we received to keep on learning the rest of our lives; thanks for the opportunities God has given us to express His love in so many different ways; let us go with JOY as we give God thanks for life itself, with all its opportunities. Amen."

During the Commencement Ceremony the next afternoon we were all introduced, and when I came on the President mentioned that I had been the only woman in the class, and everybody clapped. I will admit it felt good to have the early work appreciated.

A big change came at Wesley when Ron Klipping, our Executive Director, retired. Our new one was Kevin Anderson, who was about 45, and appeared younger than he was. He was a Lutheran and had been the Executive Director for a Retirement Center in Minnesota. Many groups had an opportunity to interview him, including the Resident Councils. He had some ideas new to us, and we thought we could work with him. Soon we found him more "Resident Friendly" than Ron was. Two important and frustrating rules have been changed. One was the subject of dogs and cats in the cottages. Small dogs and cats were allowed. How I wished I could have brought Penny with me! Also, cottagers did not have to move into one of the apartment buildings when they became 85. Instead, this was done by assessment, beginning when it seemed necessary. Some of our good managers moved, but we got some good ones in their places.

Several times at the FOR Conference at Seabeck I had the Sunday morning worship service. One year when the Oregon group was finishing the plans for the Conference, they found that they did not have anyone for the Sunday morning service. One of them suggested I might do it. The man who called me said they wanted to have an Inter Faith service, but I told him I could not do that in one week. He said he would do the Buddha section, and would ask a Jewish woman to participate. I worked out a service, and when it was time for him to present the Buddhist contribution he quoted Sister Teresa. I was shocked and as he turned to sit down I told him he should say something about Buddha. He did for a moment or two. The Jewish woman did better as she gave a short talk about the Jewish faith. Then I told the story of Jesus, bringing out some of the peace ideas. I read a poem, then had them sing a verse of "Let There Be Peace", and continue singing as they went down the hill. The whole group responded beautifully, but I wished that the Buddhist part had been better and the Jewish a little stronger. Mike Yarrow, our Seattle FOR leader put his hand on my shoulder and said he was impressed. That felt good.

In April 200l I became 90 years old! People said they could not believe it—nor could I. After all, I was still chasing around, still driving to Olympia, and not feeling that I was old. I decided that as that happens only once in a lifetime, why not celebrate. I did, with five birthday parties. One was the general one here when all the people with birthdays in that month have a special dinner. One was a small one with the Program Committee, partly because I would be giving that up in June. As we had for many years, Judy and Lillian and I were together. I made a small birthday cake and we went to Lillian's apartment at Hearthstone Retirement Center at Green Lake. I drove to Lillian's, and Judy's daughter, Karen, brought her. We had a good visit. I decided that the 60+ Club, the retired ministers group at Puyallup, would enjoy a party. One of the women in the group ordered a cake for me from Safeway. I explained that in the Philippines it was the one who had the birthday that furnished the food, and as I was still sometimes doing things a Philippine way, it was appropriate for me to furnish the cake. They accepted that. The fifth party was the family. We had a special room at the Des Moines Creek, the restaurant just down the hill. Ruby, Forrest, and Cheryl came from Vancouver. Frances and her son Earl, his wife and two children came from Seattle. Ann and her daughters, Julie and Lisa and their children were there. As it was a Saturday, neither of their husbands could come. One should reach 90 oftener, I thought.

TEXAS ELDERHOSTELS, 2001

Faith and I had decided to go to Texas for two Elderhostels back-to-back. This was her first time to go to Texas and I had only stopped in San Antonio for a short time once and walked along the River Walk, an individual walking alone by the side of the river. In San Antonio we were housed in the Emily Morgan Hotel. It is a beautiful building with carvings on the outside, built in 1920. It had been a hospital, then an office building. Then San Antonio decided to become a tourist town and remodeled it into a hotel. It had large, beautiful rooms.

The main attraction was the Alamo, which was just across the street from our hotel. It was smaller than we had expected it to be and it was empty inside, which surprised me. Originally it was a Franciscan Mission built in 1718. Later it became a fort. In 1835 the American rebels fought the Mexican government for independence. 187 rebels were holed up in the Alamo, with one cannon, thinking they would be safe. All were killed. "Remember the Alamo" became the freedom call, even though they did not get their freedom. A beautiful monument has been built on the spot where the bodies were heaped and buried. Sam Houston was not far away and this gave him time to organize an army and defeat the Mexicans in just 18 minutes. The Republic of Texas was born, and two years later it became a part of the United States. San Antonio did not join the Confederate army during the Civil War and thus the city was not destroyed.

The River Walk was far different from the time I had been there before. There were shops all along the sides and many small restaurants. We took a boat trip and discovered how beautifully the walls were constructed. We ate lunch at one of the little restaurants. The entrance now is through the lobby of the Hilton Hotel, extremely beautiful.

Peace Demonstration

With dolls

Ringing bells at age 90

One of the studies was the inter-cultural aspect of the city. Meals were eaten in several ethnic restaurants. Even though I do not care for Mexican food, the Mexican restaurant was most interesting. We went through several dining rooms that had baskets and other native crafts hanging from the ceilings. We ate in a room with the walls completely painted in Mexican style. An artist was painting on one of the walls while we ate.

One day we went to visit the Mission San Jose, the only one preserved of the five Franciscan Missions built in the early 1700's. The purpose was not only to convert the Indians but also to colonize the area. Also there was the need to protect the area against the French. There was considerable housing for the Indians who came to the Mission for security and also for the treatment for their diseases. The Indians had to learn two new languages, Spanish for speech, and Latin for worship. They even changed their names. The old Mission building had many beautiful carvings. We were surprised to see it used as a backdrop for a modern model in a lovely long dress being photographed.

On our way to the Lyndon B. Johnson Ranch we stopped at Fredericksburg. At a park we saw an interesting metal maypole with figurines. Using it, a guide explained the history of the city. In another park we saw stone figures which told of the never-ending treaty with the Comanches.

The LBJ Ranch is four miles long and has been given to the State as a Museum. Most interesting to me was the little red schoolhouse. We were told that LJB ran away from home when he was four years old and came to this school where his siblings were. It was in front of that building that he signed the bill authorizing the Head Start Program.

At the final dinner Faith and I sat with the same group we had been with all week. Usually we tell our ages either at the final dinner or in the morning, but we decided to tell them to only those we had known. They were pleasantly surprised, as Faith at 97 years did not look or act it. I was slower at 90.

Faith and I had made arrangements for one night in a motel near the airport, so we could leave easily in the morning. My friend Adair Myer, who had been a companion that first year in the Philippines, lived in San Antonio. When I contacted her I suggested that I take her out for dinner, as in correspondence it seemed she had little income. A friend of hers brought her to the motel and took us to the restaurant which Adair had chosen. We had a good visit until her friend returned about 9:00 P.M. to take her home. This was the worst motel I have ever known. Even the manager could not get into our room using his reserve key. He had to unscrew a part of the door to let us in. The bathroom light was so noisy that we left it off and used the hall light. Early in the morning we were happy to find that the younger assistant had things going as planned—coffee and continental breakfast and ride to the airport.

We flew to Houston and transferred to Brownsville for our second Elderhostel. In the airport we road an electric cart which ran around considerably picking up and delivering other people before taking us to our right gate. We never would have found it. Our hotel was a Ramada Limited, not luxurious but comfortable. To get to our meals we went behind the Holiday Inn through a lovely spot with hundreds of very small parrots flying around in the trees. This was the first time I had ever seen a parrot outside of a cage.

We had a day between the Elderhostels. We rested in the morning, then in the afternoon we walked the three blocks to the bridge that took us over to Metamaras, Mexico. This is a tourist center with arts and crafts, many pharmacies selling medicines at lower prices, and the inevitable vendors.

The first morning of the Elderhostel we got acquainted with Brownsville. It was originally Fort Brown, as a support to the U.S. claim to the Rio Grande border. During the Civil War, Brownsville prospered as the Confederacy's cotton port, shipping material out of Mexico to dodge the Union blockade.

Pearl, our leader, showed some of the beautiful clothes she had made for her daughter's "coming out." This was a Mexican custom, and she was indicating the blending of cultures which goes on in the towns so close together, yet in different countries.

We went to a very large shopping center in Matamoros and Faith stayed there. She had difficulty with directions and she was afraid she would get lost following me around. She could do most of her Christmas shopping there. I went with others to the market. I came back to the store and also did most of my shopping for Christmas presents. I also bought a leather purse for myself.

We chartered a bus to El Paraiso, a resort on the San Rafael River near the Gulf. It was about 40 miles north of Tampico, where I had ventured years before. The double cabins had thatched roofs, giving them a Mexican look. They were well built, and had private baths. There was excellent food, an outdoor swimming pool, and horse-riding. Most of our time was spent in the two small boats going down the river looking for birds. As neither Faith nor I were birders this was a new experience for us. I had taken my binoculars, but I did better without them. Usually, by the time I found the tree, the bird was gone. Some of the group understood our lack of knowledge and helped greatly. Faith's daughter is a birder so she made a list of all that were seen, about 50. I would question another birding trip but this was a new and delightful experience.

The biologists who were with us had another species for us to study: the sea turtles. As we walked along the shore of the Gulf one of the leaders pointed out the holes in the sand where the turtles had laid eggs, but sea gulls or other predators had eaten them. The leader of the group, looking for a live sea turtle, walked very fast and far, leaving all except one behind. I turned back before Faith did. The next day we went in a different direction, but also to the shore. There we were shown a protection for the sea turtles. A large section of the shore was cordoned off with a high chicken-wire fence, and inside were long sticks indicating where turtles' eggs had been buried. Each spot contained the eggs from one nest, 50-150. The eggs were left underground and the mother then swam away. She may come back two or three times to lay more eggs. When the eggs were hatched a door was open for them at night and the baby turtles dashed out into the ocean. Even so, some of them were caught by a predator along the way. These are an endangered species, but with that kind of help they are coming back.

Back at El Paraiso we gathered in the yard for a pinata. A number of people tried it, as I did, and finally someone hit it. As we waited for dinner, Faith decided to have them guess our ages. One man came close to mine, but he was not far behind me, and I may have referred to something that he remembered. Of course no one got close to Faith's. We had an excellent final dinner in the covered section near the pool.

We had an interesting experience as we were crossing the border. We had been eating our box lunches on the bus. Included were ham sandwiches, and for most of us it was more than we could eat. We had no way of throwing them away. We all had to get off the bus, stand behind a barrier, and put our purses out in front of it. The woman in charge had a beautiful dog who sniffed at all the purses, and pointed one out. The woman had to search it, finding a piece of something from the lunch. The woman and the dog went into the bus and they were inside quite awhile. She came out laughing. "You must have had ham sandwiches." The dog had stopped at every seat and would not move until she had thrown out the box. We were not aware that we could not bring ham into this country. Why? Later we thought it might be because of the mad cow disease? There was no explanation, but we loved the dog.

◆   ◆   ◆

Faith persuaded me to attend the Senior College at Highline Community College. Classes were held in the morning and the afternoon. In between I heard a bell choir play as they were wanting people to join them. I suppose I compared them to the Methodist group for I thought they were terrible. One woman played only one note all through a piece, while the woman next to her tried to show her where they were. I had been thinking that, at 90, I wanted to do something that I had never done before. I decided that at least I could play as well as that woman and I joined the Judson Park group. We had an excellent teacher who got the four of us new ones off to a good start. He got a good job and could not continue. I then joined the Morning Bells at the United Methodist Church. Margaret Van Gasken was very patient with me for there was much to learn. I was glad that at my old age I could learn something new.

◆   ◆   ◆

A new project kept many of us very busy for several months. The head of the Maintenance department, Brian, wanted a video that would explain the working of our new telephone system. Instead of taking the handle off the phone if we were in trouble, we had a wrist band. If we fell and could not get to the phone, we would push the center of the band, and it activated the telephone. This sent a message to the nursing and security departments and help would arrive immediately. That was the primary safety feature. Brian wanted the residents to be familiar with the use and purpose of this telephone.

We who volunteered formed committees. Paul Beeman, the pastor I worked for in Olympia, was asked by Brian to be the chairman. The committee chose me for the narrator. We had people who had done everything so of course we had a former telephone company executive who could borrow telephones dating back through the years. In that way we could have a brief history of telephones.

The script was written by two people, both of whom included delightful humor. And it was all made much more attractive by a clown, a woman who had moved in just two months before we began. It was really a group project, and we all worked together as a team. When we saw it projected, we were surprised at how good it was. Then Brian admitted that he had not expected us to put that much work into it. He didn't know Paul, or any of us, who would not have been happy with anything less. He said he wanted several videos, and we all groaned. It had been fun but it had taken a lot of time. He had one or two others done, illustrating other things, but he asked other employees to do it, and we have not seen them. They were much less intensive.

Our church had begun to serve coffee at the highway rest areas to raise money for the Habitat for Humanity trips. I had fun meeting people and talking with them about Habitat, or the church. At one time we were serving at Smokey Point, the last stop before the border to Canada. There seemed to be quite a line waiting for coffee. As I looked I saw a man who looked familiar. "That can't be Forrest, my nephew from Vancouver," I said to myself. I looked again and found him looking at me questioningly. I left the serving for someone else to do, and went outside. As we recognized each other without a word we hugged one another. "What are you doing here?" I asked. "What are you doing here?" he asked. I was serving coffee; he was on a church trip to Victoria. As I walked to their bus I passed Mark and Shelley, who did not seem too surprised to see me or perhaps did not recognize me. Ruby was talking to a group of women in front of their bus. I stood in front of her for a few minutes before she saw me. Then she was shocked. Her friends looked on as we hugged and got straightened out as to why we were both at that spot at that time. We laughed about that episode for a long time.

SOUTH WESTERN PARKS ELDERHOSTEL 2002

Faith and I went to an Elderhostel hosted by the Dixie State College at St. George, Utah. We were studying the geology of Bryce, Zion, and the Grand Canyon. We had a geologist with us, who tried to teach us about all the types of rocks, but it was more than we could absorb. However, it was better than just looking at the formations and not understanding anything.

St. George was in the southwest corner of Utah. During the Civil War a Mormon was sent there to grow cotton because it could no longer come from the South. As the city grew a Mormon College was started, which has now become a State College. The Orientation was held before dinner which was held in the College Banquet room.

After dinner we went on a field trip to Snow Canyon, only a few miles away. This was Navajo Limestone, a beautiful red color. We found small very round rocks, which had been formed by wind. The whole area of Utah and Arizona had been uplifted by compression millions of years ago, then became covered by a lake. In due time rivers formed from it, and erosion then created the formations of the area.

Our first all-day trip was to Zion National Park, 41 miles away. This is Utah's oldest national park, with cliffs rising to 3,000 feet into the air. We drove slowly, stopping often to look at the formations: the Watch Tower near the entrance, and the Great White Throne where the iron oxide in the Navajo Limestone had bleached out, making it stand out as very different from the others. We went to the Zion Park Lodge to eat our lunch. A group went on a rough hike for about a mile and half. Faith went along, with her beautiful walking stick to help her. I had almost fallen over my cane several years before, and thought I might do the same thing with a walking stick. At any rate, Barb Handel, a friendly woman, said to me, "Let us walk a ways." We did for awhile, then saw a large muddy spot and we both felt we did not want to try that. For several hours we were free to walk around, rest and enjoy the scenery. Because roads had been changed since the 30's when I had been there before, I could not be sure of the place where we had heard the Easter Cantata. A speaker during the week told us about the history of the area and afterward I told him about being there for the concert. He said a college had presented it for five years, but World War II interrupted it. He said hundreds of people came for it from all over the country and this was the first time he had met someone who had come to it accidentally.

As Utah had Daylight Saving Time and Arizona did not, it was quite a feat to keep us all where we were supposed to be at the right time. Actually we did quite well, with the help of the leaders. At Page, 160 miles from St. George, we crossed the Glen Canyon Dam. The bridge was 700 feet above the Colorado River.

We visited a Navajo Indian Village. A Mormon missionary had spent two years among the Navajos, and married one of the women. He had set up this "village" to help tourists understand something of the culture. We were broken up into three groups in order to see and hear better. Our group went to the sauna first, which was very low, and it was necessary to duck to get into it. Most of us did not go inside; we just looked in. The hogan was not like the homes I had seen for this one was all new. The ceiling was crisscrossed, but perhaps that was a new way. We all went in and sat down around the edge as the man explained that this was the home of many of the people. Then he said he and his wife lived in a modern two-story home, I presumed it was in Page. When we went out we had to go in single file clockwise. He pointed across the way and said "There is a Navajo village." I did not challenge him for I knew that Navajos did not live in villages. I presumed these worked at the dam, which would make a big difference. We went to a shed where a weaver showed us how she made raw wool into a thread to weave. Also we visited a jeweler who talked about the type of silver and turquoise jewelry I had bought earlier. However, I noticed he was wearing the newer type which I bought in Santa Fe at the time of the Indian Market several years before. I did not say anything, though I considered it. I think all of us bought necklaces made of cedar with various colored stones. While we had lunch with these Navajos they told us about the Code Talkers. A white man who had grown up with the Navajos knew how complicated the Navajo language was, and when he was involved in World War II he suggested that it be used for a Code. The Japanese were never able to break the Code.

Lake Powell was the second largest man-made lake in the United States. At that time it was 57 feet below its normal level. As a result we were told we would have to walk part way to the Rainbow Bridge. This was the largest natural bridge in the world. It was salmon-pink sandstone and resembled the arc of a rainbow. As we rode on the lake between the canyons I was comparing the water line with what I had seen when Randy, Jean, Ann and I rented the houseboat in another section. It was much lower. We got off the boat and walked about three-fourths of a mile to the Bridge. We had thought we should see more beyond it, but the view seemed dark. We were about half way back when we heard thunder. Suddenly the rain came in a downpour. We walked as fast we could, but Faith and I were the last ones. The way to the boat was on a wooden platform, first with a railing, then without any sides and without anything to hold on to. The wind was strong, and Faith might have been blown over if it had not been for her walking stick. The leader came from behind and walked with me. Together we could break the wind. When we got on the boat, Faith went upstairs where we had been sitting, and tried to hide from the wind with others who were there. She was very cold. I went to the downstairs section, thinking it would be warmer. A man gave me his seat, and when I got my breath I took off my jacket which I discovered was not water-proof. It was soaking wet. I was soaked through. One of the women in our group told me she had an extra sweater if I would like it. She loaned me a sweatshirt and I put it over me as a blanket. As we got up to leave, I was about to return it when her husband said, put it on. I did, and it was warm. We had been told that we would be taken up the hill, which was steep. It was one at a time in a strange contraption. I waited for it, then at the top of the hill waited a long time again for the bus to take us to the restaurant. I was sure I would have just about frozen if I had not had the sweatshirt on. I thought I would be late for dinner, but when I got there I found it was a buffet and there were quite a number in the line ahead. This was an upscale restaurant, Wahweap Lodge. Fortunately we were on a slightly upper lever from others. With all our smelly wet clothes and all of us looking bedraggled, we did not feel we belonged in that place. After dinner we went to Kanab and checked in at the Shilo Inn. As I took off the sweatshirt I realized that she had just bought it at the college, and that she had never worn it. Can you feel guilty and grateful at the same time?

Bryce Canyon was pink sandstone, the youngest of the stones, making the erosion even more erratic than in older rock. Faith and I walked along the top rim, while most of the others took the very narrow steep trail to the bottom. One of our friends sent me a picture taken from the bottom. It would be great to see those configurations from that angle, but the extremely beautiful view from the top satisfied us. It was not cloudy, but the sun was not bright while I was taking pictures. Then the sun came out bright, and I thought the pictures would be better. I walked back and forth again taking more pictures. When I realized I should be getting to the bus, I thought I could walk through the grass and get to it quickly. I discovered I was hindered by a fence which I could not climb over or through. I had to go around it, then find the bus. I was the last one on, but they were patient. Actually those last pictures were not as good as the others.

On the way back to the hotel we went to a Western Ranch for dinner. Long tables were set up outside, with the dinner being cooked in heavy iron kettles over small open fires. A covered wagon held the necessary kitchen equipment. The chicken was delicious, as was the rest of the meal. The coffee pot had to stay on one of those hot coals to keep hot, so to get a refill was a bit difficult. The apple pie for dessert was also delicious. It was a different kind of dinner but welcome.

On the way to the North Rim of the Grand Canyon we had a rest stop at Jacobs Lake. We did not see a lake, but the stop gave us time to wander around the little store and pick up a snack or two. The North Rim was very different from the South Rim. The Grand Canyon Lodge was built in 1920. It had massive walls and timbered ceilings. The Dining Room was large and we were surprised at how many people were eating. We had a reservation for lunch, but only a few of us could go in at a time. It was about 1:30 P.M. before we all were served. The food was good, but we thought not exceptional. The Lodge gave us good views of the Canyon.

After lunch we walked around. There was a very narrow path just below the Lodge, where a few of our group walked to see down to the bottom of the Canyon. Faith and I decided against it. We walked around, and Faith decided to sit down in the Lodge and I continued to wander. I found a stairway going toward the path, and realized it had a railing at the bottom. There I could look down into the lower part of the Canyon. Those who took the path said I could see just about as much as they could. The cliffs on the other side were beautiful but we could not see the river. We were told that 5 million people came to the Grand Canyon every year, and only 10% came to the North Rim. We left about 5:00 P.M. and drove the 180 miles back to St. George. We could have gone to an outdoor play but we were too tired.

In the morning we went to the North Section of Zion National Park, the Kolob Canyon. This was a winding road between the cliffs. We stopped to take a good look at the Checkerboard Mesa. We went through the tunnel and up to the top of an area new to us. We had our group picture taken and pictures of the leaders with a huge vermilion sandstone in the background. There was a valley between two cliffs, and I wanted to take a picture, but the sun was shining in my eyes. The woman who had loaned me the sweatshirt had her photographic equipment with her. She came over to me and said she would help me. She put her hand over my camera at the right spot and I took two pictures. One came out just right. I wondered if I could do that again.

On the way home we passed a town where polygamy was still practiced. At that time the Mayor was being sued by the national government. He claimed freedom of religion. Back at the College we ate box lunches and then we were on to Los Vegas and home.

◆   ◆   ◆

The Olympia United Methodist Church celebrated its 150th Anniversary in 2002. It was the longest continuous Methodist church in the State. The first celebration was at the Church, and during the service those of us who had been former pastors were introduced. I was introduced as the "inspiration for the Energizer Bunny that goes on and on." After the service the entire congregation walked about a mile to the center of town where the first service was held. There was a bar there at that time and it was the only place in town where people could gather. When the gun went off as a call to come they thought perhaps the Indians were fighting and instead they found a preacher! Those of us who were older were taken in old cars. Someone put a disabled person in the car I was to ride in. I could then choose a cute yellow 1950 Dodge. They had arranged for a bus coming back to the church.

The second celebration was about a month later. This was a dinner for everybody. Present members chose people to sit at their tables. Both Faith and I were seated with the Woods, who had been good friends. This was held in the gymnasium of the St. Martin's College, as it was the only place in town large enough to hold all the people. All the former pastors were introduced and we said a few words. I saw a great many friends, and had lots of affectionate greetings and hugs.

The doctor I had for ten years seemed to think I was so old that I should just turn over and die. After an unpleasant encounter I decided to change doctors. The Wesley nurse recommended one who agreed to take me. He started right out with a heart exam to find out just what was happening. Then because he found some blood in the urine, there was a kidney test, then a bladder test. The specialist giving the latter said, "I recommend we do nothing." The other doctor had told me that my cholesterol, which was border-line, did not matter at my age. This new one said he paid no attention to age, it depended on how one was functioning. He said I was functioning like a 70 year old. The cholesterol could lead to small strokes. He had kept the same pills I had before, and another pill, which was quite expensive, was added to the others.

Why did President Bush decide to go to war with Iraq? Was it oil? Or was it a "regime change" because Saddam had tried to kill the Senior Bush ten years before? He gave other reasons, of course. Once a week for five months a number of us joined with some others from Burien and stood in the park on our corner where the roads cross, holding up NO IRAQ WAR signs. We were there even after the war started, with such signs as Peace Takes Courage and Democracy Includes Dissent. We were surprised at the favorable response of a large number of people, very different from those of 1991. On February 15, some of us went to Seattle and joined the thousands marching to oppose the war. A couple of us did not want to march all the way, so we took the Monorail into town, then stood on the sidewalk until our group came. Our signs as we stood there gave lots of people who were marching a realization that there was support from the watchers. We joined and marched a few blocks, then took the bus home. There were marches in every city in the country, and all around the world, adding up to millions. Bush said he did not have to listen to those little caucuses. We were angry. Since he said that he did not read the paper nor listen to news, he depended on his staff to bring him the reports. When he went to London and thousands demonstrated against him, and they had to keep him away, he said that he realized that the war was unpopular. I wondered if his staff never told him it was unpopular with us and all around the world. I counted up that it was the seventh war I had known. I was too young to know anything about the first, but from World War II on I have opposed them. We have called ourselves a Christian nation, but I could see nothing in war that is Christian. It bothers me when churches support one war or another.

Faith and I had been getting acquainted with Marj Westfall, one of our newer Gardens residents. She had been with us on the corner with our anti-war signs, quite surprised at herself. She had recently come from New Jersey because she has grown children near here. There she had not been involved in politics, but she was so opposed to our invading Iraq that she joined us. She expressed a number of anti-church feelings but became attached to us—a former pastor's wife, and a missionary. We loved it.

THE TORONTO ELDERHOSTEL 2003

In September Faith, Marj and I went to an Elderhostel in Ontario, Canada. I had read that I did not need a passport, just a credit card would do. Marj did not have the proper identification either. We both called back to the office, and the housekeepers went into our rooms, found what we needed, and Judy, who drove the car for personal needs, brought them to the airport. It cost us $4 each, which we thought was not excessive considering the work it took.

We planned to arrive a day early to tour Toronto. When we discovered that the Elderhostel would do that for us, we decided to go to the museums. We checked in at the Metropolitan Hotel, then Marj asked at the desk for a bank. She had thought she could get her Canadian money at the airport, but she wanted it on her Visa, and that was not possible there. The bank the hotel sent her to would not take a Visa. Fortunately both Faith and I had changed our money before we left, so we could loan her what she needed. We walked on trying to find a place for dinner. Most of them were Chinese, but not up-scale. Finally we found an American restaurant, and decided on it. Later we found if we had gone in the other direction we would have found many.

We had hoped for good weather, but a hurricane had come to the southwest, and the tag end of it came up to Toronto, bringing strong wind and rain. We took a taxi to the Royal Ontario Museum, and found a good part of it under construction. We were not much impressed. However, it had a small but nice gift shop, and I bought a present for Fran and a butterfly magnet for myself. We ate lunch there. As the rain had stopped, we walked on to the Art Gallery of Ontario. Some special modern art was supposed to be there, but it had not arrived. White forms were there instead. Both Faith and Marj appreciated the modern art more than I did. There was a large gift shop and we spent quite a bit of time in it. On the way back to the hotel Marj was determined to take a taxi, but we could see the hotel sign just ahead. Faith and I said no, and we laughed to ourselves about it. She was from the East, not accustomed to walking from one place to another. However, on the way we came to a bank where she could exchange her money. She felt quite relieved.

After the orientation we were free to take a walk, or do nothing. I opted for the walk which was a few blocks away to a large mall. Our leader pointed out the little spaces that in many cities would be left in gravel, here they were in flowers. The Toronto Eaton Center, a large mall, was like the Eaton Center of Vancouver I had wandered in.

In the morning we broke up into two groups, one to walk, one who chose to ride a bus. The three of us chose to walk, though we suspected that Marj would have preferred to ride. We walked about several blocks to the Underground, a large section of shops, various professional services, etc. The entire section was about five miles, but we did not go to all the side sections. We walked perhaps half a mile. We walked on some distance to the St. Lawrence Market. This was like our Pike Place Market where farmers, fishermen, and others sell their fresh food. Some of us went up the elevator and looked down on the first floor, but evidently we missed some interesting things in the basement. The people who had opted to ride joined us there. We sat outside awhile until time for us to take the bus to go to Queen's Quay where we ate lunch. We had time to wander in the shops a bit, and to see some of the Canadian arts and crafts.

We had an opportunity to sit outside near the water, and then on to the Soulpepper Theatre Company to see "The Play's The Thing" at the Harbour Front Centre. In this comedy a playwright has a play within a play to keep two lovers together and prevent his own financial ruin. We thoroughly enjoyed it. We were taken to the Famous People Players for dinner. The young people preparing the dinner and serving it are "slow learners." A few others are hired to help them. The large room was highly decorated with paper cutouts they had made. There were about two hundred people there we thought. Actually we waited at least half an hour before we were served, but they tried to serve us all at once, which was a little difficult. They did extremely well. The dinner was well cooked and very good.

After dinner we were sent upstairs to the Black Light Show. The leader told us that she had been a "slow learner" and one time when she was talking to her mother about the teasing that she experienced, her mother told her to take a puppet play to school. She did and the whole class clapped and cheered, and did not tease any more. She showed us the large scene she had made and said it all began there. As she grew older she made it her purpose in life to help others who were slow. We did not see the young people at all. They were dressed in black, in front of a black background. Light was thrown on paper hats, walking sticks, and shoes. After playing with these awhile, they brought out other designs; and accompanied by rock music, they seemed to play back and forth for a long time. Some of the young people sitting in the row ahead of us got caught up by the music and the playing on stage, and would stand up until some one asked them to sit. Finally their leader motioned to them to stop. This whole performance took about an hour and a half. Then the actors all came out and bowed, and the applause was great. It was 10:00 P.M. before we left for the hotel.

For the morning field trip, again we broke into two groups. Our leader took us to the tunnel; we took a train, then transferred to a street car. When we got off we walked about four blocks to The Distillery. There were a number of vendors at the tables selling things: jewelry, purses, and various other things. We walked around and sat for quite awhile until the other group came. They had taken a different route and missed the street car we took, and had to wait a long time for the next one. We were ushered into a small room to eat our box lunches. Afterward we were taken to the building which had been the Distillery. We were given a history of the Distillery as we stood inside the first floor. Then we had a lecture on the arts and culture of the area, but I found it rather boring. As we were leaving, some of the group called for taxis, but Faith and I knew we could walk the four blocks to the street car. Marj admitted later that she wanted to take the taxi.

We went directly to Ryerson University for an Acting Workshop. We worked in couples to act a scene. Some were quite good, others not so good. I got acquainted with a woman I had seen but not talked with.

Dinner was on our own. Marj chose the place this time. She chose the Chinese restaurant in the Hotel, an expensive high-class place. The food was good, but I was not too impressed. Marj loved it. In the evening two of the women from the Acting Workshop gave two reading plays. The idea was that we should go home and do something like that ourselves.

We had a city tour without getting out of the bus. They took us to various areas of the city. Then we went to Niagara Falls. Faith had never been there before, and I had been only on the American side. I had not realized that the Canadian side is so much larger and more beautiful. We had lunch overlooking the falls. It was raining slightly, and most of the group stayed in the bus. Faith and I told them that was Seattle rain, and we and a few others left the bus and went to the edge of the falls. We drank in the beauty.

We were taken on a tour of Niagara, then on to Niagara On The Lake, a town about ten miles north. It is a small quaint town, and our reason for being there was for the Shaw Festival. This was held for eight months in three theatres in town, presenting eleven plays and attracting several thousand people each year. Our leaders had planned a trip for the afternoon but it had not materialized. Many of us went to an afternoon play by a Canadian woman, at our own expense. It was the "Coronation Voyage," which really did not have anything to do with the Coronation, except that it did take place on a ship on the way to it. The "Coronation Voyage" took us across the Atlantic on the Empress of France. On board were a Mafia Chief who must make a bargain to secure freedom for himself and his family, and three girls named Elizabeth who have won a competition to be at the Coronation. "These characters come to life in a complex, humorous and provocative exploration of colonial politics and family betrayal."

The evening performance was Misalliance, by Shaw. The Tarleton and Summerhays families were at a sedate country-house party in Surrey, all set for an amusing exploration of family dynamics. Suddenly an airplane drops from the sky, making a nose dive into the greenhouse. All is plunged into chaos as we meet Lisa, the Polish acrobat. Now the conversations are with the gloves off between friends and lovers, husbands and wives, children and parents.

We traveled about 175 miles to Stratford, on the River Avon. The Shakespearean Festival was opened in 1953 in a tent. There are now four theatres, all indoors, and it has a six-month repertory season. We were divided into two groups. One walked around the beautiful parks while the other went to the Festival Theatre Costume Warehouse Tour. This was interesting for me because at Ashland we see only a few costumes, not the warehouse. However, there was not the backstage tour which is always so interesting at Ashland. We had lunch at Falstaff's, then had some free time to wander about the town. We had a guided excursion of Stratford with an historical background of the Stratford Festival.

Like at the Shakespeare Festival in Ashland, one can see other plays. We saw "Birds," by Aristophanes (414 B.C.): Two men were complaining about Athens. They were tired of the wars between Athens and Sparta and the dictatorship they lived under. They decided to leave and build a town of their own. They went to a place where a former leader of theirs had been turned into a bird and lived among other birds. They were dressed in very unusual costumes, which almost looked like colored crepe paper. These men become birds, and the town they built begins to be at war with another group of birds, and the one man becomes a dictator. The moral was that you will build the kind of town you know. Many of the group were not impressed, but I was, for I have seen countries which fought against colonialism become almost the same when they became free.

The next morning we went back to Toronto. We stopped at the Airport and left off those who were flying out in a few hours. Then on to the Hotel for those who had left their cars there. Then because we did not need to be at the airport until about 4:30, we were taken to the Shoe Museum, at our request. There were four floors of shoes, with one floor on two sides. I was fascinated, more than Faith and Marj. The basement had shoes from early Egyptian times until modern times; the next floor had Canadian shoes, and the making of boots of the Yukon; the next floor had wedding shoes, most of which were of silk and for very expensive weddings; and the top floor on that side had beautiful wedding costumes with shoes from around the world. One floor had exhibits on the other side showing shoes of important people, Hollywood actors and actresses, and those of some athletes were huge. Before we got very far we realized it was time for lunch, and the sales people recommended a little cafe across the road. It was Eastern European and quite good and inexpensive. Faith and Marj finished looking around quite a while before I did and they did quite a bit of shopping in the little gif shop. I did a little shopping, but not much. I saw in a case a pair of shoes that were a little pin, and I thought they looked like the ones that Cheryl had given me, so I took a good look. I wish I had priced them, for Cheryl told me she got them from the Girl Scouts. Finally we called a taxi and got to the airport a bit early for our check-in. Then we went home in the one non-stop plane between Seattle and Toronto.

◆   ◆   ◆

A sad time was the death of Judy Kreger in the fall of 2003. She and Phyllis Hoogan and I had stayed in close contact through the years. Both had told me for years that they wanted me to do their Memorial Services. I used to try to remind them that I might go first, but they were adamant. I did the Memorial for Phyllis in 2001, and now also for Judy. It was in her Woodland Park Presbyterian Church and her relatives and many cousins and friends were there. One of Phyllis' sons read a long paper about her life. I used Romans 8:38-39 as a Scripture and just brought her into it as one who lived the message of this Scripture. I stayed for the reception, but I knew the two daughters and a few of the cousins. Some of the cousins had not seen each other for a long while. I hovered around the edges, then helped the woman folding the table cloths. I showed her how we folded the round ones at Olympia, and evidently she was impressed for she told the daughters about it later. I suppose she thought a minister would not do such a thing, but little did she know! Later Judy's daughters sent me a generous check, with instructions to do something with it that I particularly wanted for myself. I bought tickets to the last three operas of the season, starting with Carmen in January. I thought I could go by myself on the public bus.

CUBA 2004

The International Association of Women Ministers had been meeting overseas every two years, as women ministers in other countries were isolated. When I received the information that the meeting would be in Cuba, I decided to attend. Many people questioned my going there, but just that I had not been there was enough for me. In order to go to Cuba it was necessary to go with a group approved by the U.S. government. Religious groups, as well as some others, were allowed, after getting permission from the Secretary of the Treasury. This involved much paperwork on the part of our leader. Extra expenses involved were immense. While all this was being done, President Bush made new rules for Cubans living in this country. They could travel to Cuba only once in three years, and could send money only to parents. As Cubans could not travel as before, the airlines did not have many passengers. Had we returned a week later we could have been stranded as some other Americans were.

We stayed at the Ecumenical Theological Seminary, about a two-hour trip from Havana. The women faculty and students planned our three day meeting, doing an excellent job. They used art in ways new to us. Discussions were a little difficult in small groups as there were some students whose English was poor, yet we got along well. One young woman was especially encouraged to know that I had waited six years for full clergy rights and admission to a Conference, for her denomination had not yet given that status to women.

Fidel Castro was in power, but getting old. President Bush seemed to think he could choose Castro's successor. However, our friends told us that they did not want someone who had been in the U.S. since the Revolution, but rather they want someone who had lived with them through the succeeding years. They said they would like a little less "Fidelismo" but that they did want to keep three things: Free education through College; free health care for every one; and free housing and food for everyone. They pointed out that they had no homeless, and no one starving, even though the food was not sufficient.

During the time that Russia helped Cuba, atheism was the rule. However, house churches had always been allowed and there had been about 5000 of them. When the Russians had to release their economic and other influences, changes were made. With pressure from the Council of Churches and the Pope, Castro released most of the restrictions on the churches. Although very small, they were growing rapidly.

Although the health care was not sufficient, we were impressed by their treatment for AIDS. The government was arranging for treatment from the time they were diagnosed with HIV, and this had resulted in many fewer deaths from AIDS. They thought they were close to discovering a vaccination, but the embargo goes both ways, and they had no opportunity to share their knowledge.

Although it was a socialist country, it had made a number of compromises with capitalism. They had invited foreign investors, and had a large tourism business. We went to one of the tourist sections, which had 30 luxury hotels. The government received 51% of the proceeds. It was impossible to keep everyone on the same level economically, as there were many entrepreneurs who set up a tent and sold things, often home-made. Those who worked in the luxury hotels made much more than the government paid its workers. Some families received money from relatives overseas. Then there are the large number who receive only the government subsidy, leaving them in poverty. We did wish the Congress would cancel the embargo and that President Bush would leave Castro alone.

◆   ◆   ◆

The Retired United Methodist Missionaries, who met every two years, came out to a Methodist Conference Center in the woods near Portland. Many had not been west before, so it was an opportunity for seeing relatives and friends, and sight seeing. We who persuaded them to come west were surprised that we had as many as we had two years before in Nashville.

Faith Callahan really celebrated her 100th birthday. Three hundred friends and relatives came from all over the country. What amazed me was the one worry she had—she could not remember the name of one certain couple. She knew them, but their name evaded her. Only one couple? I think if I could remember a few I would be doing well. To remember almost 300 indicates her lively spirit, and why she is so much fun to be with.

A surprise came when the two daughters of Judy took me out to lunch for my birthday, keeping up the tradition that Judy and I had for so many years. They told me that they realized the richness of friendship that Phyllis and Judy, their mother, and I had.

I am 95 years old, living longer than anyone in my family. And what a life it has been! I think back to those early decisions, and realize they must have been a way of the Holy Spirit leading me. Other friends did not have money to go to College, yet my decision and the opportunity were there. It was His leading that convinced me to see the Baptist Chaplain just the day that Dr. Bailey was in town, a professor looking for Seminary students. And those years at Westminster College, and the summers where His Way brought me years of growth. When I seemed to be going here and there He led me into new experiences which were needed later. His leading me into the ministry; then those years in the Philippines; and the unexpected work after retirement at the Olympia church, and His leading me here to Wesley Homes. And He continues to lead day by day. Oh, I thank you, God.

I look at the shelves of dolls and remember the wonderful countries I have been in and their beauty. I remember the wonderful people who have enriched my life. And I look out at the rose garden below. My cup is overflowing!

BIBLE STORIES

✦

IT COULD HAVE HAPPENED

Note: If you use these stories in any way, please give credit to the author.

MARY, THE WIFE OF CLEOPAS

My sister, Junia, and I, Mary, had lived in Caperneum most of our lives. It was after I was married to Cleopas that he and I moved to Emmaus. She and I wrote occasionally but not often. One day when I heard from her she was excited about a young teacher named Jesus. In the days that followed she went often to hear him speak. After some time she heard he was coming to Jerusalem. He was to redeem Israel, she said. Would he bring an army, I wondered, to fight the Romans? We knew that the Messiah was to defeat any ruler that Israel had. Would that finally be true now?

Cleopas and I went to see Jesus enter Jerusalem, and there were many people waving branches and hailing him as the one who would free them. But as we watched him come, he did not come in as a ruler, on a horse, but on a donkey. This seemed strange, but we knew him to be a holy man, so we welcomed him, too.

Cleopas was also wondering about the situation in the Temple a couple of days later, when Jesus overturned the tables of those selling animals for the sacrifices. These weren't Romans, but Jewish leaders. As he heard Jesus speak in the temple, though, he was convinced Jesus was the Messiah. Back in the women's section, I got acquainted with his mother. Actually she had been in Jerusalem for some time, and now she was near him again. Jesus' whole spirit was so powerful that we walked the seven miles every day to hear him. The night before the Sabbath Jesus had a special dinner with his twelve close disciples, and a few of us women served the dinner. I saw Jesus breaking the bread and wine in a way that was unique. It was a special, distinctive way. It was beautiful.

Then the morning after that dinner we walked to the city earlier than usual. But this morning some of the followers whom we knew well, Alexander and Rufus, told us that Jesus had been tried by Pilate overnight, and that he was to be crucified that day. What? Not our Jesus? They said their father was coming into the city that day to hear him, and he would be so disappointed. The horror of it engulfed us all.

Before long a group of Roman soldiers came along the road, and sure enough, there was Jesus. He looked terrible, for he had been beaten horribly. Rufus had found his father, and together we all followed as closely as we could. Suddenly a guard took the cross bar from Jesus and seeing Simon, Rufus' father, looking as though he had just come from the country, with a sneer, he told him to carry it. Simon did so proudly, knowing how much Jesus had meant to his sons.

I can't tell you how awful it was to stand there hour after hour and watch Jesus suffer. Mary, his mother, and Mary Magdalene and I (known as the three Marys), were together. His poor mother said she had never understood him. And yet he did so much for many people, and she had come to realize that he was very close to God. But now, had God forgotten him? He knew his mother was there, and he told John to take care of her. Afterward many of us stayed on in Jerusalem, staying together, locking the door for fear that our lives were in danger, too. After three days Cleopas and I decided we should be going home. Then some of the women came from the tomb and said Jesus' body was not there. Peter and John had gone to the tomb, then, and found it empty. What was the meaning of it all?

Cleopas and I went on home, very puzzled. The Messiah was supposed to free Israel from Roman rule, or any other rule. It was to become a country as it had been during the Prophets' time. We had not heard anyone coming behind us, but a man caught up with us, and talked with us. He asked us why we were sad and puzzled. Then, as though he had been a follower, he brought out the teachings of the Prophet Isaiah, how the Messiah was to suffer and he would bring people closer to God. When we got home, the stranger began to go on, but we invited him for dinner and to stay overnight. It was getting late and we were sure he had more to teach us.

I got dinner ready in a hurry, just frying some fish, and cooking some bread quickly. Then in that distinctive way Jesus had, the stranger broke the bread. I looked at Cleopas and he looked at me in astonishment. We looked back, and the stranger was gone. It had been Jesus! Why didn't we recognize him? We rushed back to Jerusalem to tell the followers our experience. While we were there Jesus appeared to us all. It was so comforting and so beautiful. But we knew we had work to do, to tell everybody we knew about Jesus, the things he had taught, his compassion for the sick and for everyone, poor and rich, and just knowing that when we were with him we were with God, closer than we had ever been before.

Isn't it ironic that people picture me as a man? I would have had a name if I were a man. And John remembered that I was with Mary at the cross. Why wouldn't I walk home with my husband and invite the stranger to dinner? Wouldn't you have done the same?

PHOEBE: A MINISTER OF THE CHURCH AT CENCHREA

I am a business woman who owns a little shop in the town of Cenchrea. This is the port city for Corinth, and I am accustomed to having travelers from the ships come to my shop. Sometimes I go to Corinth to buy things for the shop, and one of the men I buy from is a Jew. We often talk about his God. I like the idea of the one God instead of all the gods we have in Greece. And this one God of his not only fashioned the whole universe, but also is interested in his people. That has been a whole new idea to me, and I like it. But I am not going to become a Jew. I don't like all those laws about eating, and I'm certainly not going to have my son circumcised.

Sometimes my Jewish friend and I go together to hear the different speakers who talk about the issues of the day. They stand right there, on that hill top, and we are below, so the voices carry beautifully. One day my friend told me that there was to be a speaker in the Synagogue whom I might like to hear. He was a follower of a man named Jesus. He had heard about him from some of his friends up north so he was curious to hear him. And so I went with him.

Before this man began I thought he was not a very professional-looking person, not really very attractive. When he began to talk there was something in his bearing that made me want to listen. His name was Paul. There were quite a few there that day, and he talked to them about the Messiah that their prophets had told them would come. Soon he turned his attention to us Greeks. He talked about Jesus, and his message of the love of the one God.

Right away Priscilla came over to me and introduced herself. We became good friends. Thus it was that I went back many times when I wasn't busy with the people from the ships. Sometimes Paul got into arguments with the Jews, because he said he had been sent to the gentiles (that is what the Jews called us) to tell us about Jesus, and that we did not have to keep all their laws, and that circumcision was not necessary. I liked that. I decided I wanted to be a follower of this Jesus. Not that I understood everything. I could see that his life had upset those in authority, both Jewish and Roman. He had a large following which made them wary of his intentions. The Jews seemed to think he was making himself to be God, and the Romans thought he might cause trouble. So his death on the Roman cross was not difficult to grasp. But I could not understand the talk about his appearing to the followers and then to Paul a year and a half later. Paul assured us that Jesus could be with us in spirit. I did not understand that, either. However, I came to like Paul and this Jesus he talked about. Sometimes I brought people from Cenchrea with me to hear him, and they became interested, too. We decided we would gather together in town about once a week. Sometimes after we heard Paul we discussed what he said. Sometimes he wrote letters to other cities where he had preached, and the man who did the writing for him let us read them. As I had more education than some of the others, I was the one who read these letters aloud. We learned to have prayer for one another, and for Paul and his work. But we did not have any emotional experience about it. I think we expected something earth-shaking, like Paul falling off his horse.

Aquila, Priscilla's husband, was a tent maker, and as Paul had been one, too, he was staying with them, and making tents in order to earn money. One day, out of curiosity, I asked him how much he paid for the tent material. He told me, and I told him that was too much. I went to see my Jewish friend, who wasn't coming any more because his friends from the north had threatened him if he continued. He told me to have Paul come to him, and he would sell the material to him for a much lower price. Paul and Aquila were grateful for that.

After Paul had been in Corinth for a couple of years, and had formed a church there, he wanted to go to Ephesus. He intended to go by way of the northern cities for the people of Philippi had sent him money whenever he needed it. I knew my Jewish friend had heard from some of his friends in the north, so I checked with him. "Oh, no," he said, "that is too dangerous. Some of the Jews will be sure to kill him, for they think he is spreading a heresy." When I told Paul that, I also told him that there would be a ship leaving for Ephesus in about two weeks. He decided to follow my friend's advice. Before he left he came to Cenchrea and spent a few days with us. When we gathered our group together he said we were already a church, and named me as their leader.

My son was very ill, and nothing seemed to help him. When Paul came he gathered us together and he prayed fervently for my son. We all experienced an unusual peace, and we began to realize what Paul meant by the spirit of Jesus being with us. In the morning my son was better. It was a long time before he shared with me his experience of that night. He said he relaxed, no longer afraid of death, and there was a calmness and peace he had never known before. He thought it was as though the spirit of Jesus was with him.

Paul went on to Ephesus, and wrote notes to us sometimes, just to encourage us. I wish I had saved them. Priscilla and Aquila had joined Paul in Ephesus, as the work was growing rapidly and he needed them. Some of the leaders from the church in Jerusalem had come to Corinth and told them that Paul was wrong, that they had to keep all the Jewish laws in order to follow Jesus, because he had been a Jew. We were glad they had ignored our little group. This caused a lot of disagreement in the Corinthian church, and they could not agree with each other. Paul wrote to them about it several times. We read those letters, and found much in them for our own growth. Finally, after Paul had been in Ephesus about three years, he came back to Corinth to help them settle their difficulties. Paul was gathering money to help the poor Christians in Jerusalem, to help us feel that we were all still one family. We helped as much as we could. While he was with us waiting for the ship to Asia, my Jewish friend came to my shop, and told me that some Jews from Corinth were planning to kill him as he was on his way to the ship. So Paul took the northern route which seemed safer at this time. In Philippi, Luke, the doctor, joined him. They went partly over land, and partly by ship, until they reached Caesarea. We were horrified when we heard about his experiences when he got to Jerusalem. Fortunately Luke was with him all the while.

Like most people who could afford a trip I very much wanted to go to Rome. After all, it was the capital city of the world. By now I had quite a few friends there, for some I knew from Corinth and also from Cenchrea were there. I was anxious to meet the other Christians, too. So I decided to take a vacation and of course pick up a few things for my shop. While Paul was in Corinth this second time he wrote a letter to the Christians in Rome. We had not seen it, but when I got to Rome and read it, I found he was explaining his desire to visit them, and share some very wonderful teachings about Jesus. Was I surprised when I came to the last chapter! Of course, the Christians had told me that Paul had told them about me, and they had welcomed me as he told them to do. But I was shocked—he called me a minister of the church. It was the first time he had called me that. I knew he used the masculine form of the same word for a man who was leader of a church. And now he used that same word for me. Some of the Christians in Rome asked how that could be, but when I told them about our little church, they understood. They thought it was a good title, too. It made me feel good, but it also humbled me, for I knew I must return and keep that little church together, and help it grow so that as people came and went on the ships they could hear about Jesus.

In The Woman's Pulpit, The International Association of Women Ministers, 2002.

"IN THE CASE OF A WOMAN"

My name is Helen, and I live in Corinth, Greece. My father is Jewish and my mother Greek. Many of the Jewish boys went to the Jewish school, and read the Scriptures in Hebrew. My father hired a Jewish teacher, who taught my brothers to read the Scriptures in Greek. My sister and I insisted that we learn, too, and father agreed. I especialy liked the Psalms, when they told about the loving kindness of God. I liked our Jewish God better than those Greek gods. I did not find any loving kindness in them.

I was about twelve when a strange-looking man came to speak in the Synagogue. Of course all the women and girls were in the back, and when we saw him we girls started to giggle, but our mothers quickly quieted us. We did not understand much of what he was saying, except that he talked about the Messiah.

Priscilla and Aquila had come from Rome and were leaders in the Synagogue. As they had been baptized by John, they quickly learned about Jesus and became helpers of Paul. One evening Paul talked a long time, and some of the women got tired and began to talk among themselves. We girls were tired, too, but we knew better than to start talking. These friends had not grown up in the Synagogue; maybe they didn't know. Paul scolded us, sternly, and said, "Let women be silent in church…If they have questions to ask, they must ask their husbands at home." I saw Priscilla quietly go over and put her arms around one of the women so she would not feel hurt.

Many of the Jews did not agree with Paul and after awhile they told him to leave the Synagogue. Those of us who wanted to learn more about this man Jesus left and went to the house of Justus, next door. It was crowded, but we didn't mind. Sometimes Priscilla would come over to our house and gather some of the women together and answer our questions. Sometimes she just came to visit us, for my mother and grandmother loved her. She would tell us about Jesus and he became very precious to us.

Paul stayed in Corinth for about two years. The traditional Jews became so angry with him that they plotted to kill him. Father heard about this and warned him and helped him get away. Paul went to Ephesus and later asked Priscilla and Aquila to join him because the work was growing so rapidly.

When I was sixteen I married Fortunatus, a man in our group who had not been a Jew. He had grown up with all the many Greek gods, and he quickly accepted this idea of one God and his son Jesus who brought this God of love to the world.

It seemed that our church people were always quarreling. Some of the Jews who followed Jesus thought everyone, even my husband, could not be a Christian unless he was circumcised. Fortunatus not a Christian! Imagine that! And they followed the strict Jewish food laws, and they thought we should, too. But my mother had never followed them strictly.

Because Mary and I had listened to Paul, we would talk over the things he said, and then one of us would say a prayer during the service, or give a message. But John said women should not speak in church. My husband defended us because he said that anyone who had an understanding of the Way should share it.

We were having so many disagreements that Paul sent word to us that he was worried. My husband and two of the other men went to Ephesus to talk with him, and he sent a letter back with them. We were reading the letter aloud in church. My Fortunatus was reading the section about men being superior to women. He handed the letter to me, with a wide grin, giving me a little punch. That is all the affection we could show in public.

So I began to read. "Thus it follows that if a man prays or preaches with his head covered, he is, symbolically, dishonoring him who is his real head. But in the case of a..." I squealed! "Helen!" Fortunatus was mortified. "Listen—if a man prays or preaches...in the case of a woman if she prays or preaches. If a man does. if a woman does...it is all the same. He should not have his head covered. A woman should. Ohh." I quickly put my shawl over my head. "John, Paul is not telling us to stop speaking in church, he is assuming we will continue." After the meeting, I went over to John and said, "We can still be friends, can't we?" He dropped his eyes for a moment, then said, "Yes, we all appreciate what Paul says."

And so it was that in Corinth we women occasionally prayed, or preached. Being at home with the children we sometimes brought in different ideas, and most of the men liked that. They agreed with Fortunatus that we welcomed all who could contribute ideas about this Way of Jesus which was new to all of us.

In "Courageous Spirit, Voices from Women in Ministry." Upper Room Press, 2005. Used by permission.

ESTHER, A DAUGHTER OF TIMOTHY

I am Esther, the youngest daughter of Timothy. Perhaps you did not know my father, but you have heard about him. Paul was visiting the churches of Asia Minor which he and Barnabas had started on an earlier trip. When he came to Lystra he visited with Lois and her daughter Eunice, who were Jewish. Eunice had married a Greek man and they had become leaders of the Lystra Christians. My Daddy, Timothy, was their oldest son. He was thrilled to really meet Paul, for Eunice had often talked about him. Daddy followed Paul everywhere he went. Daddy and my Mama had known each other all their lives, and Eunice had chosen my Mama for his future wife. She did not want him to go away with Paul. But Daddy begged, and with the encouragement of the leaders of the Way, Paul decided to take him along. Because of the demands of the Jews, Paul had him circumcised. It was so painful Daddy never encouraged anyone else to have it done.

Paul didn't know how long they would be gone. Actually it was years. They intended to go through Asia Minor and over to Troas, and then, if it seemed advisable, to go to Ephesus. However, they stopped in Troas because it seemed that Ephesus was having trouble. While they were there, Luke met them and persuaded Paul to go with him to the towns of Macedonia. The word about Paul had spread, and there were people wanting to know about this God and Jesus he was talking about. So Paul, Silas and Daddy went with Luke.

They had trouble with the Jews in all those towns. One bright spot was the day they found Lydia and her husband worshipping at the river. They quickly became followers of Jesus, and Paul baptized them. Paul discovered that Lydia was a trader in purple cloth, worn only by the wealthy. She invited them to stay in her home, which Daddy said was the most beautiful home he had ever seen. Lydia became the center of a strong group which in future times helped with Paul's needs.

However, the Jews became so angry that they were planning to kill Paul, so he, and Silas and Daddy went on to Athens as Luke thought some people there were open to new ideas. Luke was right; there were people who liked new ideas, but there was no depth, so they went on to Corinth. Here they found Pricilla and Aquila, who had been baptized by John. They were thrilled to hear Paul, and as they were tentmakers, as was Paul, they worked together. In that way the group was not dependent on the generosity of the people who could afford to house them. Daddy wished he could learn a trade, but Paul said he needed Daddy to work with him.

After Paul had stayed in Corinth for a couple of years, things seemed to clear up in Ephesus, so they all set sail and went there. The work grew fast, and this became home to Daddy. Daddy always had trouble with the Greek food. Paul was so concerned about him that he told him to drink a little wine with his dinner, but it did not agree with him. So he just drank water, which sometimes was not very clean, and that disturbed his stomach, too. After some time he became ill, and went home to Lystra. Eunice took good care of him, and while he was there he and Mama were married. Paul was disappointed; although he thought that it was alright for a man to marry, if he was giving his time to spreading the good news of Jesus, he should not be worried by a family. While Daddy was in Lystra, Eunice taught Mama a great deal about food that would help keep him from getting sick.

Back in Ephesus again Mama was no worry, as she worked with Daddy all the time, especially with the women and children. My brothers and sisters were born, and after awhile I came along. I followed Mama everywhere, and very early learned about Jesus. All of us children went to school so that we could help in the work. It was a little easier after the Christians in Jerusalem told Paul that the new Christians did not have to be circumcised, but they should keep the food laws. Paul had to agree, but laughed to himself as he thought of all those Greeks with their own ideas of food keeping those strict Jewish food laws.

Daddy wanted to go with Paul when he and Luke started out for Jerusalem, but Paul told him no, he was needed in Ephesus. The trip proved to be dangerous, and Paul was put under house arrest in Caesarea for two years. Luke was with him but not confined. He was free to talk with the Christians, and he learned many things from them. There were many stories about Jesus, some of them magical, not at all like what Jesus actually did. Luke would tell them to Paul, who told him not to believe all those myths, but to stay with what he had been taught. And then Paul went to Rome. He wrote Daddy a short letter, wanting him to come, as Luke was the only one with him. But Daddy was ill and could not go. And then Paul was killed. Daddy grieved a great deal. It was hard for him to lose someone who had been so close to him since he was young and who had taught him so many truths. He thought about the changes in the way Paul had referred to him: Timothy, my beloved child; my true child in the faith;

my son; my fellow worker; and finally as an equal, Paul and Timothy, servants of God. How wonderful this had all been.

The work in Ephesus, as in all the other centers, became harder and harder, as various rulers demanded everyone to worship them, which of course the Christians could not do. The business leaders were angry because the Christians refused to work on Sundays.

My brothers and sisters married and lived in their own homes, continuing to spend all the time they could helping in the church. I was a teenager when one night we were awakened by men coming into our house and shouting. Daddy got up to see what was going on, and they grabbed him and took him away. Mama didn't know if it meant prison or death. I cried, and Mama cried, too, then she prayed, and told me that it would be alright for Jesus' spirit was with Daddy and with us, too. The next day the church held a prayer meeting, and we prayed all day and continued in the night. There was a calm that came over us all, as we were aware that the Spirit of Jesus was with us and with Daddy. Mama became the leader of the church. We all helped her and she became a beacon for all who had become Christians, and for many who had been worshipping the Goddess Athena, but who now came for information about the Christian way. They were inspired by the faith of this family whose lives could be taken because of their beliefs. The Goddess Athena did not inspire them like that.

Daddy was in prison three years and when he got out he was very ill. He was almost starved, as he had been given very little food, just enough to keep him alive. Also, much of it disturbed his stomach. Mama thought he was going to die. The church decided that he should leave Ephesus and go to Lystra.

Being in his old home again lifted Daddy' spirits. But he grew weaker and weaker and died. Mama began to work hard. She was older, and I began to take part of the leadership. Then a young man, who had been in prison only a short while, came home and took over his old job. His mother had already decided that I should be his wife, for she had been looking for an educated girl for him. We were married and Mama lived with us.

The churches had grown in so many towns that it became necessary to have a leader called a Presbyter to tie small groups of churches together and a Bishop over a larger area. One day a Bishop came and talked to Mama about the letters that Paul had written. They were making a list so that it could be sent to all the churches. She and I looked through Daddy's letters and gave him what we had. After he left I found a short letter Paul had written to Daddy, quite affectionate, to encourage him. I asked Mama why she did not include that one. She thought it didn't have any teaching in it that would help others.

Mama was getting too old to continue working in the church, and the group persuaded me to take over as the leader as they knew I had learned a great deal from Daddy about Paul's teachings. My husband had good work and we hired a woman to help with the babies as they came along, so that I could have time to visit people and find new converts.

And so the years passed. People were having strange, secretive, ideas about Jesus, and some of the leaders were not very good people. A Bishop came and as we talked I told him about this other letter that Paul had written to Daddy. In fact there were two of them, I had discovered. He was very interested, and asked if he could have them. They could be very useful, he said. It was some time before he came again. He showed me a new letter. I understood, of course, that using Paul's name, and putting it as though Paul had written it, would give more people a desire to read it. Many people did this. Although it was based on the original letter, including some of the bits addressed to Daddy, it was very different. It told the kind of life the Presbyters and Bishops should be living—they didn't have those in Paul's day—and also a great deal about staying with the correct teachings about Jesus. Paul's problems with the Jews were with the food laws and circumcision, not what he taught about Jesus. Then I read on: "The women should dress themselves modestly and decently in suitable clothing, not with their hair braided, or with gold, pearls, or expensive clothes, but with good works as is proper for women who profess reverence for God. Let a woman learn in silence with full submission. I permit no woman to teach or to have authority over a man."

I was dumbfounded. Did that mean that we who were the church leaders, and there were a number of us, had to stop and let the churches die? "This is not Paul's teaching," I told him. "Times have changed, my dear" he said, as though talking to a child. "Yes, of course they have changed. Men have gone to prison and others have been killed. What would have happened to these churches if women had not carried on the work during those times?" "It is a little easier now," he said. "And you are saying that women are no longer needed?" "Well, you women are getting a little out of hand." I was indignant. "Whose hand, yours? We women are not going to stop. If there is a need to lead a church, we will continue to do so." He left, quite disgusted with me. One of the other Bishops who was more understanding worked out a little service to honor the leaders, largely to keep Paul's teachings in focus. The other women and I were included. He called it "Ordination." It was a wonderful moment for us.

I am old now, and my son and his wife have taken over the work of the church. Women are still leading some of the churches. My only worry is that in the future as people read those words in that letter they might think this was Paul's teaching, and the way it really should be, and women might be put down. Oh, I hope if that ever happens, that the women will read Paul's words that it doesn't matter if you are man or women, all are in Christ together. I hope they will know they are needed, and become determined as we were to continue working for the God of Jesus.

978-0-595-39590-3
0-595-39590-2

Printed in the United States
54120LVS00002B/166-204

9 780595 395903